The New Heidegger

Also available from Continuum:

The New Heidegger

Miguel de Beistegui

continuum
LONDON • NEW YORK

Continuum International Publishing Group
The Tower Building
11 York Road
London SE1 7NX

15 East 26th Street
New York
NY 10010

www.continuumbooks.com

British Library Cataloguing-in-Publication Data
A catalogue record for this book is available from the British Library.

ISBN: HB: 0-8264-7060-2
      PB: 0-8264-7061-0

Library of Congress Cataloging-in-Publication Data
Bestegui, Miguel de, 1966–
    The New Heidegger / Miguel de Bestegui.
        p. cm.
    Includes bibliographical references and index.
    ISBN 0-8264-7060-2 — ISBN 0-8264-7061-0 (pbk.)
        1. Heidegger, Martin, 1889–1976. I. Title.
B3279.H49B433 2005
193—dc 22   2005041398

Typeset by Servis Filmsetting Ltd, Manchester
Printed and bound in Great Britain by MPG Books Ltd, Bodmin, Cornwall

Contents

List of Abbreviations

Works are cited in the original German pagination, and followed by pagination in translation, where there is one. Translations have often been modified.

BDT. 'Building Dwelling Thinking', translated by Albert Hofstadter, *Poetry, Language, Thought* (New York: Harper & Row, 1971).

BW. *Basic Writings* (ed.) David Farrell Krell (New York: Harper & Row, 1977).

EM. *Einführung in die Metaphysik* (Tübingen: Max Niemeyr Verlag, 1953); translated by Ralph Manheim (New Haven: Yale University Press, 1959).

G. *Gelassenheit* (Pfullingen: Neske, 1959); translated by John M. Anderson and E. Hans Freund, *Discourse on Thinking* (New York: Harper & Row, 1966).

GA 6. 1. *Nietzsche* (Frankfurt am Main: Vittorio Klostermann, 1996), pp. 1–220; translated by David Farrell Krell, *Nietzsche*, Vol. I. *The Will to Power as Art* (San Francisco: HarperCollins, 1991).

GA 13. *Aus der Erfahrung des Denkens* (Frankfurt am Main: Vittorio Klostermann, 1983).

GA 19. *Platon: Sophistes*, Gesamtausgabe Band 19 (Frankfurt am Main: Vittorio Klostermann, 1992); translated by Richard Rojcewicz and André Schuwer, *Plato's Sophist* (Bloomington: Indiana University Press, 1997).

GA 21. *Logik. Die Frage nach der Wahrheit*, Gesamtausgabe Band 21 (Frankfurt am Main: Vittorio Klostermann, 1976).

GA 24. *Die Grundprobleme der Phänomenologie*, Gesamtausgabe Band 24 (Frankfurt am Main: Vittorio Klostermann, 1975); translated by Albert Hofstadter, *The Basic Problems of Phenomenology* (Bloomington: Indiana University Press, 1982).

GA 29/30. *Die Grundbegriffe der Metaphysik. Welt – Endlichkeit – Einsamkeit*, Gesamtausgabe Band 29/30 (Frankfurt am Main: Vittorio Klostermann, 1983); translated by William McNeill and Nicholas Walker, *The Fundamental Concepts of Metaphysics. World, Finitude, Solitude* (Bloomington: Indiana University Press, 1995).

GA 45. *Grundfragen der Philosophie: Ausgewählte 'Probleme' der Logik*, Gesamtausgabe Band 45 (Frankfurt am Main: Vittorio Klostermann, 1984); translated by Richard Rojcewicz and André Schuwer, *Basic Questions of Philosophy: Selected 'Problems' of Logic* (Bloomington: Indiana University Press, 1994).

GA 53. *Hölderlin's Hymne 'Der Ister'*, Gesamtausgabe Band 53 (Frankfurt am Main: Vittorio Klostermann, 1984); translated by William McNeill and Julia Davis, *Hölderlin's Hymn 'The Ister'* (Bloomington: Indiana University Press, 1996).

GA 54. *Parmenides*, Gesamtausgabe Band 54 (Frankfurt am Main: Vittorio Klostermann, 1982); translated by André Schuwer and Richard Rojcewicz, *Parmenides* (Bloomington: Indiana University Press, 1992).

GA 55. *Heraklit. Der Anfang des abenländischen Denkens Logik. Heraklits Lehre vom Logos*, Gesamtausgabe Band 55 (Frankfurt am Main: Vittorio Klostermann, 1979).

GA 56/57. *Zur Bestimmung der Philosophie*, Gesamtausgabe Band 56/57 (Frankfurt am Main: Vittorio Klostermann, 1987); translated by Ted Sadler, *Towards the Definition of Philosophy* (London: Athlone, 2000).

GA 63. *Ontologie (Hermeneutik der Faktizität)*, Gesamtausgabe Band 19 (Frankfurt am Main: Vittorio Klostermann, 1982); translated by John van Buren, *Ontology – The Hermeneutics of Facticity* (Bloomington: Indiana University Press, 1999).

GA 65. *Beiträge zur Philosophie (Vom Ereignis)*, Gesamtausgabe Band 65 (Frankfurt am Main: Vittorio Klostermann, 1989); translated by Parvis Emad and Kenneth Maly, *Contributions to Philosophy (From Enowning)* (Bloomington: Indiana University Press, 1999).

GA 66. *Besinnung*, Gesamtausgabe Band 66 (Frankfurt am Main: Vittorio Klostermann, 1997).

GA 67. *Metaphysik und Nihilismus*, Gesamtausgabe Band 67 (Frankfurt am Main: Vittorio Klostermann, 1999).

GA 69. *Die Geschichte des Seyns*, Gesamtausgabe Band 66 (Frankfurt am Main: Vittorio Klostermann, 1998).

Hw. *Holzwege* (Frankfurt am Main: Vittorio Klostermann, 1950/1980); edited and translated by Julian Young and Kenneth Haynes, *Off the Beaten Track* (Cambridge: Cambridge University Press, 2002).

KL. 'Kassel lectures', *Dilthey-Jahrbuch*, Vol. 8, 1992–3.

OA. *De l'origine de l'œuvre d'art. Première version (1935)*; edited and translated by Emmanuel Martineau (Paris: Authentica, 1987).

SD. *Zur Sache des Denkens* (Tübingen: Max Niemeyer, 1969).

SDU. *Die Selbstbehauptung der deutschen Universität* (Frankfurt am Main: Vittorio Klostermann, 1983); translated by Lisa Harries as 'The Self-Assertion of the German University', in *Martin Heidegger and National Socialism* (ed.) Karsten Harries (New York: Paragon House, 1990).

Supplements. From the Earliest Essays to Being and Time *and Beyond* (ed.) John van Buren (Albany, NY: SUNY Press, 2002).

SZ. *Sein und Zeit* (Tübingen: Max Niemeyer, 1927); translated by John Macquarrie and Edward Robinson, *Being and Time* (New York: Harper & Row, 1962).

TK. *Die Technik und die Kehre* (Pfullingen: Günther Neske, 1962); translated by William Lovitt as 'The Question Concerning Technology', in

Martin Heidegger, Basic Writings (ed.) David Farrell Krell (New York: Harper & Row, 1962).

UK. 'Vom Ursprung des Kunstwerkes. Erste Ausarbeitung', *Heidegger Studies*, Vol. 5, 1989, pp. 5–22.

WhD. *Was heisst Denken?* (Tübingen: Max Niemeyer Verlag, 1954); translated by Fred D. Wieck and J. Glenn Gray, *What is called Thinking?* (New York: Harper & Row, 1968).

Wm. *Wegmarken* (Frankfurt am Main: Vittorio Klostermann, 1967/1976); translated by William McNeill et. al. *Pathmarks* (ed.) William McNeill (Cambridge: Cambridge University Press, 1998).

Introduction

On one level, the aim of this book is quite simple: it is to give a sense of the magnitude of the philosophical earthquake that Heidegger's thought represents. Also – and as an immediate consequence – it is an attempt to communicate the excitement that so many of us have felt and continue to feel whenever we discover a new lecture course, a new text by Heidegger or when we open *Being and Time* for the thousandth time. I hope to communicate the significance of this earthquake, this vertigo to anyone who has a minimal knowledge of the history of philosophy (or perhaps not even). No prior knowledge of Heidegger is required. Heidegger is a notoriously difficult thinker (all thinkers are, in my view), not least because of his experimental use of the German idiom, which is a direct expression of the novelty of his thought. These difficulties are often intensified when translated into a different idiom, such as English. On the issue of language, of concepts and neologisms, let me simply say this: every great thinker is an inventor – an inventor of concepts. Why? Not for the sake of inventing concepts (as if this were an easy thing to do), of clouding issues and making things difficult for the reader, but simply because, driven by an inexorable need to take problems further, or in a different direction, the great thinker thinks precisely at the limit of what has been thought up until then, and so at the limit of conceptual language itself. Why *concepts*? Because this is the tool with which philosophy thinks. Mathematicians 'think' with numbers and symbols, artists 'think' with colours, shapes and materials, poets 'think' with images and metaphors and philosophers think with concepts. Because philosophers operate at the limit, because they feel compelled to push further and to broaden the horizon of thinking, they often find themselves at odds with language. This doesn't mean that they don't write elegantly. The history of philosophy has its share of elegant writers, as well as clumsy ones. The elegant writers (Plato, Descartes, Hume, Nietzsche, Bergson, Foucault, to name just a few) are deceptively 'easy', though. They too are pushing language to the limit, although differently – much in the way of great novelists. The work that is required of the reader is certainly as great as when reading the most heavily conceptual writer. Heidegger's prose evolved from the very conceptual (in which he forges a whole set of concepts and creates neologisms) to the (apparently) more 'literary'. Beginning in the 1930s, he works in the direction of a certain purity of language, resorting to aphorisms, fragments, and turning increasingly to poetry as a resource for thinking beyond classical metaphysics. To say that, as a result, the 'later' Heidegger is more immediately accessible than the 'early' would be a serious mistake. Anyone who has read him has experienced the increasingly radical and demanding evolution of his thought. All of this to say that there is an *irreducibly* experimental side to any great philosophy, much in the same way that there is something experimental in Cézanne or Picasso, Debussy or Joyce. All try to invent a new idiom. This experimental dimension is precisely where thinking at the limit takes place, where the singularity of a given thought is being shaped. It is the place at which the greatest effort is demanded on the part of the reader. It is also where the greatest reward is obtained. Anyone who claims that an immediate, effortless access to the *genuinely* new is possible, anyone who claims that the substance and core of, say, a philosopher's thought can be extracted and communicated without treading the difficult path of his or her own negotiation with a tradition and its language is but a charlatan. That being said, I have tried to keep the technical vocabulary to a minimum in what follows, and have introduced it only progressively. I hope not to have shied away from the most challenging aspects of Heidegger's thought. But I also hope to have presented them in a way that is clear and accessible. This is an introduction to Heidegger's thought. It is not, however, an attempt to dilute it to the point of betraying its complexity and subtlety.

Let me now turn to the title of this book, *The New Heidegger*. By 'new', we need to understand the following: of the roughly 100 volumes planned in Heidegger's complete works, 'only' 50 have been published so far. Heidegger died in 1976. Since then, his texts (lecture courses, books, public lectures) have been slowly released (too slowly, many of us believe). There is, so far as I know, no clear date by which the whole of his work is supposed to have been released. But we have every reason to believe that the first couple of decades of this century will continue to see the publication of works by this thinker who entered the philosophical scene in the most spectacular way in 1927, the year in which *Being and Time*, to this day his most widely read and significant text, was published. All of this to say that, by virtue of Heidegger's own literary estate, there is always something new 'about' – by – Heidegger. The Heideggerian continent is still being charted. Over the years, we have gained a reasonably good knowledge of it. Much of it still needs to be discovered, though, as each volume that is being released reveals its share of surprises. This is a continent that, in many respects, is still in the making. And so, in writing this introductory book, I have tried to incorporate as much of the newly released material as possible – with the following limitations, however: since I hope to direct the reader to the original texts discussed, I cannot presume that he or she knows German, and so have deliberately focused on those recent texts that are available in translation. On a few occasions, however, and only briefly, have I taken the liberty of referring to untranslated texts.

So, what's new in this continent that we can call *Heideggeriana*? The last decade or so has witnessed the publication of some of Heidegger's most important (and most challenging) work. Almost all of it dates from the late 1930s.

These volumes are particularly illuminating as regards Heidegger's views on nihilism and 'machination', the (post)human and the divine, the death of God and/or the flight of the gods (or Nietzsche and Hölderlin), language and poetry, space and time and, above all, truth. At the same time, some of his very early lecture courses and various texts have been translated, thus providing the English reader with a deeper and clearer understanding of his relation to Greek and medieval philosophy, the so-called 'life-philosophy' of Dilthey, Protestant theology and Neo-kantianism. As a result, we have a more precise picture of his itinerary leading up to the publication of *Being and Time*. I shall draw on the earlier work to the extent that it allows me to shed light on questions and problems that are recurrent in his thought.

This approach does not mean that I have neglected the 'old', hugely influential and now canonical texts. But since there are already quite a few general introductions and commentaries available (on *Being and Time*, for example), I have not felt the need to add to those by focusing on *Being and Time* alone. Instead, I have decided to privilege a thematic approach to the content of Heidegger's thought, there again emphasizing those aspects that most clearly come out of his recently released production. In dealing with such themes, I have adopted a principle of continuity: by looking at how a given question recurs time and again in his thought, I am able to shed light on the evolution, the twists and turns of that thought. Every theme discussed is a valid point of entry into the whole of his thought. Ultimately, they all lead to one another and refer back to the same problem, or the 'matter' of Heidegger's thought (the question of being). The reader should feel free to explore this book in whichever order he or she deems fit. The first, introductory chapter is perhaps the only exception to this rule, and should be read before all the others. That being said, there is a definite continuity between the various chapters, each starting where the previous one finished. Whilst laying the philosophical foundations for the book as a whole, Chapters 2 and 3 are also the most complex and demanding and could, as such, be left to the end.

A second way in which I understand the title includes, as would be expected, the most significant developments in the literature on Heidegger. For the most part, these amount to substantial advances in the area of Heidegger's biography, and in the genesis of his thought. The works of scholars such as Ott, Safranski, Kisiel and Sheehan have allowed us to reconstruct Heidegger's early years as a thinker, casting light on his relation to Catholicism and Christianity, Neo-Kantianism, logic, mathematics and the natural sciences and Husserlian phenomenology. But they have also allowed us to understand better the details of Heidegger's action as rector of the University of Freiburg in 1933–4 (as well as, to a an extent, the motivations behind his initial and unconditional support of National Socialism). This introduction to Heidegger's philosophy will not involve a biographical chapter as such, but a short appendix (Appendix 1), in which I stress the aspects of his family background, his education, his influences and his teaching, leading up to the publication of *Being and Time* in 1927. Drawing on

Heidegger's own insistence that every thought is factically embedded, that is, rooted in one's being as existence, and in one's own history, however, I shall show the extent to which aspects of his thought can be illuminated from a historical and biographical perspective. For example, the first chapter, devoted to Heidegger's conception of philosophy's relation to life, and to the genuinely philosophical life, will allow me to incorporate elements of his early years; the chapter on politics will quite naturally include references to his action and his speeches as the first Nazi rector of the University of Freiburg. At the same time, however, and precisely to the extent that, for Heidegger, his life as a thinker was indistinguishable from his life in general, it cannot be a question of falling into the trap of clarifying his thought by turning to historical, biographical or sociological analyses. His philosophy sheds light on the most crucial aspects of his biography, as much as the latters helps us to clarify aspects of the former.

Finally – albeit perhaps less explicitly – *The New Heidegger* aims to give a sense of the extraordinary impact of Heidegger's thought on twentieth-century philosophical and non-philosophical life. His is a thought that opened up entire areas, and helped to think afresh more classical ones. These include: phenomenology, deconstruction, hermeneutics, ontology, art and architecture, human and artificial intelligence, psychotherapy and ecology. Many of the great European philosophers of the twentieth century, such as Arendt, Gadamer, Levinas, Merleau-Ponty and Derrida, are closely associated with this thought; other contemporary thinkers, whether inside or outside philosophy, are finding their inspiration in it. I do not get into the detail of any of these thoughts. I simply mention some of them, and include bibliographical references for those interested in pursuing them. They are windows (introduced in a series of Appendices) into a landscape at the edge of *Heideggeriana*. Ultimately, *The New Heidegger* is an invitation to explore a continent that is still being charted and the boundaries of which, some of you, one day, will perhaps push even further.

Most chapters are followed by a bibliography and by recommended further readings available in English.

Chapter 1 ('A Matter of Life') introduces philosophy as an activity or a possibility of life (or existence) itself, as what we could call a 'vital' activity. In that respect, it is like any other human activity. Philosophy's activity, though, differs from others in that it is directed towards life *itself*, and bears on life as the support (or the condition of possibility) of all activities. There is, therefore, an intertwining of life as the object to which philosophy directs itself and life as the subject on the basis of which philosophy is made possible. This is where the singularity of philosophy lies. Philosophy is the reflection or the bending of life back onto itself. In and through philosophy, life reveals itself to itself. As such, it also amounts to an intensification of life, to an increase in its potential. By contrast, science is seen as a process of de-vitalization (*Entlebnis*), however important and interesting it may be: the life that is presupposed in science is not the life that science thematizes. In passing, this chapter addresses the delicate question of life's access to itself: if the object of investigation is my 'I am', in all its facticity and complexity, that is to say, as *lived*, how can I hold it in view, thematize it without distancing myself from it, and so turn it into an object, a mere *thing*? How can philosophy avoid devitalizing life itself when turning itself into a theoretical object? The answer involves an explanation of hermeneutic phenomenology as the true *method* of philosophy. Beyond this methodological question, this chapter reveals how Heidegger slowly came to identify life with the pre-theoretical, pre-epistemological sphere of concrete, everyday existence. It is as existent beings (Dasein) that we relate to the world, that the world affects us and matters to us. This relation constitutes the very essence of who we are. In isolating and describing rigorously this unrepresentable, unmathematizable layer of experience, Heidegger reveals a sense of being beyond (or rather beneath) that of naturalism. Philosophy becomes *fundamental* ontology.

Chapter 2 ('The Truth that Lies Beneath') deals with the question of truth. This is a question that, in many ways, coincides with the very subject matter of Heidegger's thought. But what does he mean by truth, once life or existence can no longer become an object of *scientific* investigation? What is truth outside its scientific frame of reference? The truth that Heidegger seeks to thematize is *pre*-scientific. This means less that it is indifferent to truth in the modern sense of the term, and more that it grounds it or makes it possible. Yet precisely to the extent that this modern sense has become dominant and goes largely unquestioned, the more primordial sense of truth, whilst always operative, remains covered over. Heidegger wants to retrieve this always presupposed, yet never acknowledged sense of truth. At stake in the question of truth is the possibility of understanding the way in which being is *there* (and this, from the start, is what Heidegger had in view with the word *Da-sein*). At stake is the possibility of describing the dimension of the 'there is', this dimension, at once everywhere and nowhere, that is implicated in the very place and time in which things find themselves. This chapter traces the evolution of Heidegger's thought on that question, from the early Sophist lectures (1924–5), through *Being and Time* (1927) and into 'On the Essence of Truth' (1930) and *Contributions to Philosophy* (1936–8).

Chapter 3 ('Of Space and Time') turns to the question of space and time from the point of view of life. Very early on, Heidegger arrives at the conviction that factical life, or existence, as the pre-theoretical 'ground' of metaphysical and scientific life, presupposes a different conception of space and time. Prior to the division of the world between two 'things' or 'substances' (*res cogitans* and *res corporea*, mind and body), there is another, deeper sense of world, which involves its own spatiality, and its own temporality. We moderns have come to identify space with geometrical space; the world is now equated with nature as it is represented in Galilean and Newtonian physics – a Euclidean surface in which 'things' are granted a position and a velocity, thus marking points along a trajectory. Similarly, time – still within the confines of classical mechanics – is but the *measure* of the distance between two such points. But,

Heidegger asks, is this space as we *live* it? Is this time as we *experience* it? Of course, we can ourselves be *turned* into such objects and our movements as bodies be modelled mathematically. But, in doing so, do we not also cover something over? Do we not forget that, from the start and necessarily, we always relate ourselves to this life that is being reified, precisely to the extent that we *are* it? So, we need to ask: Does this mathematical, physical description of our own position within a set of coordinates properly express our experience of 'where' we are? Does time as the measure of movement accurately describe our experience of ourselves as entities living in the world? This chapter explores the spatiality of the world from an existential–ontological perspective and reveals time (ecstatic temporality) as the unity of existence as 'being-in-the-world'.

Chapter 4 ('The Grip of Technology') extends the analysis of truth in its historical dimension by asking the question: What is the configuration of truth that befalls us *today*? What is the light in which things manifest themselves today? Heidegger's answer (namely, 'technology') is well known, but often misunderstood. In this chapter, I show the extent to which Western metaphysics and history are *essentially* technological, that is, governed from the start by an unquestioned conception of reality that is intrinsically *productivist*. What we are witnessing today, in the age of techno-science, cybernetics and the (intelligent) machine is nothing other than an acceleration and a revelation of a process initiated a very long time ago. By questioning technology with respect to its *essence*, and not only its various aspects, Heidegger concludes that it displays our destiny. It is at the end of that process, once it is revealed for what it is, that thought is perhaps in a position to initiate an altogether new beginning, and intimate a turning within history. The question is: What is the attitude that is going to replace that of technology? What sort of relation to the world – and to others – demands to be freed? Heidegger's response can be summarized in one word: letting-be (*Gelassenheit*).

Chapter 5 ('The Saving Power of Art') deals with Heidegger's conception of art and poetry as the antidote to technological and calculative thought. Art, for Heidegger, is the other, often hidden side of the essence of technology. It is a form of knowing, and of truth, yet one that does not unfold as production and machination, but as poetics. This singular conception of art presupposes that philosophy breaks with aesthetics, which remains bound to a productivist conception of art, and to a concept of truth that is intrinsically metaphysical. Heidegger's freeing of the *question* of art from the *philosophy* of art takes the form of a meditation on the work of art as the site or the place of an event that is quite literally counter-productive. This has nothing to do with celebrating a purely 'useless' conception of art ('art for art's sake'). Rather, it has to do with the possibility of identifying a space within which the essence of truth can be seen to be taking place. Drawing on a number of sources, I show how much of contemporary art is framed by the technological System that Heidegger describes, and so is indebted to a conception of truth that remains unquestioned. At the same time, however, I show how other works of art develop the free relationship to technology that Heidegger advocates, precisely by turning to that which, structurally, technology itself cannot know. Art – a *certain* art – reveals the possibility of a different relation to the world, and to language as the primary medium in which this relation is played out.

Chapter 6 ('Politically Adrift: The Affair with National Socialism') deals with the most delicate and controversial aspect of Heidegger's thought and life. Heidegger's life was that of an academic and a philosopher. Given what he says concerning the facticity of life and the connection between life and philosophy, his political engagement cannot be set aside as a merely marginal episode. To say this, though, does not mean that Heidegger's thought is intrinsically fascistic, as some have argued. In 1933, he became the first Nazi rector of the University of Freiburg. He resigned ten months later. In this final chapter, I refer to his speeches and actions from that period. I then try to present the reasons behind his political engagement. It is primarily as an academic that Heidegger enters the scene of politics, and as a thinker that he supports the Nazi revolution, in which he sees (although he was soon to realize the extent of his mistake) the unique possibility of a radical, historical change that would bring about a total transformation not only of the university, but also of the relationship between the university and society in general. It did, indeed, but not solely in the way in which Heidegger had anticipated, thereby forcing his resignation and his disillusionment with what, until the end of his life, and with a touch of regret at not having seen it develop its potential, he referred to as 'the movement'.

I

A Matter of Life

. . . {m}an himself has become more enigmatic for us.
We ask anew: What is man? A transition, a direction, a storm sweeping
over our planet, a recurrence or a vexation for the gods?
We do not know. Yet we have seen that in the essence
of this mysterious being, philosophy happens.[1]

For many years, as a child, I had a recurrent nightmare. Slowly, but inevitably, I was drawn into what at first looked like a dark room (except that, in another version of the dream, the room was filled with white light). The dark grew darker (or the white whiter), until I realized there was no room whatsoever, and certainly nothing to be identified within it. My gaze was entirely absorbed by the ever-deepening black or white into which all things would dissolve, including my own gaze, threatening to engulf my entire self. I would not die, though. In fact, I was acutely aware of my own presence and my whole being, albeit in a way that was utterly painful. There was nothing to see, nothing to hold on to, to recognize or discover – not even the scariest of things. At that point, the presence of a thing, of anything, no matter how ominous, would have seemed infinitely reassuring in comparison with this pure light that was wrapping itself around me like a heavy cloth, wearing me down and threatening to choke me. My dream may not seem like much, but it was utterly terrifying. I would wake up in a sweat, petrified, and with just enough strength to call for my mother. 'What's wrong? What's the matter?' she would ask, rushing into my room, shocked by the expression of terror on my face. At first, I tried to tell her about the dream, but couldn't find the right words. Part of my unease, and my general state of dread, was due to my inability to formulate my state of mind. It was as if, in the face of this faceless threat, language itself was of no avail. My description of the dream was bland, and totally unable to match the extreme nature of my emotional state. Language – this means of communication that, over the years, I had learned to master and trust – was failing me, as if forcing me to describe actual, concrete things, which my mother could understand as the cause of my disquiet, when, properly speaking, there was *nothing* to describe. And so, despite my obvious distress, but also quite naturally, my mother thought there was very little – if anything at all – to the dream, which she never could take seriously. How right she was! There was indeed *nothing* to it. Nothing at all: none of the monsters and creatures I sometimes dreamed of, no loss or death of a beloved, no separation, no arguments – *nothing*. But wasn't this precisely the point? Could a dream about – and so an experience of – nothing be infinitely more dreadful, infinitely more unsettling and uncanny than a dream about something, however terrifying? There was indeed nothing to be afraid *of*. Yet was the absence of anything *specific* reason enough to dismiss the experience itself? Or was the absence of all things, the fact that I was denied access to anything in particular, not the clue to the meaning of the experience itself? Wasn't it the indication that, however paradoxical it may seem, we human beings can experience nothingness itself? But then, where does such an experience come from? What is the link between the *being* of being human and my experience of nothingness? And if this line of questioning is at all legitimate, why would it be a matter for philosophy (as opposed to, say, psychology)? What must be the definition, destination and purpose of philosophy, if it is to have anything to do with one's experience of nothingness? Could the possibility, as well as the destination of philosophy, be revealed to us in something as deeply personal, unsettling and existential in nature, as the experience of the nothing? Could philosophy be at all concerned with – and even triggered by – our experience of the abyss, in which our everyday familiarity with the world, and our very identity, come under threat?

Naturally, these are questions I was unable to formulate as a child. At the time, all I could do was wait for the deep unease and anxiety that would linger on for interminable moments after my mother had left me to recede, and eventually go back to sleep. Yet I had experienced, and somehow also discovered, the ground, or, better said perhaps, the abyss, from which, many years later, these questions would spring. It was only when, as an undergraduate, I first came across a lecture by Heidegger entitled 'What is Metaphysics?' (1929) that I was finally able to make sense of my old recurrent nightmare, the meaning of which my reading of Freud had not helped to clarify.[2] The literature on dreams and their signification is now abundant. Dreams are always understood as coded messages, as signs written in a mysterious language, which the specialist and expert alone is equipped to decode. No matter how indirect or veiled, dreams are always thought to be about something, and especially about our hidden, repressed desires and fears. They are essentially metaphorical. Heidegger, on the other hand, says virtually nothing about dreams. But he does take the possibility of the experience of 'something' we call 'nothing' seriously. Seriously? How can we take *that* seriously? How can we even begin to talk about nothing, when nothing is precisely the absence of anything to talk about? Should we not dismiss this outright as pure speculation, or metaphysical nonsense, as a famous logical positivist from the Vienna Circle once did?[3] Heidegger does not just take seriously the possibility that there is something to nothing. He takes this possibility as a decisive clue for investigating who we are, and so unveiling the meaning of our being, which he takes to be the very goal and *raison d'être* of philosophy. Far from minimising the significance of my dream, it was as if Heidegger's text allowed me to envisage it as an entirely legitimate and, as it turned out, privileged point of entry into this mode of questioning, and this infinitely varied universe we call philosophy.

Not until I had come across Heidegger's short lecture from 1929, then, was I able to gain concrete insight into the relevance of an experience – a dream – that I knew was of great significance even as a child, and that had the power to reveal something essential about myself. When reading Heidegger's text, it was as if words were finally coming to my rescue, such was their evocative power and their scientific rigour. Step by step, little by little, Heidegger introduces his reader to the reality of nothingness, which he locates in the state of mind or, better said perhaps, the 'mood' or 'attunement' (*Stimmung*) we call anxiety. Unlike fear, which is always fear of something, anxiety is the feeling generated by the experience of the withdrawal and the vanishing of all things. But in the withdrawing of all things, does everything really vanish, or is there something that remains? Is there something in addition to, or, better said perhaps, in excess of, things – a residue, as it were, but a decisive one, insofar as it would point to that to which we human beings find ourselves exposed, and so destined, as to our own, singular essence, a remainder that, moreover, would set philosophical thought on its course? How can we begin to articulate this residue, this elusive 'something', which is not a thing, if not as the 'something in general', as the 'there is' from which all things emerge? But this 'there is' in general, does it not also coincide with myself, independently of anything to which it can be directed? After all, was it not myself, and myself alone, who remained in my dream, despite and beyond the vanishing of everything else? Was my sense of dread not born of this most unusual and, in fact, uncanny situation, in which I found myself alone with myself, and came face to face with myself, my pure, naked self as it were, as opposed to the task or the thing at hand, which characterizes my habitual relation to the world? But who is this 'self', and can it be envisaged independently of the world it experiences? After all, isn't the world that I experience and that surrounds me something like an extension of myself, and isn't my self constituted through its many relations to that world?

The experience of my dream was one in which I was suddenly faced with myself as this being that is ordinarily surrounded by a manifold of things, for the most part familiar, and immersed in a world (*Welt*), or an environment (*Umwelt*), which I normally navigate quite effortlessly, and quite naturally call *mine*. In fact, this world that I call mine, and that is so utterly familiar, is familiar to the point that, for the most part, I am not even aware of its presence. I carry it with me everywhere, as it were; I cannot dissociate myself, or my own being, from it, and for that very reason its presence is never an issue. It is as if, as a distinct phenomenon, as something we could interrogate and describe philosophically, it was always covered over in those very dealings it enabled, always concealed in the very habits and automatic operations of everyday life it made possible. This world, *my* world, or this world that I do not so much possess as *am*, this worldliness that seems to designate who I am, is in fact not unlike Poe's famous purloined letter: so obviously there, so evidently, patently present before my eyes, so close to myself, that I cannot actually see it for what it is, that I actually fail to see it. This purloined world is the positive phenomenon which, Heidegger suggests, philosophy must turn to as a matter of urgency, and learn to *see*. To see what always and from the start stands before our eyes is perhaps the most difficult task. To direct our gaze, which, naturally as it were, directs itself towards objects and things in the world, back towards ourselves, and describe conceptually what and how we see the world, amounts to a very delicate operation, and one that raises complex, methodological questions.

Had it not been for the resources made available to him by Husserl and his phenomenology, Heidegger would have never been able to carry out the task he set for philosophy. Phenomenological training is all about learning to *see* the things themselves, and seeing the world and our position within it exactly as it is. Reading Husserl, and putting the phenomenological method to work in various contexts, Heidegger once argued, was like having scales fall off his eyes, and discovering the world as if for the first time. At this very early stage of our enquiry, we need not develop a proper exposition of phenomenology as the method providing the correct access to the phenomenon under investigation. Anticipating this exposition, we can simply emphasize the part that this method played in Heidegger's ability to direct philosophical thought back towards our own concrete being, allowing him to see things in the way in which they present themselves, from themselves as it were.

Returning to my dream, let me simply stress how the absence of familiar objects and beings, or the dissolution into nothingness of the things I had learned to rely on over the years as an extension of myself, and had invested with my emotions, my hopes and desires, my habits, how, in other words, the lack of anything – no matter how fantastical – to relate to, had the mysterious power of revealing my self to myself, of bringing to the fore the very worldliness that is normally covered over in my everyday dealings. By depriving me of anything familiar, and so by revealing myself as a stranger to myself, my dream had uncovered an essential trait of my being, if not its basic truth, namely, the fact that this being that I am cannot be dissociated from the world that surrounds it. Paradoxically, by suspending my relation to anything concrete in the world, by neutralizing the world as the task at hand, or as the local situation in which I usually find myself, and with which I must deal, my dream had brought me face to face with myself as this being that is irreducibly *in* and *of* the world, as the being to which worldliness belongs essentially. In certain experiences, which we could call limit-experiences, this familiar and reassuring life we call ours dissolves into nothingness, leaving ourselves in a state of existential nakedness and generating in the process a feeling of deep anxiety. This is the very loss I had experienced as a child on many occasions. What traumatized me was in fact the opposite of what I had initially taken it to be, namely, a loss: it was the experience of an excess, an irreducible residue, and the uncanny sense of coming face to face with my own being. What my dream had uncovered was the phenomenon of world itself, as well as the extent to which I do not exist independently of it. It had done so by allowing me to experience the world as something that exists, yet not as the sum of all existing things.

Now this phenomenon is one that might strike the reader as obvious. And in a way, Heidegger's sole ambition was to make this obvious phenomenon conceptually transparent. Yet if it seems obvious to most, it is all the more surprising that, at least according to Heidegger, the philosophical tradition seems to have gone to so much trouble to bury it under a series of metaphysical abstractions. As a result, the tradition in question must itself be subjected to the most rigorous critical analysis or, more appropriately, to a systematic *Destruktion* (a 'destruction' that is more a deconstruction or a destructuring than a straightforward annihilation). Through this deconstruction alone will the phenomenon in question be allowed to (re)surface and occupy centre stage.[4] Among the many abstractions of the philosophical tradition which hindered a proper access to the being of the human being stands the distinction, almost immediately fixed into a dualism, between man and world. This dualism has run deep ever since Descartes introduced it at the dawn of modern philosophy. It establishes a crucial distinction between who we are, or the being of the human, understood as a 'thinking thing' (*res cogitans*), and the being of the world, understood as 'extended matter' (*res extensa*). The human, this metaphysical construction stipulates, is a self-posited and autonomous thinking substance, which exists independently of the world it faces. The being of the human is ontologically distinct from that of the world. As a result, man can access the world through his own essence as a thinking substance only, or at least primarily and most significantly. Thought is itself understood as the ability to represent and formalize, and knowing as a metaphysical and mathematical–physical enterprise. This is the basis on which an encounter with the world takes place. In turn, the world is itself subordinated to its ability to be known, or represented, whether physically or metaphysically. And it is for that very reason that it can only be envisaged as extended, inert matter. This corresponds to the view of the world that is implicit in the physics of Galileo and Newton, and marks a turning point in the manner in which nature, and man's position in its midst, is envisaged. Heidegger's reaction to this metaphysical conception of the world and of ourselves is to say that we exist only in and through our relation to the world, that we, as human beings, are nothing independent from, and in addition to, our being-in-the-world. This means that we are not a substance, and not a thing, but, precisely, an existence, always and irreducibly open to and onto the world, always moving ourselves within a certain pre-theoretical *understanding* of it. Openness to the world is what defines our being, not thought. Thought is one way – and indeed a distinct way – of 'understanding' the world, or of comporting ourselves towards it. But it is certainly not the only way, nor indeed the primordial one.

To the extent that my reader is already familiar with aspects of Western philosophy, and with modern philosophy in particular, he or she will have already noticed the singular nature of Heidegger's approach. Some of what he says may resonate with aspects of Kierkegaard and Nietzsche's philosophy, or with the fiction of Dostoevsky. But for the most part, it would seem that he is far away from the main concerns of classical philosophy. Take the following, so-called 'epistemological' question, for example, which is thought to run through the whole of modern philosophy, from Descartes to Kant and beyond: 'How can I know that I know?' This is not Heidegger's question. Why? Because, as I've begun to show, the question of knowledge, and of the conditions under which it can be obtained, must be subordinated to a prior, more fundamental question, namely, that of the essentially worldly character of our being. The privileging of the question of knowledge stems from a certain interpretation of our essence (as thinking substance), which Heidegger rejects. Consider this other question, through which philosophy enters the domain of morality: 'What must I do?' This is not Heidegger's question either. Why? Because who this 'I' is has not been clarified to his satisfaction. Based on what I have said so far, it would seem that his question is more something like: 'Who exactly is this being that I am, this being whose being is called upon in each and every one of my experiences, in my dreams as well as in my everyday dealings, in my scientific endeavours as well as in my *rêveries*? Can we describe precisely and define rigorously what it means *to be* for this being?'

The way in which we need to go about answering such questions is by interrogating the manner in which the world is there for us, or the way in which it is disclosed to us. In this endeavour, limit-experiences, such as the one revealed in my dream, and our ability to analyse them, may prove invaluable. For is it not precisely at the moment when our familiar world, and so our very self, seems to dissolve into nothingness, leaving us in a state of utter perplexity, if not anxiety, that we may catch a glimpse of who we really are, and what we are really about? Furthermore, by revealing an aspect of our being (if not our being in its totality) hitherto unsuspected, do such experiences not have the power to set us on the way to philosophical thought? Do they not reveal the very purpose of thought, and ourselves as destined to thought, in revealing ourselves to ourselves? Throughout, Heidegger insisted on this intimate and necessary connection between who we are, between the *being* of the being human, and philosophical thought: not because thought is a capacity that we have and that can direct itself towards a number of objects, including ourselves, but because philosophy is born of this life itself, and expresses it. Heidegger wants to show how philosophy, when properly understood, stems from this life that we are. This is what he calls the metaphysical destination (and destiny) of the human being, which the limit-experiences I've been alluding to have the power to disclose. By 'metaphysical destination', he means the fact that our own being is an issue for us, at all times, but especially in those rare moments when we catch a glimpse of ourselves, or when we come face to face with our own being. Then, we are disclosed to ourselves, as the being for whom there is always more at issue than just things. We are revealed to ourselves as the being that is open to – and this means experiences and understands – this residue or this remainder I began by evoking. This residue is precisely the 'there is' in general, the fact and the event of pure presence that cannot be reduced to any present thing. Heidegger calls it the 'there' (*Da*), 'being' (*Sein*) and even 'truth'. What I had experienced in my dream, Heidegger was telling me in his lecture, was something like pure being; it was a metaphysical experience. And this is precisely the sort of experience that reveals the destination and purpose of philosophy. Naturally, the oppression, the suffocation, the sweat and paralysis I felt in my dream were quite physical. Yet the origin of the sensation was itself metaphysical. What caused it so to speak – at least this was the hypothesis Heidegger was asking me to consider – was the brute (and brutal) fact of existence, or my being as being-in-the-world.

Existence (*Dasein*) is the unifying concept that Heidegger eventually retains to designate this being that we are, and which is revealed in anxiety. Initially, though, and in the early 1920s in particular, he referred to the human *being* as 'life', 'facticity' and 'factical life'.[5] In 1925, for example, he opened a series of lectures on the life-philosophy of Wilhelm Dilthey with a reference to 'a fundamental problem for the entire history of Western philosophy: the problem concerning the meaning (*Sinn*) of human life'.[6] The *meaning* of human life, or that of the *being* of our being human, is what Heidegger focuses on initially. By facticity, we must understand the fact that the human being is essentially open, open-onto or ex-posed to something (*das Aussein-auf-etwas*). The being of who we are is characterized by this structure of openness and exposedness. And it is precisely this structure, which, Heidegger believes, Husserl was able to isolate and describe so rigorously through his concept of intentionality. To say that the human Dasein cannot be dissociated from the relation to the various objects of its world, as Husserl did, means that the structure of openness belongs to it in a way that is irreducible. But what is most singular about the human Dasein is that it is open (on)to itself, open to its own openness, and so can, up to a point, become transparent to itself, and thus be in a position to grasp its ownmost possibilities. This is the *Durchsichtigmachen* of life itself, its self-clarification, or explication. Factical life, or existence, then, points, first of all, to the fact that we are always and from the start ex-posed to the world and thrown into it, always outside as it were, without any interiority that we could call our own, and that would be independent from the world. Second, it points to the fact that this being in the world that characterizes us is where 'being' takes place, where the key to understanding the event of presence is to be found. The 'ex' of existence also signals the fact that our being is not brute, material being. It is not the being of a table, a stone or even an animal. Why? Because – and this, once again, is something my dream revealed, possibly causing the extreme anxiety that accompanied it – this being that I am is not one that I am *once and for all*, and that I am *simply* (in the way in which we could say that the table simply 'is'), but this being that I must continue to be, this being that I have no other choice but to be, this inescapable 'having-to-be' (*Zu-sein*). This is the difference between simple, brute being and existence. The having-to-be of existence is also and at the same time a 'being-able-to-be'. The former points to something like the necessity of existence: so long as I am,

I must continue to be. But this being that I must continue to be is precisely not the being of inert matter. Rather, it is the being that is in the mode of being-able – to do this or that, to be this or that and even to reject its own fate, and to live as if it were not 'able', as if it weren't free. This latter attitude, this temptation, really, far more widespread than we might think, is what Sartre called 'bad faith' and Heidegger 'inauthenticity'. It amounts to a refusal of one's being as freedom, a desire to flee one's fate as the being that 'can' (*Seinkönnen*). As we shall see, this is a temptation that is widespread, and which stems from our very essence. Contrary to popular belief, we do not long to be free, but to nullify this freedom through a certain type of existence.

I cannot stress enough the significance of Heidegger's decision to restrict the concept of existence to the being of the human being alone. All other beings *are*, naturally, but they do not *exist*. Why? Because they do not have this irreducible connection to the world, the openness to the world *as* world that defines the human being. No doubt, a stone, a table 'are'. But they do not have to be this being, they do not have to carry on being. They can be merely or objectively present, as in the case of man-made things, or certain physical phenomena. They can even have a world, as in the case of animals, although Heidegger insists that the world of the animal differs essentially from that of the existent being.[7] In each case, however, those beings do not comport themselves to their own worldliness, and are not exposed to the reality of openness as such. Unlike the human Dasein, they do not have to *be* it. Unlike the being of, say, this table on which I am writing, my being is this being that must be, this being that *can* be this or that (an architect, a writer), that *can* do this or that (make friends, marry, go for a walk), precisely to the extent that it *must* be, that it always has its own being to be. Whenever I speak of this life as *my* life, what I presuppose is this: that I am this life, or that this life is the one I have no choice but to live. Sartre, an innovative reader and interpreter of Heidegger, summarized this condition (the human condition) by saying that we human beings are *condemned* to be free. By that, and in a spirit faithful to Heidegger's insight, he meant that, at every moment, we have to be our being, to live our life and to keep confronting what Heidegger called the facticity of existence. This facticity is the source of the greatest joy and enthusiasm, as well as the greatest anxiety. It is what propels us and motivates us. And yet, at times, it is also what triggers in us a longing for brute (and not free) being, for being a mere thing. At times, existence can be too heavy a weight and too much to bear. At times, we just want to withdraw into pure nothingness, to disappear altogether or simply to evade existence by acquiring the being of a stone.[8] This is the paradox of our being human: so long as we are, we must continue to be; being, for us, is not so much a fact as it is a striving. We are this being for whom its own being is always an issue for it. This is our strength, and this is our burden. It is our fate. We can never say: I am, once and for all, I am done with being. Insofar as our being is always open and outstanding, the question of our being is, for us, never quite settled. It is always ongoing. This being is not something we can ever set aside, and move on to something else. Only when we are dead can we be done with having-to-be (with existence). Alive, we can only be by existing. Existence is the very meaning or mode of our being. Existence is our essence. And by virtue of this essence itself, we are responsible for our own being. This responsibility demands that we embrace existence not as a burden, but as a chance. We must convert our fate – the fate of freedom – into deeds and words that reflect the openness of our being to the future and indicate that, for us, life is something that is still to come, still outstanding.

This fate – our fate as free, metaphysical beings – is what the experience of nothingness reveals. By revealing ourselves as open and exposed to what, from the start, is in excess of things in the world, the nothing reveals our metaphysical nature and destiny. If we are destined to philosophical thought (to metaphysics), it is because of our meta-physical being. The need for philosophy – one could go as far as to call it a drive – is born of the metaphysical destiny of the being human. We, as human beings, are exposed not just to things in the world, but also to the world itself, not just to a corner or a slice of it, but to the world as such and as a whole. We are the being that reaches outwards, not just towards things, but also towards itself as the ultimate horizon from which the things themselves emerge. Existence is this being-outside oneself, this being at the limit, this mode of being that, from the start, has exceeded beings, and exceeded them towards itself. It is in this excess that the world itself is opened up, and from out of this primordial clearing that all questioning, including the most rigorously scientific questioning, becomes not just possible, but inevitable. At the same time, however, for the most part, the world is given, or experienced, not in its totality, not on the basis of myself as being-in-the-world, but only partially, in this everyday, practical familiarity that covers it over. If human existence is indeed destined to metaphysics, this possibility requires a radical and demanding conversion on our part in order to be realized. Philosophy is, in a way, counter-natural: it goes against our natural tendency to avoid ourselves, it advances counter-stream. At the same time, though, it is a possibility of life itself – and indeed the possibility in which life itself is revealed and made transparent to itself, appropriated in a unique and singular manner.

Hopefully, we are now beginning to understand why, as early as 1922, Heidegger declares 'the human Dasein insofar as it is interrogated with respect to the character of its being' the primary object of philosophical research.[9] This 'thing' that I am, and which, Heidegger tells us, an entire tradition, from Greek philosophy to the Old Testament, New Testament Christianity and Greco-Christian thought, designated as 'life' (*Zoë, vita*), must now be interpreted in existential terms.[10] Only as *Aussein-auf-etwas*, that is, as being outside itself and towards something, what Heidegger calls 'world', can life be understood properly. It is only as *factical* life that human life can be distinguished from inert, lifeless presence. As the explicit taking up of factical life itself in what Heidegger calls its 'fundamental mobility' (*Grundbewegtheit*), and by that he means precisely the fact that life is not a mere thing, philosophy is itself a modality or a possibility of life, in which life is given a singular expression. Philosophy is this attempt to grasp life as it unfolds, in its essential mobility, before any theoretical representation or interpretation of itself. This task is a very delicate and complex one, as life is always involved in some pre-theoretical understanding or interpretation of itself (it is, Heidegger says, 'concerned' about its being), yet one that is informed not by its highest and most genuine possibilities, but by its natural tendency to *avoid* itself. It is precisely to the extent that life finds it difficult to bear its own facticity, that is, to live according to its highest possibilities, that it is naturally drawn to making it easy for itself, to withdrawing from such possibilities. In the light of this difficulty and this tendency of life, philosophy can be seen as the attempt to make explicit in life what is only ever implicit, to turn existence into an explicit issue for it. Philosophy is a doubling of life back onto itself, an attempt to take itself up again in its essential structure of 'being outside itself and towards something'. In doing so, philosophy does not make it any easier for life. On the contrary: philosophy runs against life's intrinsic tendency to avoid itself and make it easy for itself. It is, if you will, life turned hard, or existence intensified, in and through this doubling back of life onto itself as essentially 'out there'.

I have just alluded to the fact that, in the short text from 1922 as well as in *Being and Time*, Heidegger describes the unity of factical life, or existence, as 'concern', or 'care'. With this word, Heidegger wishes to characterize the 'fundamental mobility' of factical life. We human beings *are* in such a way that, in being, we are concerned about our own being. This amounts to saying that our being is always at issue in the fact and the manner of our own being. We are concerned with ourselves. The concern of life is directed towards life itself. Yet to the extent that life is essentially factical, that is, always open to something, its concern is directed at the *world*. As a result, the movement of caring is characterized by the fact that factical life goes about its dealings (*Umgang*) with the world. And the world itself is always there, in this or that way, as having been taken up or addressed and claimed (*logos*) in care in one way or another. There are many ways in which factical life can be concerned about the world: it cares about needs, jobs, peace, tranquillity, survival, pleasures, practical as well as theoretical knowledge, etc. Every way of caring about the world amounts to a certain *understanding* of it: life moves itself in a horizon that is already understood, transmitted, reworked or reshaped. What Heidegger calls 'circumspection' (*Umsicht*) is the way in which life 'sees' its world for the most part: its world is already understood on the basis of perspectives, priorities, aspirations and specific circumstances. From the start, the world is organized as an *Umwelt*, an environmental milieu, and not as a theoretical (especially mathematical) 'reality' that stands opposed, not, therefore, as 'nature' in the modern, scientific sense that we have come to take for granted, and which continues to inform today's debates around realism and idealism, naturalism and the philosophy of mind. No doubt, the world can be envisaged from the point of view of its 'look' (*eidos*), or 'form' (*idea*), in which case it becomes an object of wonder and curiosity (*curiositas*) – an object of scientific investigation. At the most primordial level, though, the meaning of the world is pre-theoretical: we do not understand

and navigate the world as a result of its theoretical representation, but of our pragmatic comportment towards it.

Yet, precisely to the extent that the movement of caring is a living *inclination* towards the world, life tends to lose itself in the world, to be sucked into it. It takes the form of a *propensity* towards becoming absorbed in the world, and 'forgetting' its own being (and freedom, as I was suggesting a moment ago) in this absorption. There is, in other words, a basic factical tendency in life towards *falling away* from itself (*Abfallen*), a fall through which life detaches itself from itself and falls into the world. Life is naturally decline (*Verfallen*) and *falling into ruin* or self-ruin (*Zerfall seiner selbst*). Terminologically, Heidegger writes, we can describe this basic characteristic of the movement of caring as 'the *inclination* of factical life toward *falling*' or, in abbreviated form, simply as '*falling into* . . .' (*Verfallen an*). *Verfallen*, Heidegger writes, is not a mere occurrence, something that happens occasionally to life. Rather, it is a *how* of life itself, a basic 'intentional' modality, or a fundamental manner in which life is open to the world. In fact, this propensity (*Hang*) is 'the most intimate fate (*Verhängnis*) that life factically has to endure within itself'.[11] What does this mean? That this characteristic of movement is not an 'evil feature of life'[12] appearing from time to time, or structurally there as a result of some primordial sin, which, one day, we could hope to atone. We must resist diabolizing this natural declivity, despite its obvious biblical resonances (and most probably initial source of inspiration for Heidegger). This state of life does not point to a higher, more perfect 'paradisiacal naturality' — whether in the old, biblical sense, or in the more recent, say Rousseauist, sense of a 'natural state' of innocence and goodness amongst men before the introduction of culture and society. In short, it cannot be a question of eradicating life's propensity towards falling. What it does mean, though, is that life tends to understand and interpret itself on the basis of its own fallen state, that is, on the basis of its own practical, concernful absorption in the world. This is a natural tendency, and an alienating (*entfremdend*) one, insofar as it drives life to avoid itself, that is, to pass by its other, more genuine possibilities. At the same time, however, this tendency is reassuring and *tranquillizing*: it allows Dasein to carry on with its life without further questioning or complication. Heidegger will want to contrast these circumstances, or this state of affairs (*Lage*), in which life is somehow lost in its own fallen state, with the Situation (*Situation*) in which life makes itself transparent to itself in its own fallen state, takes a stance with respect to itself, cares about itself in a concrete manner and takes itself up as a possible *counter-movement* to its fallen state. This is a possibility we shall return to in some detail in the following chapter.

What lies in the inclination towards falling is the fact that factical life, which is in each case the factical life of the individual, is for the most part not lived *as such*. It is lived, of course, but only as something else, as something other than life in its ownmost and most extreme possibility. It is only an *average* life. It moves itself within the *averageness* (*Durschnittlichkeit*) that belongs to its caring, its going about its dealings, its circumspection and its understanding of the world. This averageness is that of the *publicness* that reigns at any given time. It is the averageness of the *entourage*, the dominant trends and opinions, the 'just like everyone else'. But this 'everyone' is at the same time no one in particular, an anonymous 'I' that factically lives the life of the individual: everyone is concerned about such and such, everyone sees it, judges it to be so, enjoys it, does it, asks about it, etc. For the most part, factical life is the life that is lived by '*no one*', or by what, in *Being and Time*, Heidegger calls 'the one' (*das Man*). In this way of being (often considered a way of life), life *conceals* itself from itself in the world in which it is absorbed and in the averageness in which it goes about its dealings. In the tendency towards falling, Heidegger insists, it is as if life goes out of its way to avoid itself.[13]

Ultimately, this early analysis finds its way into *Being and Time* (Division One, Chapter IV), where the phenomenon of 'falling' or 'decline' (*Verfallen*) does not signify the fall of Dasein from a more original, purer and higher position, but its usual 'concernful absorption' (*Besorgen*) in and identification with the world. Such fallenness does not imply that, in falling, Dasein somehow departs from its essence. Rather, fallenness is for Dasein an essential way of being-in-the-world: not being-one's-own-self is still a positive possibility for Dasein. Yet this positive possibility is only made possible on the basis of Dasein's avoiding or fleeing itself in the face of itself – of itself as an 'authentic' ability to be itself.[14] It is clear, on one level – the level Heidegger calls 'existentiell', or 'ontical' – that life's own possibility of being itself has been closed off in falling. On another level – the 'existential', 'ontological' or structural level – however, this closure is merely the privation of an essential and primordial disclosedness that manifests itself in the fact that Dasein's fleeing is a fleeing *in the face of itself*. In other words, it is not because, 'proximally and for the most part', as Heidegger says, Dasein lives in a state of decline, it is not because the ordinary, average way of being of Dasein does not realize its ontological potential *fully*, that the possibility of such a realization does not actually precede and exceed the fallen life of Dasein. Dasein can flee in the face of itself only if it has been disclosed to itself. To flee in the face of one's self, to avoid oneself, is still to be confronted with one's self: 'That in the face of which Dasein flees, is precisely what Dasein is 'after'.[15] But this confrontation is not one that life grasps or perceives. Why? Because it is primarily felt: it is the result not of a representation, or a decision, but of a disposition, or an attunement, such as the one I began by evoking. For why, Heidegger asks, would life avoid itself, or existence flee in the face of itself, if not because, somehow, it is afraid of itself? Isn't it only insofar as one fears something that one decides to flee from it? But what is there to be afraid of in life itself, and this in such a way that factical life would turn away from itself and into the world, allowing itself to be entirely absorbed in the world, and forgetting itself in it? The answer Heidegger provides, and that constitutes the cornerstone of his entire existential analysis, as well as the key to understanding the meaning of the being of existence as time, is *death*. I shall return to his analysis of death in detail in the following chapter. At this point, let me simply emphasize the fact that, having analysed fear as a mode of *disposition* and so as a way in which life can find itself situated in the world or disposed towards it (*Being and Time*, § 30), Heidegger now wants to distinguish it from anxiety. The two dispositions are very similar. Returning to my dream, I would say that I was afraid whenever it occurred. At the same time, I could never say what it is I was afraid of. And this, Heidegger tells us, is precisely where the difference between fear and anxiety lies. Fear is always directed towards a precise object, towards a being that is approaching from a determinate region of the world. Now, in the fleeing that characterizes Dasein's fallenness, Dasein flees in the face of itself, and not in the face of an innerworldly entity. Furthermore, this fleeing has a very specific character, since it consists in a turning to the world and an immersion into it. Hence it is not fear (*Furcht*) that is at stake, but anxiety (*Angst*). Later on, I shall want to show how death, or the way in which death signals the singularity of life itself, can cause life to want to turn itself into something that is absolutely not singular (the One). And I shall want to ask, too, whether there are moments in which life can confront itself on the basis of its own death, and so disclose itself to itself, make itself transparent to itself.

Leaving aside the question of death for the time being, then, let me focus on anxiety itself, and on the way in which, in the lecture from 1929 I began by evoking, Heidegger establishes its connection with nothingness. The nothing, Heidegger argues in 'What is Metaphysics?', is experienced, albeit at a level that, for the most part, remains pre-theoretical, in certain types of dispositions, such as anxiety or boredom. He is precisely interested in the reason why we seek to flee those dispositions we call 'negative', why, for example, we cannot endure boredom, which can become physically painful, as we all know.[16] Naturally, we seek to avoid them because of their painful character. But what brings this pain about? If these moods are negative, it is first and foremost in the sense that they negate, or suspend, the world as we normally experience it. But they are perhaps also negative in the photographic sense of the term: they are like the negative of a positive phenomenon that is to be the ultimate object of philosophical investigation. They seem to interfere with ordinary life, to bring it to a halt, thus creating this sense of deep unease that we experience in anxiety (and boredom), thus broaching the abyss we all fear, and that I was made to face in my dreams. But what is this world that we 'normally' experience, and which anxiety comes to disrupt? What is this 'life' that boredom threatens, this positive phenomenon philosophy must interrogate? It is precisely our ordinary life, our everyday, familiar world. This is the life in which we find ourselves for the most part. It is 'our' life, so familiar that it has become inconspicuous. We don't need to think about it for it to 'work'; we just live it. This is the *positive* phenomenon that Heidegger describes in great detail in the first division of *Being and Time*, and which I have already briefly sketched out. There is nothing remarkable about this average life. But this lack of singularity is precisely what makes it such a decisive, positive phenomenon, one from which we have everything to learn, since we *are* it. What this ordinary, familiar existence reveals is the extent to which we are one with our world. We do not possess a world: we *are* one. Everything we do, from the most mechanical, habitual tasks, to the most unusual ones, everything we think, from the most mundane of thoughts to the most original, testifies to the fact that we are a world. Not only that. It also testifies to the fact that this world in which we live is a coherent, meaningful totality, in which things and others have their place. It is a world I inhabit and navigate. I know my way around it. Of course, I can suddenly be transported into an entirely alien culture, one of which I know nothing, in which case I will feel lost. But this only confirms the fact that I am my world, and that this world that I am cannot be exchanged for another, like one word, or one currency, for another.

But what happens when this world that is mine, or this world that I am, is interrupted, or worse still, vanishes? Am I not then totally lost? Do I not move from a state of familiarity to one of total uncanniness? Suppose my car breaks down when driving to work. Until then, the car as car, that is, as the mode of transportation that was to bring me to work in order to meet up with this or that colleague to discuss this particular project, was unapparent. Because the car is supposed to run, I don't need to think about the context in which it runs. But when breaking down, this context becomes painfully present, as does the car itself. Something similar – albeit far more radical – takes place in those experiences in which the nothing is involved. For then, as in anxiety, in boredom or in my dream, it is not just the car that breaks down, but also the world as such and as a whole. It is as if the whole network of meaningful connections, the whole machinery that I call my life, and rely on ordinarily, broke down. We talk of nervous breakdowns and mental collapses. For Heidegger, such phenomena are perhaps not best described in immediately psychological or neurological terms. In anxiety, boredom and even depression, perhaps, what we experience is a breakdown of our connection to the world as this *familiar* world. In such instances, we find ourselves with nothing to do, with nothing and no one to turn to. Everything seems to have retreated, receded, to the point of disappearing altogether. It is as if our whole being had been engulfed, gobbled up. What was left? Nothing, nothing at all – only this residue I began by evoking, and which is precisely not a *thing*, which is precisely no thing. But this nothing is not insignificant. On the contrary: it reveals existence to itself (albeit painfully), much in the way that the breakdown of the car brings it to my attention, reveals it as such. What's left, then, when all things have vanished, when my usual grip on the world has failed me, when I can no longer hold on to it and rely on it, is the *fact* of the world itself, that is, the fact that I am nothing outside this worldliness, or this being-in-the-world. What's left, then, is myself as this pure openness and exposedness, my worldly, vulnerable and abyssal self, and, with it, the awareness of something within me that I cannot master. This, perhaps, is the reality that art, literature and philosophy seeks to explore.[17] It is difficult indeed to face life, to look at it straight in the eyes, and it is painful to bear the nudity of our factical, existential condition. No wonder we feel like fleeing anxiety or boredom. No wonder my dream left me wanting to find reassurance in my mother's arms, longing to hold on to something familiar and comforting. We would rather return to this familiar world, in which our true essence is covered over, hidden under layers of occupations and preoccupations, than face the task of existence. Yet, Heidegger insists, from the point of view of someone interested in discovering who we really are, and so the meaning of the human *being*, these moments are rare documents and testimonies, which the phenomenologist must interrogate. One thing is becoming progressively clear: the nothingness that is here in question, that one experiences in anxiety, the sort of pathos to which my dream as a child testified, is born of a certain confrontation with the uncanny, or with something that is utterly unfamiliar, and dreadful. But this uncanny, and the object of our dread, coincides absolutely with who we are. It is ourselves that we experience in anxiety, as if for the first time – the very self we go to so much trouble to avoid and cover over in our everyday dealings and concerns.

Thus far, I've been trying to clarify the soil from which philosophy grows, and the task that befalls it. Although I alluded to the method by which this task can be achieved, and the matter of philosophy turned into an object of philosophical investigation, I postponed an explicit discussion of it. The time has now come to tackle this issue, and address the problem of *how* this life with which we are one can access itself, and come face to face with itself, without transforming itself into an inert, de-vitalized object. How can it make itself transparent to itself, without immediately turning itself into a lifeless thing? How can it avoid the twofold trap of passing itself by as a result of its absolute proximity with itself, and that of turning itself into a mere thing through its own theoretical, scientific investigation? How can philosophy deal with the meaning of life *qua* lived? With this question:

> We are standing at the methodological crossroad that will decide on the very life or death of philosophy. We stand at an abyss: either into nothingness, that is, absolute reification, pure thingness, or we somehow leap into another world, more precisely, we manage to make for the first time the leap into the world as such.[18]

The question, then, is one of knowing which method philosophy must adopt in order to clarify the fundamental meaning of life. By what means, exactly, shall we be able to grasp the precise way in which life experiences its own world? Through a twofold method involving self-interpretation (hermeneutics) and rigorous descriptions of life-experiences (phenomenology).

Traditionally, and reaching back to the eighteenth century, hermeneutics (from the Greek *hermeneuein*, to interpret) is the science concerned with those situations in which we encounter significations that are not immediately understandable, but require an effort of interpretation. It is concerned with the way in which interpretation works as a necessary *supplement* to understanding, whether in the form of the alien (the other person, culture, era, etc.) that we are striving to understand or the familiar world we already understand. As such, its field of application is very wide: traditionally, it has encompassed many of the social sciences, such as theology and scripture studies, law, history, the study of literary texts and philosophy. Its object can be a text or a document, a historical 'fact' or a concrete, human situation. Gadamer, a student of Heidegger in the early 1920s and a hermeneutic philosopher in his own right, claims that until Heidegger, and in the works of Schleiermacher and Dilthey in particular, hermeneutics envisaged the contemporary situation of the knower trying to access the situation of the text or the situation under investigation as an obstacle, and as the source of possible misunderstandings.[19] As the source of 'prejudices' and distortions that block understanding, the knower's own present situation was precisely what the interpreter needed to overcome. The overall aim was one of an attitude purged of all prejudices. What the interpreter negated in this scientific ideal, however, was his own *present* as an extension of the past, and so as a vital access to it. With Heidegger, hermeneutics no longer refers to the science of interpretation, but to the process of interpretation that is an essential characteristic of life or existence itself. 'Dasein', says Heidegger, 'is a being which, in its very being, comports itself *understandingly* towards that being' (SZ, 52–3). The mode of access to being is through this understanding of being that Dasein already has. Heidegger's discovery of the *ontological* significance of understanding is a major turning point in hermeneutical theory. All *deliberate* interpretations take place on the basis of Dasein's primordial facticity, that is, on the basis of a pre-reflexive understanding of being from within a concrete situation that has intrinsic relation to the interpreter's life and personal as well as common history, to his past as well as his future. Thus Heidegger shows that every interpretation – even scientific interpretation – is governed by the concrete situation of the interpreter. There is no interpretation that is without presupposition, or prejudice, for while the interpreter may free himself from this or that situation, he cannot free himself from his own facticity, from the ontological condition of always already having a finite temporal situation as the horizon within which the beings he understands gain their initial meaning for him.

To interpret, for Heidegger, is to exercise an activity of exegesis or explication (*Auslegung*) and comprehension (*Vernehmen*). The task of the interpreter is to *see*. And this seeing is directed towards a particular matter (*Sache*). Heidegger's concept of hermeneutics is essentially intuitionist, and very close to the ideal formulated by Husserl. 'Seeing' or, more generally, 'intuition', is the access to the *Sache*, and the guarantee of its givenness: from a phenomenological perspective, a matter or a phenomenon is 'given', and so manifest as a phenomenon, when it is grasped in an intuition. The ideal of intuition, and of hermeneutics, is transparency – not just, and not primarily, of philosophical texts, but of life itself. The ultimate goal of hermeneutics is to render the interpreter transparent to himself *as* factical life. Hermeneutics is directed towards the living present, or the 'fundamental mobility' of life. The emphasis on seeing, intuition and the living present means that hermeneutics is phenomenological through and through. Heidegger's own version and practice of hermeneutics is inseparable from his commitment to phenomenology.

What about phenomenology, then? It is the rigorous science that does not

have the theoretical character of the natural sciences, and at the same time
avoids the twofold philosophical trap of realism and idealism, both of which
reify life by reconstructing it, or turning it into an object. Phenomenology
alone, Heidegger claims, is 'the absolute *sympathy with life* that is identical with
life-experience [*Erlebnis*]'.[20] As a method, phenomenology allows one to do
something quite remarkable. Specifically, it gives us eyes (or the conceptual
tools) to 'see' a lived experience in the very way in which it is lived, or experienced, that is, without adding or subtracting anything to it, without transforming it in any way. Phenomenology, then, situates itself at the level at which
the experience takes place. This level is that of the pre-theoretical. When I see
the lectern upon entering the lecture hall, Heidegger says, I do not see a combination of brown surfaces, put together at a certain angle, made of wood, of a
certain height, and so forth. I see a lectern, as the place I must go to in order
to deliver my lecture. This is how the lectern is experienced, and phenomenology investigates the various ways in which things, which it calls phenomena,
can be experienced or 'given'. Phenomenology is concerned with the *how* of the
various modes of experience, not their actual content. Ultimately, for
Heidegger, it is the discourse whose task it is to clarify the one, fundamental
meaning that underlies all lived experiences, irrespective of their content. It is
the one discipline whose effort is directed at the meaning of the 'something in
general' that is presupposed whenever and wherever 'there is something' for
consciousness. The meaning of 'something in general' is just 'the experience-
able as such'. But doesn't this mean that the hidden sense of life itself lies in its
being open to . . . and that it implies the moment of being 'out towards' (*auf
zu*) something? This is the movement Husserl identified as 'intentionality'.
Intentionality characterizes the basic modality of consciousness, or the way in
which we are essentially and irreducibly open to the world. In the same way in
which Heidegger 'translates' (that is, reinterprets) consciousness (*Bewusstsein*)
as factical life and then as existence (*Dasein*), he also translates intentionality as
openness-towards-something. But towards what? How is it that the world I
experience is always imbued with signification? Where does it come from?
Does it derive from the various things (desk, papers, books, computer, or cath-
edral, bas-relief, nave, spire, etc.) that constitute my experience, or does it
somehow precede them? If the latter is the case, does it mean that I impose
meaning onto the world? But I myself, am I anything outside or in addition to
this world, in which I live? Ultimately, for Heidegger, phenomenology is to
provide an access to the fundamental meaning of life, or to the horizon on the
basis of which this world that I call mine, and that I am, comes to life. As a
method, phenomenology remains subordinated to the possibility of solving the
mystery of the *being* of the human being, and, as a result, of the meaning of
being in general. It is with the help of phenomenology that philosophy can
become a rigorous science and establish itself as *fundamental* ontology.

From the start, and throughout, Heidegger will have understood and practised
philosophy as a form of fidelity to life. Life, for him, is both the object and the

subject of philosophy. Philosophy is *of* life in the double sense of the genitive. It is a process of self-clarification and explication of life itself, and so a way of living itself to the full. In returning to itself (back from its own forgetfulness and its slumber), life doubles back on itself and awakens. Too often, in what amounts to a grave misunderstanding, philosophy is associated with escapism, with a flight into the world of abstract thought and ideas, and the creation of a world that has little in common with the 'real' world. Heidegger is attempting to show how it is the exact opposite, how life is never better served, that is, understood, and so intensified, than in philosophy, how philosophy is concerned with the world itself – and nothing else. Contrary to popular belief, philosophy is not this superfluous activity with which only the happy few have the luxury of engaging. It is not a peripheral occupation for the idle. Rather, it is the most sustained attempt to face life, to turn it back on itself in order to make it transparent to itself and grasp its ownmost and highest possibilities. Philosophy *is* this longing to understand what life is capable of, to delimit its potential and to make ourselves worthy of it. The categories of philosophy don't reflect personal views or opinions about the world, but fundamental structures of existence ('existentials') and actual, concrete possibilities of life. The concepts of philosophy are not abstract categories, empty generalities that we would somehow impose on life. They are not even 'logical forms' disconnected from the reality of factical life. If philosophy is a form of logic (*logos*), it is not in the formal, mathematical sense it has today. Rather, it is in the sense of a 'logic of the heart', or a 'logic of philosophy' directed towards 'pre-theoretical and practical' existence.[21] It is, in other words, a logic of life.

According to Heidegger, this conception of philosophy, in which life itself is at issue, is fundamentally Greek. From the very beginning, his interpretation of Greek philosophy, and of Plato and Aristotle in particular, was a way into this primordial phenomenon of factical life. At stake in his relation to the Greeks and in his attempt to repeat them in a manner that was radical and original, an attempt through which he first gained his reputation as a thinker in his own right, was an access to our own being as living, existing beings.[22] Returning the practice of philosophy to its Greek, specifically Platonic origin and inspiration, Heidegger understands philosophy as an awakening of life itself. In this regard, his attitude reflects that of Plato who suggests that the difference between the philosophizing human being and the one who is not philosophizing is the difference between being awake and sleeping.[22] The human being who does not philosophize goes through his existence as if he were asleep.[24] In another, earlier text, Heidegger contrasts the activity of the philosopher, which consists in grasping life in its vitality, as *Er-lebnis*, with that of the scientist, which consists in an operation of de-vitalization, or de-vivification (*Ent-lebnis*).[25] Because science relies on representations of the world, its picture of it is always a reification of the world. Philosophy alone can grasp the fundamental mobility of life itself. Philosophy alone can awaken life from its torpor and abandonment and from what Heidegger interprets as a separation from itself, and so a form of alienation. Heidegger wanted to bring

philosophy back to life by bringing life back into philosophy. Why does –
should – one philosophize? Simply – but this simplicity is the work of a lifetime – 'in order once again to 'see' all things more simply, more vividly, and
in a more sustained manner'.[26]

Because philosophy is rooted in life itself, because life itself is at stake in
the way in which we philosophize, there is something extreme and radical, and
perhaps uncompromising, about the philosophical enterprise:

> Philosophy – as we are presumably superficially aware – is not some arbi-
> trary enterprise with which we pass our time as the fancy takes us, not
> some mere gathering of knowledge that we can easily obtain for our-
> selves at any time from books, but (we know this only obscurely) some-
> thing to do with the whole, something extreme, in which an ultimate
> confrontation and dialogue takes place for man.[27]

The extreme and radical quest of philosophy is analogous to that of the explorer,
who longs to discover remote and uncharted territories, to push the horizon
further back and stretch the limits of life itself. Like the explorer, the philosopher is drawn to the ever-receding horizon, for this is the point from which the
world unfolds and opens up. It is the place from which we can look back at the
world, and embrace it in a single gaze. It is the place at which the world is gathered in its totality, and life appears in its meaningfulness.

And if, Heidegger tells us, the Greeks came to value philosophy to the
extent that we know, it is because, for them, the philosophical attitude meant
this ability to dwell amidst things as amidst a meaningful totality, this
extraordinary capacity to be in the world in such a way that the world as such
and as a whole could become an issue for man. More still: the Greeks understood that the very fate of man, what 'man' meant and was capable of was
entirely a function of the way in which he was affected by, and related to, the
whole of that which is. From then on, what the Greeks called *philosophia*, or
theoria, had nothing to do with a pleasant and intellectually sophisticated form
of leisurely activity. It was activity in the strongest and most noble sense. In
an attempt to clarify the meaning of the Greek concept of *theoria*, Heidegger
writes the following:

> But what is *theoria* for the Greeks? It is said that it is pure contempla-
> tion, which remains bound only to its object in its fullness and in its
> demands. The Greeks are invoked to support the claim that this contem-
> plative behaviour is supposed to occur for its own sake. But this claim is
> incorrect. For, on the one hand, 'theory' does not happen for its own sake;
> it happens only as a result of the *passion* [my emphasis] to remain close
> to what is as such and to be beset by it. On the other hand, however, the
> Greeks struggled to understand and carry out this contemplative ques-
> tioning as a – indeed as *the* – highest mode of man's *energeia*, of man's
> 'being at work.' It was not their wish to bring practice into line with

theory, but the other way around: to understand theory as the supreme realisation of genuine practice.[28]

In repeating the Greeks, Heidegger hoped to return philosophy to its ancient nobility, to reactivate the sense of urgency and the passion linked to genuine philosophical questioning.[29] But in what does this genuine questioning consist? In nothing other than a desire and an ability to open oneself and one's thought to the world as this world that I myself *am*, this living totality. Could one ever dream a more perfect life than the one engaged in that activity? Is it surprising, Heidegger asks, that Aristotle reserved the word *eudaimonia*, or happiness, for the sort of attitude that would bring us closer to ourselves and to the world that surrounds us?[30] 'Everyone agrees', Heidegger writes in a lecture course from 1924–5, that 'the purest joy comes from being present to beings *kata ten sophian*',[31] that is to say, according to thought. This 'pure abiding-with', this 'pure presence-to', Heidegger adds immediately, 'is in itself the purest disposition'.[32] It is primarily in this that Heidegger is Greek: in his concern to *live* philosophy as the most decisive and most extreme type of existence, that is, as the type of existence in which existence as such and as a whole is at issue and at stake. We should perhaps not be surprised, then, to see Heidegger reintroduce the world 'ethics' to qualify the type of existence engaged in 'theory'. Throughout, he will remain absolutely committed to the idea according to which the philosophical life, the life open to the 'meaning' or the 'truth' of being as such, is the truly ethical and active life – the 'good' life. For it is the life that *acts* the essence of man.[33]

NOTES

1 GA 29/30, 10/7.
2 Freud's 'The Uncanny' (*Gesammelte Werke*, XII, 229–68), published ten years before Heidegger's lecture, and the second section of 'Beyond the Pleasure Principle' (*GW*, XIII, 3–69), in which the founder of psychoanalysis distinguishes between anxiety (*Angst*), fear (*Furcht*) and terror (*Schreck*), as well as his 'Inhibitions, Symptoms, and Anxiety' (*GW*, 113–205) from 1926, provided me with a preliminary, yet insufficient insight into the nature of my dream. Whilst my dream coincided indeed with the sense of anxiety and bewilderment Freud associates with the phenomenon of the uncanny, this anxiety was not directed at any specific object, such as the fear of losing one's eyes (*Augenangst*) which, psychoanalysis insists, is indicative of the most deeply rooted and quite unbearable fear in males, namely, that of castration (*GW*, XII, 243). Interesting, though, especially in relation to Heidegger's own understanding of the unfamiliar, to which I shall turn shortly, and at a purely structural level, is Freud's insistence that the uncanny, or the unfamiliar (*das Unheimliche*), is in fact nothing other than the experience of what is originally familiar and with which we feel at home (*Heimlich-Heimisch*), the ordinary and commonly shared sexual desires and fears, which appear in disguise. In another, earlier text (1905), Freud claims that anxiety in children – often in the form of fear in the dark – is nothing other than an expression of the fact that they are feeling the loss of the person they love. At a purely symptomatic level, and in an earlier text still (1895), devoted to what he calls *Angstneurose*, or anxiety neurosis, Freud describes quite accurately the dominant traits of the *pavor nocturnus*, or the nocturnal dread, to

which I used to be subjected, and which, according to him, is symptomatic of this type of neurosis (see 'On the Grounds for Detaching a Particular Syndrome from Neurasthenia under the Description "Anxiety Neurosis"', *GW*, I, 315–42). Throughout, though, and whatever the text, Freud traces the origin of anxiety, and the feeling of uncanniness that accompanies it, to an unresolved sexual conflict. Remarkably, though, and on two occasions at least (in a letter to Fliess from 14 November 1897 and in Lecture XXXII from his *New Introductory Lectures*, 1933), Freud seems to have been assailed by doubts on the subject, evoking the possibility that anxiety may not be caused by the libido after all, thus opening up the possibility of another interpretation.

3 See Carnap's critique of Heidegger's 'What is Metaphysics?' in 'The Elimination of Metaphysics through Logical Analysis of Language' (1931), trans. A. Pap, in *Logical Positivism* (ed.) A. J. Ayer (Glencoe, Scotland: Free Press, 1959). A good and lively discussion of this critique can be found in Simon Critchley, *Continental Philosophy. A Very Short Introduction* (Oxford: Oxford University Press, 2001), pp. 90–110. In a lecture from 1920, Henri Bergson, the famous French philosopher, had already criticized the problem of nothingness, and the famous question, first formulated by Leibniz, of why there is something rather than nothing, as a pseudo-problem, that is, as a problem to which no reality actually corresponds. 'Nothing' (*rien*), Bergson suggests, is only a word, not an idea, and one that is the mere negation, and so the ultimate confirmation, of the fact that there always is something. See H. Bergson, 'The Possible and the Real' (1930), in *The Creative Mind* (New York: Citadel Press, 2002), pp. 95ff.

4 I return to the method of de(con)struction in Chapter 3, as well as in Appendix 6 'Derrida and Deconstruction'.

5 See 'Phenomenological Interpretations in Connection with Aristotle. An Indication of the Hermeneutical Situation (1922)' in *Supplements*, and GA 63, *Ontology – The Hermeneutics of Facticity* (1923).

6 The lectures in question, delivered in Kassel, Germany, are known as the 'Kassel lectures', and were published only recently in the *Dilthey-Jahrbuch*, vol. 8, 1992–3.

7 See GA 29/30, §§ 45–8.

8 See Appendix 2 'Existential Philosophy and Psychotherapy'.

9 *Supplements*, 113.

10 *Supplements*, 114.

11 *Supplements*, 117.

12 *Supplements*, 117.

13 *Supplements*, 118.

14 SZ, 184.

15 SZ, 184.

16 Heidegger discusses boredom in detail in GA 29/30, §§ 16–38. We shall return to this enigmatic mood in Chapter 3 in connection with the temporal nature of our being.

17 Virginia Woolf, for example, speaks of literature as a way of learning to look at life in the eyes, and then putting it aside. That she, like so many of the great writers, poets and artists of the last 200 years, such as Hölderlin, Nietzsche, Proust or Artaud, was physically and mentally fragile, is not an indication of their inability to face life. On the contrary: their work testifies to their experience of something all consuming, excessive and abyssal in life itself. They are all, in the words of the contemporary French philosopher Gilles Deleuze, great affirmers of life (*des grands vivants*).

18 GA 56/57, 63/53.

19 See Appendix 4 'Hermeneutics after Heidegger: The Philosophy of Hans-Georg Gadamer'.

20 GA 56/57, 110/92. It is quite remarkable that, given the breadth of his discussion in relation to this question of life, which includes references to physics, biology, neurology, psychology, as well as to the philosophical schools of realism and idealism, Heidegger does not mention the one thinker whose concerns, on this particular point,

seem closest to his, namely, Bergson. For the French philosopher is the one who made the possibility of a philosophical 'sympathy' of life with respect to itself his primary goal, and who saw such a possibility in the method he called 'intuition'. Intuition consists in thought's ability to follow and describe the continuous flowing character of consciousness, which Bergson calls 'duration'. Unlike the sciences, and philosophy itself, which spatialize, and so reify the life of consciousness, metaphysics designates this unprecedented effort to grasp it in its intrinsically temporal, flowing nature.

21 *Supplements*, 122.
22 See Appendix 3 'Heidegger and the Greeks'.
23 Plato, *Republic*, 476 c f., 520 c, 533 c.
24 GA 29/30, 34/23. Heidegger's remarks echo not only those of Plato, but also those of Descartes who, in the Preface to his *Principles of Philosophy* (1644), wrote that 'truly, it is to have one's eyes shut, without ever attempting to open them, to live without philosophising' (Descartes, *Œuvres et Lettres* [Paris: Gallimard, Bibliothèque de la Pléiade, 1953], p. 558).
25 GA 56/57, 89–90/75.
26 GA 29/30, 35/23.
27 GA 29/30, 5/4.
28 M. Heidegger, SDU, 11–12.
29 Regarding the impact of Heidegger's intepretations of Greek philosophy on a number of influential thinkers and scholars of the twentieth century, see Appendix 3 'Heidegger and the Greeks'.
30 See GA 19, § 25.
31 GA 19, 175/120.
32 Ibid.
33 Wm, 187/271.

2

The Truth that Lies Beneath

METAPHYSICAL TRUTH

1. The ordinary conception of truth

We all know, more or less consciously, more or less precisely, what truth is. We all have a sense of what the word 'truth' entails. We know, for example, that 'true' is the opposite of 'false'. '$2 + 2 = 4$' is a true statement, as is 'Caesar crossed the Rubicon' or 'the earth orbits around the sun'. These are all truths in the sense that they can be verified, corroborated, proven beyond doubt, etc. We also think of a lie as the opposite of truth, in a way that is not altogether different from the statement $2 + 2 = 5$. An error, a mistake, a lie can all lead to false or untrue statements. Fundamentally, they all point to a similar conception of truth: a lie is an incorrect statement, as is the assertion that the sun orbits around the earth. That the former involves a will to deceive and the latter not is irrelevant here, as both statements, or our appreciation of them, share a common conception of what their truth involves. They are correct or incorrect. But what does correct mean? It means that what I say, the statement I make, whether '$2 + 2 = 4$' or 'I am a lecturer in Philosophy' corresponds to an actual state of affairs, one that can be verified in a number of ways. The true statement can be made in relation to matters mathematical, physical, biographical or historical. In each case, however, what is presupposed in identifying the statement as true, or correct, is that it coincides with an actual state of affairs. In declaring something true (assuming I am not lying, and assuming this thing has been recognized as such), I am also establishing its certainty. We say of something that it is 'certainly' true. Certainty is also a measure of truth. In pursuing the truth about, say, nature, or history, or a crime, we want to be certain that what we are saying actually *is* the case, that it *is* so, beyond any (in some cases 'reasonable') doubt. Truth, then, refers to what *is*, to what really is or was the case (and not, for example, to what is merely possible, or what may have been the case). If we look back at what we've said so far, we have to acknowledge that what we ordinarily call truth involves a correspondence between a statement, or an assertion, and a state of affairs. It also involves definite criteria, such as certainty and verifiability.

There are, however, other ways in which something can be said to be true. Of a painting, for example, we say that it is 'truly' beautiful, and of our closest friends – those who know of, but do not pass judgement on, our less noble thoughts and actions – that they are 'true' friends. Of world-class football players, we say that they are 'true' athletes, of this bracelet that it is 'true' gold and of this seemingly taciturn and self-effaced character, that he revealed his 'true' self in adversity. In all such instances, we want to emphasize the fact that our friends do not simply *appear* to be our friends, but really *are* our friends, that the bracelet does not only *seem* to be made of gold, but actually is, that this person we knew *appeared* to be one way, but *really* was different. Here, 'truth' is opposed to mere appearance or 'semblance', and defines something in its 'genuine' state. But even here, it appears that what we characterize as 'true' – say, gold – involves some pre-established, universal idea of what gold is (precisely what Plato called an Idea), something with which this particular bracelet is in accordance, or to which its existence corresponds. The 'truth' of the gold bracelet, or of the friend, lies in its accordance with the idea, or the essence of gold or friendship. Appearances can be deceiving, as we know, and this is something that philosophy has always been keen to show (the distinction between being and appearing is a crucial, and founding, philosophical distinction). In many ways, Plato was obsessed with the possibility of identifying the philosophical tools by which to distinguish between the truly brave, or the truly just, or the truly wise man, and the one who only appears to be brave, just or wise. Most of all, he wanted to find out how he could distinguish between the truly wise man (the philosopher) and the impostor (the sophist), who pretends to be something that he is not. The figure of the impostor, the fraud, the forgerer or the charlatan, is an endlessly fascinating one, and one that has fuelled countless works of fiction.[1] For Plato, the possibility of such a distinction was a matter of the utmost importance. It was perhaps *the* decisive issue, and one that had immediate political consequences: it actually cost Socrates his life. We are still looking for such criteria, desperately, as the world of politics, art, science and philosophy is still – and always will be – populated with people who pretend to be what they are not. We are still trying to establish the criteria by which to distinguish between the 'real thing', the 'genuine item', and the semblance, or the fake, and to protect this distinction (in theory *and* in practice, in philosophy, art, science, law and politics). Descartes was equally obsessed with this question, and did much to secure the sense of truth as certainty. It is precisely this quest for an absolutely certain and indubitable truth that led him to doubt the existence of everything, including his own body, in what amounts to one of the most extraordinary episodes in the history of philosophy (if not the strangest of them all). Yet it is on the basis of such a truth, discovered in the *cogito*, that Descartes was able to secure metaphysics as the 'roots of knowledge', or as 'first philosophy', and establish the legitimacy of the natural science.

All the senses in which we hold things to be true, then, seem to involve a degree of accordance, or correspondence: between a statement and a state of affairs, between a particular and a universal or between an actual thing and its ideal content. Is this where our investigation ends, then, namely, in the recognition that truth consists of an operation of correspondence? Or should we ask about the condition of possibility of such an operation, about what — if anything — holds together the correspondence between an assertion and a state of affairs, and between a thing and its essence?

2. The traditional concept of truth

From Parmenides to Russell and Wittgenstein, from Plato to Descartes, Kant and Hegel, philosophy has always wondered about truth. It has always sought to discover the nature of truth and establish the criteria by which it can be distinguished from what is not or only seemingly true. In many ways, philosophy can be seen as concerned with truth first and foremost. Even Nietzsche, the greatest critic of the value we attribute to truth, recognizes truth as the distinctive terrain of philosophy, as the question it cannot do without. He calls it the 'will to truth'. And closer to us, Heidegger is perhaps the philosopher whose thought is most closely associated with a radical rethinking of the question of truth. Is Heidegger's thought in line with that of the tradition that precedes it, or does it mark a departure from it, and so also a new point of departure for philosophy?

Despite the extraordinary diversity of approaches in the history of philosophy, it would seem that philosophy has always been concerned to thematize and encompass the double aspect of the correspondence I was just referring to. The traditional definition of truth, which runs through much of its history, reads as follows: *veritas est adaequatio rei et intellectus*. Now, Heidegger claims in a text from 1930 entitled 'On the Essence of Truth', this can be taken to mean: truth is the correspondence of the matter to knowledge. Yet there is some ambiguity as to how to interpret this definition, and the history of philosophy has interpreted it in ways that are incompatible and mutually exclusive. Initially, and most often, the definition is taken to mean: *veritas est adaequatio intellectus ad rem*, or truth is the correspondence of intellect (or knowledge) to thing (or the matter). Yet truth so conceived, what's known as *propositional* truth, insofar as the site of this truth is the proposition or the assertion, is possible only on the basis of another kind of truth, namely, *material* truth. This truth, also understood in terms of correspondence, is captured in the formula *veritas est adaequatio rei ad intellectum* (truth is the adequation of thing to intellect). In other words, for an assertion or a proposition to be true, there has to be some natural affinity, some adequation, between thing and intellect. Somehow, it must be possible for the matter to be revealed and expressed in a proposition.

These are the two dominant interpretations of what could be called the correspondence theory of truth, one that, Heidegger believes, is still operative, and very much unquestioned today. Yet they are not interchangeable. Nor are they simply reversible. In fact, they correspond to two different conceptions of the way in which knowledge, and the universe as a whole, function. They reflect two different interpretations of what counts as a 'thing' or

a 'matter', and what counts as 'knowledge'. The conception of truth as adequation of thing and intellect can be traced back to the Middle Ages, and
expresses a Christian belief, and so a Christian world-view. It does not mean,
as Kant argued, and so many after him took for granted, that 'objects conform
to our knowledge *a priori*'. Rather, it implies the Christian belief that all
things in the world are created by God, and created after an idea first formulated in the divine intellect. Created things are 'true' to the extent that they
correspond to an idea generated in the mind of God. Insofar as God created
human beings in his image, their intellect can itself produce (or reproduce)
the ideas of those things created that correspond to an idea in the mind of
God. In other words, truth as adequation of (created) things to the (divine)
intellect guarantees truth as adequation of the (human) intellect to the
(created) thing.

With the collapse of the Christian, or at least the creationist, standpoint on
the universe, best exemplified in Kant's thought, the correspondence theory of
truth is given a new interpretation. Yet it is not called into question. The two
levels of truth, and of correspondence, are maintained. The theologically conceived order of creation gives way to a conception of material truth as the
accord of something with the 'rational' concept of its essence. The divine order
has been replaced by the rational order, and it is believed that the truth of the
world lies in its rationality, or its concept. As a result, the propositional level
is reasserted even more strongly: a 'true' or 'correct' statement is a statement
the content of which corresponds to the concept of a thing. An untrue, or
incorrect, proposition signifies the non-accordance of the statement with the
matter. Likewise, the untruth of the matter (in the sense of non-genuineness)
signifies the lack of agreement of a being with its essence. In each case untruth
is considered as non-accord. Untruth is the opposite of truth, and so is simply
outside the essence of truth (the reason why I say this, which seems so obvious
to us all, will soon become apparent).

Through this brief incursion into the philosophical, technical interpretations of truth, it would seem that the various, pre-philosophical senses of truth
I began by invoking, and with which we seem to operate on a daily basis, are
justified and given a theoretical basis. All the examples I began by giving
would seem to fall into one of two conceptions of truth, whether material or
propositional. Yet both presuppose a sense of truth as correspondence, or correctness. Our investigation seems to be at an end. The question Heidegger
wishes to ask, however, is whether correspondence and correctness are indeed
the last word on this question, or whether they themselves presuppose yet
another level, or possibly several levels of truth. But what would those be?
What exactly remains to be explored in the question of truth? Is there an *essence*
of truth that remains concealed in the interpretation that we all seem to be
taking for granted?

THE ESSENCE OF TRUTH

1. Essence as possibility and ground

In a famous lecture on truth delivered on a number of occasions in 1930, and subsequently revised, Heidegger begins by asking about the *inner possibility* of accordance, about what makes it possible as such.[2] His investigation into the essence of truth takes the form of an investigation into the possibility of accordance. Let's look a bit closer at what sort of thing the correspondence is, beginning with the notion of a statement. A statement, Heidegger argues, is a specific type of relation, a way of comporting oneself to something. Let us return to the example of the bracelet. When I say: 'this bracelet is made of gold', I am relating to the bracelet in a way that is quite different from when I say: 'this bracelet is beautiful', and differently, too, from when I am wondering about its cost. These are all ways in which the bracelet can be talked about, related to and presented. Where does the specificity of the truth statement lie? In the fact that it *represents* the bracelet. It is a particular way of presenting the bracelet, a specific way in which the bracelet is brought to light. In the truth statement, I am envisaging the bracelet from a certain perspective. I allow it to stand in a certain way, namely, with respect to its essence. I allow it to stand as an ob-ject, or, in Heidegger's own vocabulary, as something that is objectively present (*vorhandene*). There are other ways in which I could choose to let it stand, other ways in which the bracelet could become manifest: as an object of aesthetic appreciation, for example, or, if it is a gift, as a gesture of love. This means that my relation to the object involves a whole situation, a whole 'region', from within which it comes to stand in this or that way. To relate to something propositionally, and with a view to revealing its truth, is certainly one possibility that is open to us, but not the only one. Should we not begin by admitting that the correspondence theory of truth, whether material or ideal, does indeed presuppose something, namely, a specific kind of comportment to the matter at hand, and so a specific orientation towards the world? Should we not also admit that, were it not for the worldliness of this comportment, or for the fact that every comportment is a comportment towards an aspect of the world, there would be no possibility of any truth? And should we not, finally, agree on the fact that the phenomenon of 'world' is itself in need of clarification?

The question, however, is one of knowing whether this (more primordial) phenomenon that we call the world has anything to do with truth itself, with its essence, or whether it is simply the layer of reality that sustains truth, but that is distinct from it. In other words, do the modes of comportment other than truth understood as correctness also involve a certain operation of truth? And the further question consists in asking whether this 'other' operation of truth might itself be local, or whether it can be shown to operate at all levels of human behaviour. But if that is the case, should we not conclude that our very being, understood in terms of existence, is itself 'true' — not of course, in the sense that it would correspond to some concept of who we are (present, perhaps, in the mind of God), but in the sense that it would designate the open region itself, from which things emerge, stand within presence, in short, present themselves? Does the world of phenomena – the world as such and as a whole – not presuppose truth as the opening up or the clearing in which they take place and find their proper place?

These questions bring us to the threshold of yet another, more fundamental sense of essence, namely, 'ground'. Having identified the possibility of accordance, and so of correspondence, in human comportment, we need to ask further about this comportment. How can we characterize it? But haven't we already begun to provide an answer to this question in the previous chapter? To ask about the essence of truth as comportment, isn't this tantamount to asking about the essence of man? But we have already seen that the essence of man is existence (or, as Heidegger begins to write it in the 1930s, to distinguish human existence from the old *existentia*, ek-sistence). The connection that does need to be addressed, however, is that between ek-sistence and truth. It is to precisely this connection we now need to turn. Ultimately, we shall have to see how, despite the remarkable achievement this connection represents, it does not suffice to address the question regarding the essence of truth. We shall have to see, then, how it is the question of truth itself that forces Heidegger to take his philosophy beyond the standpoint of life, or existence, and so further away from anthropology.

2. Truth and ek-sistence

In discussing Heidegger's interpretation of the classical conception of truth, we referred to the medieval and modern traditions, and to the Latin concept of *veritas* in particular. *Veritas* is a translation of the Greek *aletheia*. Yet this translation is more than just the displacement of a word from one idiom to the next. It marks a historical turning point in the way in which truth is understood. Let me be as clear as possible on this point. Heidegger is not arguing that a so-called 'Greek' conception of truth, gathered as it were in the word *aletheia*, collapsed simply as a result of its translation into Latin. This collapse, or, better said perhaps, this transformation, was already well underway, if not entirely carried out, in Ancient Greece itself. Yet the important thing to bear in mind is how the word itself retains something of a conception, at least an experience of truth that must have dominated at some stage. This is the experience that, according to Heidegger, still orients the Platonic and Aristotelian texts, albeit only obliquely. In reading Aristotle on truth in his early work, Heidegger performs something like a rescue operation, as he tries to recover a sense of truth already under threat at the time, and certainly buried by the time of Aquinas, Descartes and Kant. This operation is not, however, a merely historical rescue. For the sense of truth that the world *aletheia* retains, and the clue for which we can find in Aristotle, concerns each and every one of us today. Why? First, because it calls into question our ordinary conception of truth, and, second, because it identifies most clearly and most precisely who we are, because it describes the human Dasein in its very being. Through his interpretation of Aristotle, Heidegger is able to understand the being of the human being *in terms of* truth. Specifically, he is able to understand the openness of existence itself, the fact that existence is outside itself and towards the world, in terms of truth.

What Aristotle reveals, especially in Book VI of the *Nicomachean Ethics* (VI, 1139b15–18), is the extent to which the human *psyche*, or, as Heidegger translates it, the human Dasein, is essentially an operation of *aletheuein*. This is a verb we could translate as 'truthing', if it existed in English. In English, we 'tell' or 'speak' the truth. But, as we shall see, *aletheuein* is not restricted to speech, or language, alone. We also speak of 'discovering' or 'uncovering' the truth, as if it had the ability to hide, or as if it was often somehow covered over. This brings us closer to the meaning of the verb *aletheuein*, which involves precisely something like an uncovering, an unveiling or a disclosing. In fact, Heidegger will go as far as to claim that uncovering, or unveiling, is the fundamental and original meaning of truth.

As we've already seen, it's traditionally been thought that truth, for Aristotle – and for the whole of philosophy after him – is a matter of judgement. Specifically, it is generally assumed that it consists of an adequation between thought and its object, an adequation that is expressed in what's now known as a proposition. What we call a proposition is what Aristotle called *logos apophantikos*, that is, a statement 'that contains truth [*alethes*] or falsity [*pseudes*] in it'.[3] Consequently, it is assumed that the question of truth is a matter for the discipline that, ever since Aristotle, has been known as 'logic'. Heidegger takes issue with this assumption, and argues that, in a way, our speech, and our propositions, presuppose the primordial sense of truth as *a-letheia*, or dis-closedness. In his first course on logic and truth from 1925–6, he defines *apo-phainesthai* quite literally as 'letting a being be seen on its own terms', and equates it with *a-letheuein*, uncovering, unveiling or removing (a being) from concealment.[4] All of this to say that if Aristotle does indeed formalize what we could call the classical, metaphysical conception of truth by establishing the nature of the link between truth and language; if, in other words, he is indeed the founder of 'logic', he does so on the basis of a sense of truth that is itself 'pre'-metaphysical. This is a sense that he intimates, but that the tradition after him – especially the Neo-thomistic one – will be quick to forget. This forgetfulness was to have decisive consequences, as it drove philosophy away from what Heidegger takes to be its ownmost object, away from what is questionable and question-worthy in the most literal sense, and into logical positivism.

Let us now turn to this primordial and threatened sense of truth that we find in Aristotle. For something to be said to be true (or false) in the now classical sense of the term, it must *be there* (*da-sein*) in a certain way to begin with. In other words, it must be present, manifest, in the first place – even if it is to be declared false or fake. In the most fundamental sense, something is 'true' (*alethes*) or 'false' (*pseudes*) to the extent that it is first made manifest, brought into presence – in a word: uncovered. Only as something that 'is there as unconcealed [*als un-verborgene da-sein*]' can it be said to be true (or false).

Now this preliminary and primordial modality of truth is remarkable in that is not a function of the human *logos*, or at least not exclusively, and not primarily. The most primordial level of truth, Heidegger argues, is not the proposition (*logos apophantikos*). 'Logic' is the not the ultimate and decisive level at which the questions of truth (*aletheuein*) and falsity (*pseudesthai*) are to be debated. Of what is truth a matter, then? Where is its fundamental level revealed? Following Aristotle, Heidegger claims that it is the human *psyche* that is the key to the question of truth. Why? Because the human *psyche*, of which the *logos* is only one aspect, consists itself of an operation or process of uncovering, through which beings are brought into presence. Does this mean that truth is a matter for psychologists? Not at all, insofar as the human *psyche*, or its Heideggerian equivalent, namely *Dasein* or existence, is nothing like a consciousness (*Bewusstsein*), or a power of reprentation. The human *psyche* is precisely defined in terms of its ability to wrest beings from concealment and bring them into the open, into unconcealment. Aristotle does not claim that the human *psyche* is primarily a matter of producing representations articulated in *logos* or language understood as true or false propositions; he doesn't claim that understanding the way it operates is a matter for psychology and logic in the modern sense. Rather, he claims that the human being or soul (*psyche*) is itself and in its entirety an operation of *aletheuein*, an activity of uncovering or unconcealing. *Aletheuein*, Heidegger writes in 1922, 'does not mean "possessing the truth" [*sich der Wahrheit bemächtigen*] but rather taking the beings meant [*vermeinte*] in each case and as such into safekeeping [*in Verwahrung nehmen*] as unveiled [*als unverhülltes*]'.[5] But what does it mean to safe keep or shelter phenomena? How does such safekeeping occur?

The passage I have just cited is actually a translation of a passage from Aristotle's *Nicomachean Ethics* (Z 3, 1139b15–18). In it, Aristotle mentions the various ways in which the soul brings and takes beings into true safekeeping. Significantly, each way is accompanied by discourse or speech; each mode of truth involves *logos*, either by way of affirmation (*apophansis*) or denial (*kataphansis*). Language is implicated in all modes of revealing, yet it is not itself one such mode. This means that language is not the primary locus of truth. Why? Because language is always about something, about something that is itself uncovered in ways other than through language.[6] And if language is 'true', it is precisely in the sense that Heidegger appeals to when wanting to define the *logos* of phenomenology. If such a discourse is 'true', it is only to the extent that it allows phenomena to speak from themselves, and so from their own situation, their own horizon of truth. It is 'true' only to the extent that it effaces itself before the things themselves, allowing them to present themselves *as* they themselves are. The *logos* of phenomenology is the discourse that allows things to manifest themselves in speech as this or that, as having this 'as-what' character. This means that the truth of the *logos* is itself entirely dependent upon – and in the service of – the truth of the phenomena it articulates. It is entirely subordinated to phenomena in the *how* of their being-unveiled. It is the task of philosophical discourse to identify the ways in which beings are 'true' in this sense, that is, originally disclosed and experienced.

Now it isn't necessary to review these ways in detail. In a moment, I shall focus on just two of them, and show the importance they play in the overall economy of Heidegger's *magnum opus*. At this point, suffice it to say that it is only because truth is understood as a bringing out of concealment and into the Open, that Aristotle, and Heidegger after him, are able to characterize the human soul as an operation of truth. At the same time, it is only because the human soul is understood as ex-istence, or as a being outside oneself and oriented towards the world, at once open to it and opening it up, that it can coincide with the unconcealing of truth. It is by virtue of its own being, or by virtue of the fact that it ex-ists, that existence can be understood in terms of the originary *aletheuein*. To say that the operation of truth coincides with our very being, or with existence as such and as a whole, amounts to saying that it is not primarily a matter for this part of the soul – today, we would say this faculty – that we call thought, whether understood as scientific, epistemic thought (where truth is located primarily), or as pure, divine, intellectual intuition (*nous*). It is only one mode of truth, and a derivative one at that. Proximally and for the most part, Heidegger claims in *Being and Time*, truth is at work in our everyday, average mode of being.

At a most general level, the connection between ek-sistence and truth begins to unfold long before it is made explicit in § 44, 'Dasein, disclosedness and truth'. To the extent that, at least in the context of the analysis of Dasein, truth coincides with existence as such, it is even operative from the very start of the analysis. Yet it is perhaps in the sections devoted to Dasein's spatiality (§§ 22–4) that the connection becomes clear for the first time.[7] The first and most important thing to bear in mind is that the spatiality that is here in question is not that of objective, measurable space, but of existential, lived space. Heidegger goes as far as to say that the sense of space we now take for granted, that is, space as an objective given, which can be represented mathematically and measured universally, is actually rooted in the spatiality of Dasein and of the world as an existential–ontological phenomenon. Far from being a point inscribed within a pre-given, objective space, identified through a set of co-ordinates, human existence is itself its own space – a space that cannot be measured or represented geometrically, but that needs to be described ontologically and existentially. In those sections devoted to the spatiality of Dasein, Heidegger describes existence in terms of a certain ability to bring things close by from out of their originary distance and to orient itself in the world on the basis of its needs, necessities and possibilities. He designates these structural possibilities of existence as 'de-severance' (*Ent-fernung*) and 'directionality' (*Ausrichtung*) respectively. In comporting itself towards beings in the world in this manner, Dasein 'frees' beings or 'lets them be' for a totality of (mostly practical) involvements. It frees their own spatiality and their function, it opens up the context or the world from which they appear as such or such a thing: as a thing of use, or as a thing for contemplation, as familiar or unfamiliar, as threatening or reassuring, etc. In other words, it makes room for them, and provides them with their own, individual space. This means that Dasein is essentially space-giving (*Raum-gebend*), or room-making (*Einräumend*). As existence, it gives or clears a space, it opens up a world inhabited by things, it discloses beings in their being. The 'Da' of Da-sein captures this originary spatiality, that is, this clearing or this disclosedness (*Erschlossenheit*) that, as we shall see later on, Heidegger ends up indentifying with existential, ecstatic time. This is what existence is and does: it opens up a world, it clears and reveals a space, it wrests beings from their originary concealment and brings them into the open. Mostly through practical use, existence abolishes the distance that separates it from beings, brings them close by, into the vicinity of its own concerns. For the most part and most often, the things that surround existence are 'ready-to-hand' (*zuhandene*), there to be used as 'equipment'. The phenomenon of disclosedness (*Erschlossenheit*), with which existence coincides, precisely as Da-sein, or as the 'there' of being, is the original phenomenon of truth, truth proper. Insofar as Dasein uncovers beings in the world, Dasein is true in the most primordial sense. The beings thus disclosed are themselves true, yet they always presuppose the more originary operation of truth that existence is: 'only with Dasein's disclosedness is the most primordial phenomenon of truth attained'.[8] And this is why Heidegger claims, somewhat provocatively, that '"there is" truth only insofar as Dasein is and so long as Dasein is'.[9] In the end, then, existence is said to have an intimate connection with truth to the extent that existence itself is the very operation of truth, the clearing or disclosing without which nothing could ever be said to be true, for it would never be encountered, present in any way. Only that which can be disclosed can be true. Only that which ex-ists or is there can disclose. Truth and being are equiprimordial insofar as being, for Heidegger, means the open region, in the openness of which things take place and find their place.

a. Practical truth

In the analysis of Dasein developed in Division One of *Being and Time*, the operation of truth is analysed in the way in which it occurs 'proximally and for the most part', that is, in everyday existence, in the most mundane and habitual activities of Dasein. Heidegger turns the question of truth, of being as disclosedness, into a matter of everyday comportment, wresting it from its privileged locus (the human logos) and its traditional definition (*adequatio rei et intellectus*). For Heidegger, the question of truth is no longer *primarily* a matter of propositions, or judgement. It is primarily a matter of and for everyday practical existence. Nowhere is this more visible than in those sections of *Being and Time* devoted to the analysis of the everyday world of Dasein.[10] What do we find there?

Unlike the concept of 'nature', which is a representation – a metaphysical construction, or an abstraction – and thus only a secondary and derivative phenomenon, the concept of 'world', and the definition of 'man' as being-in-the-world, aims to capture the essence of what it means to be human. It is an originary phenomenon, the human in its primordial phenomenality, or in its being. As such, it is more concrete, 'truer' than any metaphysical 'definition' of man, which always presupposes the being-in-the-world of Dasein, and yet fails to grasp it as a positive phenomenon. The primary task of the analysis of Dasein is thus to bring the human back to its originary and concrete soil, back to existence, from out of the metaphysical constructions that have been grafted onto it: 'rational animal', 'being created in God's image' or whatever.

Accordingly, the task of the analysis of Dasein is to show how, at the most concrete, mundane, seemingly inconspicuous level, a certain operation of truth is already at play. It is to show the extent to which everyday practical existence is itself a happening of truth, an *aletheuein* in the sense developed by Aristotle. It is to demonstrate that man 'understands' his own being, to reveal what it 'means' to be prior to any conceptualization or any representation of this being, at the pre-theoretical level of everyday existence. This first level Heidegger thus characterizes as 'everydayness'. The world it discloses is an *Umwelt*, an environment, or a world that is not so much opposite as it is all around. It is this world to which there corresponds a peculiar kind of seeing, a seeing that Heidegger defines as an *Umsicht*: the concerned, absorbed, practical gaze that characterizes our everyday dealings with the world, the circumspect gaze that is on the look out for things. But the truth is that this gaze, this peculiar mode of envisaging the world as the world that's not there before me in the mode of an object, or of nature, in other words as a reality that is simply present, awaiting to be represented, but as this world that's all around me, surrounding me, and in which I am concretely situated, always 'in position', this gaze, then, is immediately translated and actualized as *handling*: our everyday relation to the world, our way of being in the world 'proximally and for the most' is 'handy'. Thus, the gaze that is at stake here is not that of the spectator or the observer, the gaze that holds things at a distance. It is precisely the gaze by which distance is abolished, and things are brought into nearness:

> If we envisage things simply by way of a 'theoretical' look, we fail to understand them as readiness-to-hand. But when we deal with them by using them and manipulating them, this activity is not a blind one; it has its own kind of sight, by which our manipulation is guided and from which it acquires its specific thingly character.[11]

Thus, to the 'practical' there corresponds a specific kind of seeing (*Umsicht*, or circumspection) which is quite distinct from the purely contemplative kind (traditionally referred to as 'theory'), much in the same way that 'theory' itself is not simply devoid of a specific mode of concern. If my hands are the primary instruments of this everyday relation to the world, they are at the same time the very extension of my 'concerned' or practical gaze, of this gaze that envisages things with a *view* to accomplishing this or that practical task. The gaze that I throw onto the world and that guides me through it is first and fore-most a practical gaze, the kind of seeing that results from my living in a world of practical necessities. It is the gaze that orients my body according to the many needs and obstacles that it encounters, and which converge in my hands as in the tip of my being. Thus, my primary relation to the world is one of *Handeln*, of action in the sense of handling, and the things which I encounter within the world are, for the most part and primarily, things-to-be-handled, *manipulata*, *pragmata*, in short, things of use (*Zeuge*). These 'things' are not 'objects for knowing the world "theoretically"; they are simply what gets used, what gets produced, and so forth'.[12] Thus, man is first and foremost *manipulans* and *faber*, and the hands of Dasein are the instrument of this specific kind of *aletheuein*, which Aristotle designated as *techne* and which Heidegger translates back into the vocabulary of onto-phenomenology as 'know-how' (*Sich-Auskennen*),[13] or as finding one's way in the realm of practical concern and preoccupations (*Besorgen*), of manipulation (*Hantieren*) and of production (*Herstellen*). In each case, the hands of Dasein disclose a world, reveal some-thing about the concrete situation of Dasein; they are coextensive with the practical operation of truth in which Dasein is involved.

At the most basic level, then, existence is an operation of disclosure or clear-ing through which something ready-to-hand is freed for its use and function; in the realm of the practical, we let something ready-to-hand be so and so as it is already and in order that it be such. The operation of truth is a letting-be: a letting something be *for* what it is, the un-covering of something in its readiness-to-hand within the world of practical concern. And coextensive with this discovering is the 'understanding' of the world on the part of Dasein. Dasein's relation to the world, as this practical, primarily 'handy' disclosure of things within the world, reveals a world of 'meaning', where meaning is not to be understood primarily in terms of an operation of signification that takes place at the level of a faculty of understanding or reasoning. We do not inject meaning into the world 'intellectually' and *a posteriori*; rather, the world itself is meaningful by virtue of its very practicality, the chair is 'meaningful' by virtue of the fact that I need to sit down and can actually sit on it. And if, for some reason, I cannot sit, if sitting is a possibility I am deprived of, the chair remains meaningful, it remains 'present', albeit only negatively. I 'understand' the chair not by way of representation but by way of sitting; the chair that I understand properly, or primordially, is this chair on which I am sitting, or on which I would like to sit. In this situation, it is not the I of the *cogito* that understands, but the I of practical concern. My body is the vehicle of my concern, and the manner in which my practical relation to the world is carried out. It is the instrument of my freedom, the material basis of my power – not of my might (*Macht*) over the world, but of my ability to navigate it and find my way through it, my ability-to-be (*Seinkönnen*). And if Dasein is indeed a power, a *potentialitas*, it is first and foremost as this ontological power, as this power of truth understood as disclosure. The intelligibility of the world is pri-marily a function of our ability not to represent it but to *be* it, that is, to

comport ourselves towards it practically. Of course, I can still comport myself
to the chair theoretically and raise questions such as: 'What is a chair?', 'What
is it for?', 'Of what is it made?', etc. These are abstract questions, however,
questions that carry the world onto a different plane, the plane of representation, on which the chair, from its original status as a practical thing (a
Zuhandene) is being turned, or modified, into an object of questioning (into a
Vorhandene). But the point is that the primordial and meaningfully originary
relation or comportment to the chair is the one where the chair appears as
'that-on-which-I-can-sit' or, more precisely still, as 'that-on-which-I-want-to-
sit'. This is the level at which meaning first emerges. If meaning as such cannot
be dissociated from a general structure of signification, such a structure does
not refer so much to a capacity for abstraction and formalization as to existence
itself, to the very existing of existence. Dasein, and this means the assemblage
Dasein-world, is itself a structured totality of signs, or references. It is something like a proto-language, to which language as we normally understand it
remains subordinated. What the analysis of Dasein reveals, at its most concrete and mundane level, is a world of interconnected significations, and a
horizon of understanding, in which a faculty of representation plays absolutely
no part.

This, then, is what Heidegger means when he says that Dasein 'understands' its world: it does not understand it in the way it understands a mathematical problem, that is, abstractly, but precisely to the extent that it has a
world, or rather, that it *is* that world. It is only when we sever man from the
world to which he necessarily belongs and wrest him from the soil in which
he grows that the question concerning the world can take on abstract and irrelevant forms, such as when we inquire into the existence of the world, and adopt
the sceptical standpoint. It is only when he is cut off from his essence, and
turned into an abstraction, that man begins to pose the question of understanding and of signification, of truth and of presence, in epistemological and
metaphysical terms. This was clear to Heidegger as early as 1919:

When the sense of existence is investigated in terms of its origin and our
genuine basic experience of it, we see that it is precisely *that* sense of
being that cannot be obtained from the 'is' we use to explicate and objectify our experience in one way or another when we acquire knowledge
about it. The sense of human existence is to be obtained rather from its
own basic experience of having [later on, and specifically in *Being and
Time*, Heidegger will say: understanding] itself in a *concerned* manner.
This having [or understanding] is enacted prior to whatever knowledge
about it we might later acquire by objectifying it with the 'is,' and such
knowledge is in fact inconsequential for this enactment. If I seek this
objectifying knowledge, the attitude of observation will become central
for me. All my explications will then have an objectifying nature, *but they
will put me at a remove from existence and from a genuine having* [or under-
standing] *of it* (concern).[14]

The attitude that, following the vocabulary of Husserlian phenomenology, Heidegger calls 'scientific', 'metaphysical' or 'natural' becomes possible only when the sense of existence is severed from the basic experience (*Grunderfahrung*) within which it is rooted. This severing amounts to an essential *modification* of the originary phenomenon (existence). As a result, the investigation into the meaning of our being remains abstract. Following Husserl's footsteps, the task of thinking for Heidegger will have consisted in an attempt to bring philosophy back to its concrete soil, to make philosophy concrete again. And because philosophy was to be returned to the concreteness of the question concerning the sense or the origin of our being, it itself came to be viewed as the most concrete, and indeed vital of all activities.

b. Ethical truth

Having revealed everyday, practical existence as the basic operation of truth, Heidegger wonders whether it is the most complete form of truth. Does everyday existence constitute the ultimate mode in which Dasein is disclosed to its own being? To be sure, existence is disclosed in everydayness. But is it disclosed to its own disclosedness, or does it remain somewhat closed to it and closed off from itself? Is there a part of itself that is not disclosed to Dasein in its everyday disclosing of the world? If so, can Dasein *be* in such a way that it becomes transparent to itself *as* disclosedness? These are questions that have already surfaced in the previous chapter, especially in connection with the phenomenon of anxiety. The time has now come to address them properly.

Ultimately, they will find their solution in a distinct comportment of Dasein that Heidegger calls '*resolute* disclosedness' (*Entschlossenheit*). This term, and the comportment it designates, is actually Heidegger's existential–ontological 'translation' of the concept of 'prudence' (*phronesis*), through which Aristotle describes the specificity of the moral action (as opposed to, say, technical production, or theoretical knowledge). For Heidegger, it designates the phenomenon in which Dasein becomes transparent to itself through a repetition of itself, and can also be seen to coincide with the realm of genuine praxis. But Heidegger's entire struggle with respect to the sphere of praxis consists in wresting it from its moral, modern and specifically Kantian interpretation, in order to return it to 'ethics', in the originary sense of the term, that is, to an activity or a comportment in which what it means to be human becomes the sole concern and object of the activity itself.[15] In such an activity, the disclosedness or truth-character of Dasein is revealed *as such*, and thus elevated to another power. In *Entschlossenheit*, nothing 'more' is added or revealed. It is only a matter of letting Dasein's own power of disclosedness bear on itself *as* disclosedness. It is, therefore, a matter of repeating what is already the case, but in such a way that the 'thing' in question (Dasein) now becomes transparent to itself. With the phenomenon of resolute disclosedness, truth circles back on itself; the existence of truth coincides with the truth of existence.[16]

It cannot be a question, therefore, of claiming that resolute disclosedness is more or less practical than the mode of truth we began by analysing; it is practical not in the pragmatic sense of *techne*, but in the ethical sense of *praxis*. It deals not with things of use, but with existence as such and as a whole. It is concerned not with any specific thing or matter to be resolved, but with itself, and with the possibility of living according to its own essence. It is concerned with the good and happy life.

DEATH

We have already seen how Dasein is essentially defined as this capacity to be (its own being), that is, as a power of being: Dasein *can* be, and this *Können* is what distinguishes it from other beings. Dasein, we said, always needs to be its own being. In other words, Dasein can be said not simply to be, in the way in which a thing is, but to ex-ist; to ex-ist means precisely that: to be in the mode of power, of potentiality, of possibility. Dasein is essentially a pro-ject (*Entwurf*), always throwing itself ahead of itself. As long as it is, Heidegger emphasizes, 'right to its end', it comports itself towards its *Seinkönnen*, that is, towards itself as this ability to be its own being, or to ek-sist. This means that the being of Dasein is one of possibility, and not (at least not primarily) one of actuality. Dasein *is* in such a way that, for it, there is always something to come, something outstanding. It is *essentially* incomplete, *essentially* open.[17] Yet the way in which, for Dasein, there is something outstanding differs from the way in which something belonging to a being is still missing, in the way in which, for example, the debt that is still outstanding is eventually liqui- dated, or the unripe fruit eventually ripens. In this case, what is outstanding is waiting to be 'realized'. In other words, it will eventually become actual, and this actualization signifies its fulfilment. Not so with the excess or the debt that characterizes Dasein, distinct in that it is always and irreducibly out- standing: 'The "not-yet" which belongs to Dasein, however, is not just some- thing which is provisionally and occasionally inaccessible to one's own experience or even to that of a stranger; it "is" not yet "actual" *at all*'.[18]

At the same time, however, Heidegger insists that Dasein *is* its not-yet, that is, relates to it, not as something that it will eventually be, but as something *towards* which it is turned, always and from the very start. In other words, Dasein unfolds or deploys its being on the basis of a possibility in excess of actuality, in excess of the traditional inscription of the category of possibility within the logic of potentiality and actuality. As Heidegger himself puts it: 'Higher than actuality stands possibility'.[19] This possibility that is irreducibly possible, and yet the reality of which is felt at every moment; this possibility that, whilst purely virtual, nonetheless presides over the very being of Dasein, and so over the disclosedness of the world as such and as a whole, Heidegger calls *death*. Insofar as it is, Dasein is (or exists) towards its own death. This means that, as being towards its death, Dasein *is* indeed its death, yet in such a way that it never coincides with it. For the death of Dasein is always and irre- ducibly 'to come', always 'in the future' (*zu-künftig*). But if Dasein is indeed this most extreme possibility, if it is always and from the start oriented towards its own death, if it relates to itself as this possibility that is always to come, then it is itself futural, first and foremost: it is always coming towards itself, always anticipating itself. It ek-sists as projecting itself against this ultimate horizon. It *is* in the mode of the future.[20] In the following chapter, we shall have to draw out the conclusions of this claim. At this point, let me simply emphasize the connection between death, as a distinct possibility, and time, as the meaning of this possibility. Let me simply emphasize the paradox of our being, which is primarily and primordially *in* the future, and *of* it.

Death is the future, the pure form of the future, for it is a future that will never be present. Death is the event that is always impending. This may sound like a grim and pessimistic message. It has nothing to do with pessimism, though. The death that is to come is not something other than myself, something that happens to me from the outside as it were; rather, it is the very happening of existence as such, the very limit from out of which existence unfolds as disclosedness, the very horizon, therefore, from out of which the world 'worlds'. To grasp existence as this unfolding that happens from ahead, or from death itself, is to grasp the phenomenon of the world *as such and as a whole*, and not just innerworldy things. (We shall see shortly how this grasping takes place for Heidegger.) Death is not just a peripheral event, therefore, an accident, something external that befalls Dasein; rather, death, as the end *towards* which existence ex-ists, is at once the very closure of existence (for it is 'the possibility of the impossibility of existence') and its very opening up, or beginning. It is the key to understanding the disclosedness of existence, and of the world. Insofar as it reveals a pure possibility, and thus the realm of the future as the originary form of time in excess of what is merely present, death also bears witness to the ontological characterization of existence as *Seinkönnen*, that is, as this being whose being is primarily a power, or a pure virtuality. Paradoxically, then, Heidegger claims that man 'can' be being (transitively), that he *is* in the mode of the *can-be* or exists as a possibility, precisely and exclusively to the extent that he is mortal. It is the very finitude of time that is the condition of his power. Man's freedom, and the very possibility of what he calls his liberty, is a function of his own ontological structure, that is, of the fact that he *is* in the mode of possibility and potentiality. Man is the being who has the *power* to be. And this power – man's freedom – Heidegger claims, is born of his own finitude. Such is the paradox of death: without death, man would be powerless.

Yet death is the origin of my freedom only to the extent that it is mine, and irreducibly so. It cannot be passed on to anyone else, exchanged, negotiated or delayed. Because death is this possibility that is absolutely and irreducibly mine, because it is my ownmost possibility, it is the possibility in which ownness (*Eigentlichkeit*) itself is at issue: the 'authentic' existence or the 'genuine' life is entirely based on the appropriation of oneself as this being whose being consists in being towards its own end. 'Authenticity', for Heidegger, means nothing outside the possibility of appropriating what is most proper to oneself, of being or existing this possibility to the full. And resoluteness, as we shall see later on, is the phenomenon in which such a possibility is revealed. Death, then, is a power of singularization, a source of individuation. It is on the basis of death and as mortal that the 'I' becomes meaningful and possible, that 'I' make sense. If, in the context of *Being and Time*, a kind of subjectivity remains operative, it is on the basis of the thinking of death as this possibility that is ownmost. The 'I' does not precede death; rather, the 'I', as this singular 'I', emerges from out of the individuating power of death. As we suggested earlier, the Heideggerian subjectivity is not so much a subjectivity of the 'I think' as a subjectivity of the 'I can'; yet this 'can' has its source in the impending, ownmost and uttermost end towards which existing constantly throws itself.

ANTICIPATION

The question then becomes one of knowing just what sort of relation Dasein might establish with death thus understood. We must here distinguish the everyday and improper relation from the singular and proper relation that Dasein might establish with itself as with he/she who must die his/her own death, and from which the possibility of a singular self unfolds. Dasein *is* towards death. But Dasein can be this being-towards-death either properly, in which case Dasein exists or is in such a way that this possibility explicitly comes to bear on the existence of Dasein, or improperly, in which case death is operative only implicitly, and Dasein does not hold it into view. In other words, Dasein can be – and indeed, for the most part, is – so wrapped up in itself that it cannot see itself: its life amounts to a covering over of its own essence. This is the phenomenon *Being and Time* describes as 'fleeing' and 'falling', and one which I analysed in the previous chapter.[21] Alternatively, through what Aristotle called prudence, Dasein can learn to see itself genuinely, and become transparent to itself.[22] 'Prudence' or the mode of comportment in which existence is made transparent to itself as such, amounts to a twisting free from its average coveredness. Because Dasein is always in the world, it tends to be absorbed in this world that, by and large, is the world of its concern and preoccupations. So, far from constituting a direct, face-to-face relation with its own finitude, and with the operation of owning that follows from such an encounter, the average life of Dasein is a fleeing in the face of its ownmost being towards death into the familiar world of concern, the world in which existences are not envisaged as singularities but as interchangeable instances of a universal structure. I feel at home in that world, unaware of the fact that underlying this familiar relation to the world lurks the primordial uncanniness of the fact that there is a world as such and as a whole for Dasein, the primordial event of truth. This factical tendency to cover itself up testifies to the fact that, for the most part, Dasein is in *untruth*: its relation to truth, that is, to itself as this process of uncovering, is itself covered over in everyday existence.

Of course, this does not mean that death plays no role whatsoever in the average, 'fallen' life of Dasein. But there, death is precisely never mine. It is always the death of another. Not even that; it is death *in general*, or the death of anyone – which is to say no one. It is, in Heidegger's terminology, the anonymous death of the One (*das Man*): 'one dies', as if death were primarily this event that can be witnessed and verified empirically. Instead of embracing death as one's ownmost, as that which concerns me from the very start, instead of allowing one's mortality to come to the fore and to greet the anxiety which such welcoming provokes, average existence transforms 'this anxiety into fear of an oncoming event' and then proceeds to tranquillize itself by way of narratives, myths or simply by way of a prompt return to the life of concern.[23] Death, as the ownmost possibility towards which *I* am, is bypassed altogether.

But can Dasein understand its death properly ('authentically') as well as improperly ('inauthentically')? Can it develop a proper relation to that which is most proper, to its ownmost possibility and mode of being? 'Anticipation' (*Vorlaufen*) is the word that Heidegger uses in order to capture this genuine relation. In anticipating death, it is neither a matter of running ahead towards one's death, of actualizing it (for, as pure possibility, it can never be actualized); nor is it a matter of thinking about death, of 'brooding over it' or of developing a morbid relation to one's life in the expectancy of one's demise.[24] It has little to do, then, with a death drive, or with the demand to die the right death. In fact, I would like to suggest that it is quite the opposite: the holding in view of one's mortality amounts to an increase in one's life potential, in one's ability to open oneself to life, or to one's being as potentiality (*Seinkönnen*). To envisage oneself as mortal, to see oneself as this being whose being is essentially finite is to learn not to die, but to live; it amounts to an intensification of life. To allow death to come to bear on life itself is not conducive to a morbid or a sombre mood, it entails neither resignation nor passivity – in other words, it leads not to what Spinoza called a 'sad' passion but to one that is joyful and sober: 'Along with the sober anxiety which brings us face to face with our singularised ability-to-be, there goes an unshakeable joy in this possibility'.[25] Joy is not to be mistaken for the contentment which too often we identify with happiness; rather, it is the feeling linked to the increase and the 'acting out' of our ontological power (our *Seinkönnen*). To anticipate one's death, to envisage oneself as mortal is to live in the mode of anticipation, as this being which is itself only by being ahead of itself and which, in returning to itself from beyond itself, ek-sists being. Such is the privilege and the joy of being human: to be able to be (being): *Sein-können*. And if there is a single Heideggerian injunction it lies in the continuation of this *Können* into a *Sollen*: *Seinkönnen-sollen*, a having to be, or to act our own ability to be. Since one *can* be it, one *must* be it. This is tantamount to bringing it to another power. To persevere in one's being is to be in truth, or to be truth truly.

Death, then, is not the negation or the opposite of life, but the condition of its affirmation, the freeing of its potential. So, in anticipation, it is a question of comporting oneself to death as a possibility, and as a distinct possibility. And it is on the basis of the anticipation of this non-actualizable possibility that

Dasein as such has the general structure of anticipation, or of pro-jecting of itself into a realm of possibilities. These are possibilities that Dasein can actualize, projects in the ordinary sense of the term. By contrast, death is not a project, but the horizon from out of which it projects itself and frees possibilities for itself, frees itself as freedom for this or that possibility, this or that future. It is with 'anticipation' that Dasein reveals itself to itself fully, that is, becomes transparent to its own being as the fundamental and originary operation of truth whence things appear in truth, disclosed in this or that way.[26] What anticipation does, then, is to shift the focus from the result of the operation of truth – the disclosedness of things with the world – to the very operation of truth, that is, to the 'clearing' on the basis of which things are made manifest. Such is the reason why Heidegger insists that 'authenticity' is merely a 'modification' of Dasein's being: it does not amount to a change of Dasein's being, but to a different way of being this being, that is, no longer on the basis of its dilution or alienation within the anonymity of the One, but on the basis of itself as this absolutely singular disclosedness, as the happening of truth. In and through anticipation, then, Dasein is revealed to itself in truth, as truth. And so, in thus relating itself to its own self, in becoming itself through the ap-propriation of that which is most proper to it, that which constitutes it as Da-sein or as the being that 'is' or ek-sists being, existence exists more fully and transparently. By existing differently, that is, by existing explicitly the ground or the origin from out of which existence exists, man exists more intensely; for now it is exis-tence itself that is existed, it is the very disclosedness that characterizes exis-tence that becomes the explicit possibility of existence.

RESOLVE

The analyses of death and anticipation culminate in that of resolute disclosed-ness. This is the phenomenon that designates the operation through which existence decides itself for its own being, for itself as singular existence.[27] To be resolute, or disclosed resolutely, amounts to nothing other than a mode of being in which one is, or rather *I* am, necessarily and unavoidably, open to my own disclosedness: it amounts to living at the tip of existence, at its extrem-ity, where it gathers itself and 'is' truly, where its power is most visible and most penetrating. If Dasein, as being-in-the-world, designates man's relation to being, resoluteness, in turn, designates the operation through which one, or rather, *I* resolve myself to this relation to being which Dasein always and necessarily is. Resolute disclosedness is therefore a double relation: a relation to one's own relation to being. It is, Heidegger writes, *'only the possible authen-ticity of care itself, that is, the authenticity which, in care, and as care, is the object of care itself'*.[28] Heidegger calls it a 'repetition'. In this repetition, however, exis-tence repeats only its own disclosedness as existence, only this very disclosing that it *is*, and which Heidegger calls 'care'. Resoluteness is the highest degree of care as it were, the manner in which the unity of Dasein is best cared for, that is, lived *as* care.

In being resolved, existence liberates itself from its own entrapment in the absorbed life of everydayness. It frees itself for itself, as this ability to be (or disclose) being. It turns itself into an 'I' or a *proper* self. As such, being resolved amounts to 'liberating the humanity in man, to liberating the humanity of man, that is, the *essence* of man, *to letting the Dasein in him become essential'*.[29] With resoluteness, then, as the mode of disclosedness in which Dasein is presented to itself according to its essence, that is, as this power and freedom to be, we are also presented with the essence and the possibility of action. As resolute, Heidegger claims, Dasein is already *acting*.[30] And yet, he goes on to say, the term action is one we must avoid in this instance. Why? For two reasons. First, resolute disclosedness can be thought of as a certain kind of passivity, and not as a concrete action in the ordinary sense of the term. Second, the term 'action' suggests that the phenomenon under investigation is a special mode of comportment belonging to something like a practical faculty of Dasein, which would need to be distinguished from one that is theoretical. But the sort of *ontological* unity of existence that Heidegger has in mind, and which he calls 'care', precedes and cuts across any division of Dasein in various faculties. The unity of Dasein as care, which is revealed existentially and held in view as such in resolute disclosedness, cannot be dialectically reconstructed as a theory of faculties or even intimated on the basis of the classical distinction between theory and praxis. Thus, were it not that the very operation whereby existence as such, or care, becomes the very concern of care itself, simply takes place before any distinction can be made between the theoretical and the practical, between thought and action, resoluteness could indeed be seen as the movement that opens existence to itself as to the site or the place of its singularity, as to its *proper* place. Were it not for the classical opposition between theory and praxis, were it not for the way in which praxis and ethics are traditionally understood in opposition to thought, as action in opposition to contemplation, resoluteness could come to designate the origin of action proper and even to delimit the sphere of ethics itself. And so, despite Heidegger's warnings in *Being and Time*, but still keeping them in mind, let me reactivate the old, Aristotelian word of *phronesis* (prudence), which, in the years leading up to the publication of *Being and Time*, Heidegger pondered over time and again, in order to designate the mode of disclosedness in which Dasein comes face to face with itself as the site or the truth of being. At that moment, the *aletheuein* and the *aletheuon*, the disclosing and the disclosed coincide absolutely, in what amounts to a supreme degree of self-transparency of Dasein.

This 'ethical' dimension is also clearly marked out in a distinct possibility of Dasein that is immediately coextensive with the phenomenon of resolute disclosedness, namely, 'solicitude'. Far from designating a withdrawal into some pure interiority, in which *I* would no longer be concerned with others and with the world as such, resoluteness also designates the possibility of a proper or authentic relation to others, of a 'solicitude' that is genuine insofar as it is itself centred around the ownmost possibility of existence:

Resolute disclosedness, as *authentic being-one's-self*, does not detach Dasein from its world, nor does it isolate it so that it becomes a free-floating "I". And how should it, when resolute disclosedness as authentic disclosedness, is *authentically* nothing else than *being-in-the-world*? Resolute disclosedness brings the Self right into its current concernful being-alongside what is ready-to-hand, and pushes it into solicitous being with Others. . . . When Dasein is disclosed resolutely, it can become the "conscience" of Others. Only by authentically being-their-Selves in resolute disclosedness can people authentically be with one another – not by ambiguous and jealous stipulations and talkative fraternizing in the "One" and in what "One" wants to undertake.[31]

To the being-together of everyday existence, in which one forgets oneself as singularity and lives according to the mode of the empty majority, we thus need to oppose the community of singularities, the *being*-together of which would precisely be the meaning of existence as such, the community of mortal, factical existents. Returning from itself as this self that is the site of truth, as this self that discloses on the basis of a radical and inescapable finitude, Dasein turns back to the world and to others in a way that no longer resembles the kind of relation that prevails in the anonymity of our everyday dealings and relations. Man's relation to his fellow human beings is no longer one of practical, pragmatic preoccupation (*Besorgen*), but of solicitude (*Fürsorge*), in which the singularity and the ownmost possibilities of the Other are held in view and encouraged to be realized.[32]

THE TRUTH OF ESSENCE

1. Essence as unfolding

Following Heidegger's lead, we are inquiring into the essence of truth. So far, we've interpreted 'essence' as meaning possibility and ground. Thus understood, the essence of truth turned out to be existence. The possibility and the ground of the ordinary concept of truth – truth as correspondence – is the human Dasein, understood as disclosedness. Whilst itself 'true' in the most primordial sense, existence can be in untruth (in its fallen, preoccupied state) as well as in truth (in resolute disclosedness). The existence of truth, or the fact that truth is primarily a matter of existence, opens onto the question regarding the truth of existence, or the way in which existence becomes transparent to itself. In the course of the same lecture ('On the Essence of Truth') with which we began, however, Heidegger begins to understand essence differently. And what's quite remarkable is that, in transforming the sense of essence, Heidegger begins to alter radically and decisively the sense of truth itself and of its connection with being. Ultimately, it is this very shift of emphasis concerning the sense of essence that allows Heidegger to reintroduce what, quite naturally it seemed, we began by excluding from the

economy of truth itself, namely, untruth. By retrieving a suppressed and forgotten sense of essence, Heidegger is able to identify untruth as the real
essence of truth, without falling into contradiction. Now, this new sense of
essence is not arbitrary. For the German *Wesen* is not exactly the same as the
Latin *essentia*. It is a verb as well as a noun. As a verb, it means something like
to be (*sein*), to happen (*geschehen*), to linger (*sich aufhalten*), and comes from the
old High German *wesan*, to tarry, or sojourn (*verweilen*), to dwell, or inhabit
(*wohnen*), to stay (possibly overnight) (*übernachten*). It has the clear sense of
something that is ongoing, or unfolding, something that is taking its time,
something that is insisting. It also has the very important sense of dwelling.
This is the sense of *Wesen* Heidegger has in mind. But this, we recall, was
already the case with Dasein itself. The 'in' of Dasein's being-in-the-world,
Heidegger tells us in § 12 of *Being and Time*, must be understood from the old
High German *innan*, to dwell (the English 'inn' still has that meaning).
Dasein inhabits its world. It is at home in it. It is not in its world like a point
in a geometrical space. It unfolds (*west*) in its world. In that respect, the
German *Wesen* is closer to the Greek noun *ousia*, which also designates the
dwelling place, being in the durable, solid sense of the term (the Spanish
estancia, meaning the estate, and derived form the verb *estar*, to be, also captures this dimension). The question, now, is one of knowing whether there is
an essence (could we say an *esse*, or an *essencing*?), a mode of unfolding of truth,
other than existence. Does truth unfold, or in-sist, by way of ek-sistence only?
Or does it unfold also differently?

So far, we've been able to identify existence as the essence (in the sense of
ground) of truth, to the extent that it is characterized first and foremost as an
operation of disclosure, or clearing. This operation, or this way of being, we
recall, throws light on the Greek concept of *aletheia*. Yet we also recall how ek-
sistence always discloses the world from a particular perspective and in a
certain way. Ek-sistence is this light that lights up the world, yet the beings
that are so lit up are illuminated by the light of calculations, preoccupations,
needs, etc. As a result, the world is never revealed as such and as a whole (or
only in rare circumstances, such as in the dream I began by evoking). This
means that, in the very moment in which I am illuminating the world, or, to
be more precise, an aspect of it, I am also concealing the world itself, or my
own being-in-the-world. Whilst disclosing the world out of my ek-sistent,
ecstatic essence, I am also concealing my own essence as the existent being that
I am. It would seem, then, that, for the most part, my own being consists of a
double operation of clearing *and* concealing, of truth *and* untruth. It would
seem that truth and untruth are not simply opposed, and mutually exclusive,
as we thought initially. It would also seem, then, and in passing, that the old
and perennial ideal of truth as *total* transparency, or *absolute* openness, is, to say
the least, challenged. Why? Because every operation of disclosing, every
instance of truth, is *at the same time* an operation of concealing, or an instance
of un-truth. Concealment turns out to be 'the un-truth that is most proper to
the essence of truth'.[33]

Such is the reason why, in a further move, Heidegger calls untruth the 'non-essence' *(Un-Wesen)* of truth. Far from designating something like the negation of truth, or its denial, the 'non-' points in the direction of this hitherto unexplored reality at the heart of beings. The 'non-essence' is an attempt to think what's at issue in the 'un-' of un-truth in its relation to truth. As un-concealment, truth is not just the negation of concealment. For negation presupposes that what is negated is left behind – unless we think of negation dialectically, in which case it is something like a negating *and* a preserving, like a negating that preserves what is negated by taking it to a higher level. But this is not the way Heidegger understands the negative prefix of non-essence, or un-truth. First of all, and despite appearances, he thinks of it in entirely positive terms. The *non-* is not a negation, because it is a positive, and a primordial mode, of being. In fact, Heidegger argues, it is 'older' than truth itself. Truth takes place against the backdrop – one that is always there, yet always covered over, hardly ever visible as such – of un-truth. If Heidegger characterizes this essence of truth as a non-essence, it is really to emphasize the extent to which it is not an essence in the classical sense of the term, in the very sense that he has himself used up until now in the lecture, namely, as 'possibility', or 'ground'. If anything, un-truth, or originary concealment, is not a ground *(Grund)*, but an abyss *(Ab-grund)*. Why an abyss? Because it is forever receding, withdrawing. It is not a foundation, a possibility or even a condition of possibility, in the sense that philosophy, especially in its modern phase (from Descartes to Kant), has always wanted to secure. The ultimate essence, or the ultimate ground, if you will, turns out to be a non-essence. 'Essence' signals not only the condition of possibility of truth, but, paradoxically, its condition of impossibility as well, and simultaneously. What do I mean by that? The fact that, on one level, it is what makes truth possible: without this prior moment, this originary concealment, there would be no unconcealment, no presence whatsoever, and hence no world. At the same time, and on another level, this originary concealment is itself concealed as such in the world that is uncon-cealed. It withdraws from the very world it makes possible. In that respect, it is the im-possibility of the world, that which the world itself will never be. The world 'worlds' on the basis of a ground that is forever withdrawing. This means that the condition of possibility of truth is at the same time the condition of its impossibility: there never is, and never will be, 'pure', 'absolute' truth; presence is never full, total presence. It should be clear, then, why we need to understand the 'non-' of the non-essence of truth less in terms of negation, and more in the sense of a counter-movement that belongs to the very essence of truth. 'Movement' is perhaps the key word, here, as it evokes this other sense of essence I was referring to a moment ago, namely, unfolding, whiling or lingering. In fact, as a mode of essence, as a specific form of unfolding, or of being, untruth 'points to the still unexperienced domain of the truth of being' itself, and not merely of beings. This is a remarkable development, as it suggests that we have now arrived at a different 'meaning' of being. The meaning of being as time was hitherto located in the human Dasein. But now

Heidegger is discovering that there is something older than the truth of existence. He is discovering that existence itself clears or discloses 'on the basis of'
(these terms are, you are now aware, wholly inadequate) of something that is
far more mysterious, and far more elusive, than existence, namely, the truth of
being itself.

2. Truth and un-truth

In what amounts to a decisive turn in the history of philosophy (and,
Heidegger argues, in history as such), the question with which we began,
namely, that concerning the essence of truth, has undergone a radical conversion, if not a reversal. It is now the question concerning the truth of essence
(of *Wesen* in the sense of *Sein*, clarified earlier). '*The essence of truth*', Heidegger
writes, '*is the truth of essence.*'[34]

In the end, truth turns out to be not just one question amongst others, but
the way into the question that Heidegger has been pursuing almost from the
start, namely, the question concerning being. From the 1930s onwards, he will
refer to his question as the question concerning the truth of being, and no
longer that concerning the meaning of the *human* being. Why? Because the
question of truth, henceforth indissociable from that of un-truth, reveals a
hitherto unexplored domain, a dimension of being itself that the concern for
its meaning, especially as located in existence, simply was unable to attain.
This means that Heidegger now faces a new point of departure. His initial
problematic has been radicalized. Being is now to be explored primarily in
terms of withdrawal, or of an originary erasure that leaves traces (beings) in its
wake. The difference between being and beings is now to be articulated in
terms of the relation of truth and untruth. This relation is one of intertwining, not opposition. Truth and untruth are both tendencies: truth tends
towards the Open, the manifest, presence, whilst the untruth tends towards
closure, non-manifestation and the unapparent. If, in keeping with the spirit
of the early work, the concept of 'world' designates the former, Heidegger now
introduces that of 'earth' to designate the dimension of concealment at the
heart of the manifest. It is crucial to emphasize, however, that the world
'worlds' on the basis of (or, more adequately said, from out of the abyss of)
'earth'. In doing so, it conceals it: unconcealment conceals originary concealment. In their tense relation, or their strife, they arrive at a certain equilibrium. 'Presence', or the world as it is, is always a configuration of this strife.
Contrary to what the Greeks, and the philosophical tradition of the West that
stemmed from it, believed, presence is not the fundamental sense of being: to
be is not simply, and not primarily, to be *present*. Rather, what the philosophical tradition took to be the primordial sense of being is actually only derivative and secondary. Presence is the outcome, the surface effect as it were, of the
originary strife between truth and untruth. This strife is always ongoing. This
means that it is essentially temporal. Yet the temporality that is now at issue
extends beyond the confines of the temporality of existence (which we are yet

to expose). It is the time of the world itself, in its difference from earth. It is historical time. Marx believed that class struggle was the engine of history. Heidegger believes it is a struggle of a different kind that drives history, or manifests itself as history: the struggle of truth and untruth, the originary *polemos* of being. This, for him, is not an abstract view of the world. Rather, this struggle is what decides our fate at the most fundamental level. Our relation to the world, to ourselves and to others, to what we call nature and what we call culture, is played out in this strife.

Ultimately, from a historical point of view (historical in the sense I have just begun to allude to), the only interesting question is one of knowing where and how we stand *today*. How does Heidegger understand our time, our epoch if you will, in the light of this essential conflict between truth and its counter-essence? And what practical – ethical and political – consequences did such an understanding have on his life? These are questions I will address in connection with Heidegger's analysis of technology (Chapter 4) and his politics (Chapter 6). At this point, let me simply allude to what, tentatively, we could call his philosophy of history, and the way in which it informs his perception of the historical reality of his time.

We have just established that the apparent, or the manifest, is only the visible side of the invisible essence of truth. Increasingly, Heidegger's phenomenology, in becoming ontological, and in being attentive to the truth of being in particular, becomes a phenomenology of the unapparent and the invisible. It is only when the philosophical gaze directs itself towards what stands in the midst of truth, towards beings, that truth in the metaphysical sense (as correctness) becomes not only possible, but inevitable. Turning away from his positive appreciation of metaphysics in his early work, Heidegger now understands metaphysics precisely in terms of this mode of questioning that is directed solely at beings in truth, and that is structurally unable to raise the question concerning the *essence* of truth. Because metaphysics remains trapped within the limits of presence, because it is incapable of addressing presence with respect to its origin, truth for it remains a matter of correspondence, correctness and certainty. Correctness, he argues, is 'an unavoidable off-shoot of truth'.[35] If it is unavoidable, if metaphysics itself is in a sense inevitable, it is because of the essence of truth itself – because truth has always already, structurally and inevitably, begun to slip into its own erasure, and oblivion. Metaphysics will have always already begun to take place, not as an error, but more as an illusion – the visible or physical illusion according to which the world begins with beings, and thought itself with the question concerning the being*ness* of such beings.

In a way, Heidegger himself remained metaphysical so long as he understood truth simply in terms of clearing. But truth is not just clearing: it is the clearing in and through which something else, something equally originary, namely un-truth or concealment, is sheltered. Truth, then, is this co-originary event, the event of the strife itself. History, for Heidegger, is nothing other than the history of this tension, and of the 'echo' that resounds from out of the strife itself. Now, on Heidegger's reading, this history has been unidirectional thus far: the balance has consistently tilted on the side of the clearing, of what Heidegger also calls 'the world' — never encountered as such, for any such encounter presupposes that we also encounter the abyssal ground on the basis of which the clearing clears, namely, concealment (*Verbergung*) — and of what is being lit up and exposed amidst its reign. The balance has thus far tilted in favour of evidence, of the visible, of *what* towers up from within truth, thus allowing metaphysics to unfold as the questioning concerning the beingness or whatness of beings. Metaphysics' gaze is saturated with beings, so imbued with and overwhelmed by the sheer presence and visibility of the world that it cannot 'see' the invisible, which is, as it were, the other side, the lining of the visible. Metaphysics can only see what is true — what shines in the midst of truth — and so remains blind to truth itself, to the essence of truth as the clearing that shelters the concealing.

But this does not mean that the balance cannot be made to tilt in the other direction, that thought cannot become alive to the invisible and shift its attention from the innerworldy to the origin of world, to earth. It doesn't mean that it cannot dwell in this in-between, in this immemorial struggle that sustains history and the destiny of thought. This is what the 'other beginning', which Heidegger so wanted to prepare us for, announces: an absolute and radical shift, a turning within the strife itself, such that not just world, and things within it, but earth itself is brought into the task of thought. By earth, we need to understand the pre-worldly origin of world, the origin of presence that is closest to presence, its reverse or lining that is absolutely different from it. Earth will have always exceeded world. Yet earth also always falls short of world. It is simply otherwise than world, only and always preserved and sheltered within it. The unfolding of the earth is the manifestation of world, and this manifestation, the coming about of the visible, is the eclipse of earth. Earth has always eclipsed itself before world, but the very shining of world itself has its source in the invisible light of earth. Thus, it takes a special kind of eye, and a specific training in philosophical *seeing*, to see the light of earth radiating at the very edge of the world, intimating the presence, albeit infinitely discreet and non-visible, non-locatable *in* space and time, of a force of withdrawal whose retreat and refusal (*Versagung*) is far more decisive than any worldly event, and far more potent than the force of world itself.

And so, for us, on the verge of the other beginning, it is a question of knowing whether we are able to relate to beings with the reservation and tentativeness that alone can do justice to the refusal; whether, in relating to beings, we can simultaneously take over the concealing that echoes and reverberates through them, and thus transpose ourselves into its domain, and thus become something, or someone, different. It is a question of knowing whether we are able to stand in truth thus redefined, to sustain the event of truth as the clearing that shelters an originary concealing, a question of knowing whether such a stance can be achieved in thought, and perhaps also in other attitudes (in art and literature, for example, as Heidegger himself believed increasingly).

This question can only remain open. No decision, one way or another, can be made for us.

The contemporary state of humanity with respect to the truth of being is one of 'forgottenness'. This is a structural as well as a historical description of where we are. At the structural level, we need to recall that Dasein is faced first and foremost with beings from the point of view of their practicality, necessity, usefulness, etc. Structurally, we tend to cling to what is readily available, and the world in which we live is one that we tend to domesticate, organize and control. We have, in short, very little time for anything else. And today, Heidegger claims, we seem to have no time whatsoever for *questioning* in the most fundamental sense, that is, in the sense of directing ourselves towards that which, in the event of the world itself, withdraws and effaces itself. Given the specific way in which, for the most part, we disclose the world, the essence of this disclosedness, that is, concealment itself, never seems to become an issue. There is less and less space (and time) for concealment itself. *It is of the nature of concealment to conceal itself in what is disclosed.* Yet this concealment, and so the relation to the world as this open region that emerges from out of concealment, is increasingly threatened. There is, if you will, a drive to presence, and a glorification of the readily available and accessible, of planning and controlling, which drives us ever further away from the truth of being. This is state of being that, on one occasion at least, Heidegger characterizes as 'errancy', and one that he sees as far more catastrophic than the most serious error (including his own, political error of 1933–4). Despite our grasp of the world and our grip on it, what is most essential escapes us. And this essential aspect of our being is precisely the one that would guarantee a genuine dwelling on earth. We 'err' in the world, even though it now holds few mysteries for us, because we are unable to relate to the depth – the truth – that hides beneath it. We flee from what is most mysterious, and elusive, and turn towards what is readily available. By securing the available and controlling our environment, we find security, and gain a sense of purpose. But this gain is a loss, and the purpose in question the sign of historical nihilism: it is when there are no longer any genuine goals that total planning and control, consumption and production, can be presented and experienced as intrinsically valuable and eminently desirable. We believe we are achieving something real and worthwhile, when we are chasing shadows and chimera. Metaphysics devalues beings precisely insofar as it cuts them off from their own ground, from this excess on the basis of which they will always be more than the mere objective presence to which they have been consistently and systematically reduced.

Heidegger is attempting to reawaken a certain humanity, a certain history to this poverty, this defect that is nonetheless in excess of presence and of the reified representation of the world for which metaphysics stands. It is simply – but this simplicity harbours the greatest difficulty – a matter of uncovering, behind and beneath the economy of metaphysical representation and reification an altogether different economy. This is perhaps the point at which we

could begin to articulate a Heideggerian critique not just of 'metaphysics' –
for metaphysics, in Heidegger's eyes, never was restricted to the texts of metaphysics, but referred to our history and our contemporary situation, to our age
as the age of technics, the atomic bomb, unlimited industrialization, etc. – but
of the much revered and nowadays simply unquestioned 'global economy'.
This is the point at which we could begin to ask how economic priorities and
social relations could be transformed, and radically so, on the basis of this no
less radical and pivotal shift from the sheer presence and availability of a world
reduced to the flatness of its visibility to the silent, invisible and withdrawn,
and yet, at the same time, absolutely decisive and even decisional depth of the
world. The 'metaphysical' man is the 'last man' referred to by Nietzsche in
Thus spoke Zarathustra.[36] According to Heidegger, this is the man of the end
of the 'first beginning', the man who has become the slave of his own quasi-
omnipotence over the world, the man who is no longer able to understand
himself as belonging to the essence of truth. For this man, his power to *be* has
become a power to *rule* over beings as a whole, today revealed in techno-
science. His relation to the world testifies to an excess and an abuse of the
power that is granted to him by virtue of his own being. Unlike contemporary science and technology, philosophy is the thinking that refuses to give up
on being, to relinquish the concealment of being. It is the comportment that
lets go of beings in order to receive them from being itself. Nearness to the truth
of being is what makes our humanity. In this techno-scientific age, that wants
to have nothing to do with concealment, and that thinks of truth solely in
terms of correctness and exactness, we are moving further away from our
humanity. To bring us closer to it has become the historical task of philosophy. In *Contributions to Philosophy*, and in a tone that is decisively Nietzschean,
albeit shot through with references to Hölderlin, Heidegger equates the task
of thinking with the necessity of giving 'historical man a goal: namely, to
become the founder and preserver of the truth of beyng [*Seyn*], to *be* the 'there'
. . .'.[37] 'Genuine thinking' is now the 'thinking that sets goals'. Yet '[w]hat
gets set is not just any goal, and not the goal in general, but the one and only
and thus singular goal of our history [. . .], the *seeking* itself, the seeking of
beyng'.[38] As the seeker (*Sucher*), preserver (*Wahrer*) and guardian (*Wächter*) of
the truth of beyng, man can now be seen, in a way that throws more light on
what Heidegger meant by *Sorge* or 'care' in the 1920s, as the caretaker of
beyng, such a care-taking involving an irreducible operation of creation. The
man with whom Heidegger is concerned is not the man of Aristotle and of
Scholasticism, this very man of whom one can give a definition ('the animal
with *logos*'), one that is as empty as it is abstract, since no one actually *is* this
definition. It is rather the man of and for the future, who is yet to be invented.
The dividing line, then, is not between the human and the rest of the living
world. It is not a question of providing a 'definition' of the human by specify-
ing a genus common to all animated beings. It is not a matter of identifying
what differentiates the human from animal life in general. It is not for this
man, in his own name, that philosophy invokes the noble name of 'man'. It is

not so much a question of knowing *what* it is to be human, as to know *who* man is, and this means, in the end, what man is *capable of*. And to this question, to the question regarding what man is capable of, what he *can* (be), to the question regarding his potency, Heidegger will have always responded: being. Man is the being who *can be* (being), the being who has the *ability* and in whose *power* it is to ground and institute being, who lives his own being in the mode of possibility. The essence of the human consists in nothing more, but nothing else also than an originary openness to the truth of being. The overcoming of the metaphysics of nihilism, and the rescuing of the essence of man, begins with the transformation of our relation to truth.[39]

NOTES

1 See, for example, William Gaddis' *The Recognitions*, Gide's, *Les Faux–Monnayeurs*, Highsmith's *The Talented Mr. Ripley* or D. Mamet's films (*The House of Games*, *The Spanish Prisoner*).
2 'On the Essence of Truth', Wm, 73–97/136–54.
3 Aristotle, *De Interpretatione*, 17a, 4.
4 GA 21, 129ff. In passing, let me mention the fact that it is this very sense of *apophainesthai* that Heidegger is also keen to rescue when defining the *logos* (or discourse) of phenomeno-logy. See *Being and Time*, Introduction, § 7 ('The phenomenological method of investigation'), 32/55ff.
5 *Supplements*, 131.
6 *Supplements*, 131–2.
7 We shall return to Dasein's spatiality, and to the question of space in general, in Chapter 3.
8 SZ, 220/263.
9 SZ, 226/269.
10 SZ, §§ 15–18.
11 SZ, 69/98.
12 SZ, 67/95.
13 GA 19, § 7.
14 Wm, 30/26. Italics in the last sentence are mine.
15 Kant envisages the problem of morality from the point of view of a faculty, the will, and its determination in terms of freedom. The moral subject is the subject whose action is inspired solely by the *pure* will and its moral imperative, from which its own freedom derives, and not by any personal, sensible motivation. As we've already seen, freedom for Heidegger does not derive from any imperative to act according to a moral law, but from an existential–ontological structure of our being. Freedom is an ontological category, not a moral one.
16 SZ, 307–8/355.
17 SZ, 236/280.
18 SZ, 243/287. My emphasis.
19 SZ, 38/63.
20 SZ, 325/373.
21 SZ, 251–2/295.
22 GA 19, 51/36.
23 SZ, 254/298.
24 SZ, 261/305.
25 SZ, 310/358.
26 SZ, 262–3/307.

27 No matter how one decides to translate this term (resolution, resolve, resoluteness, decision, etc.), the important point is to maintain its connection with the disclosedness of Dasein (*Erschlossenheit*), of which it is an instance – indeed the highest instance.

28 SZ, 301–48.

29 Ibid.

30 SZ, 300/347.

31 SZ, 298/344–5.

32 SZ, 264/309.

33 Wm, 89/148.

34 Wm, 96/153.

35 GA 65, 345/241.

36 Nietzsche, *Thus spoke Zarathustra*, III, 'On Old and New Tables', especially § 27.

37 GA 65, 16/12.

38 GA 65, 17/13.

39 I return to the question of the completion of the forgottenness of being in technology, and of its possible overcoming, in Chapters 4 and 5.

3

Of Space and Time

The question that emerges from Heidegger's sustained engagement with Aristotle is that of the possibility of extracting a single sense in which all things, or beings, could be said to be. In other words, the question is one of knowing whether there is a unifying sense of being that underlies the many ways — or senses — in which things make themselves manifest to us. In his *Metaphysics*, to which Heidegger turns time and again in the early 1920s, Aristotle calls the different meanings of being 'categories' (and medieval, scholastic philosophy called them 'universals'). He lists them all, and asks whether they all refer back to one, privileged signification. They include being (*on*) in the sense of essence (*ousia*), being in the sense of what is good (or bad), being in the sense of what is on the basis of itself (substance), or on the basis of something else (accident), being in the sense of actuality (*energeia*) and potentiality (*dunamis*), being in the sense of what is true (or false). The one sense that, according to him, underlies all the other ones, is *ousia*, or essence. *Ousia* is the name forged after the present participle of the verb *einai*, to be; the Latin *essentia* (from the infinitive *esse*) translates it literally. In and of itself, this category does not designate much. It is only when it is interpreted further as *parousia*, or *praes-ens*, that it becomes meaningful. Presence, Aristotle argues, is the primordial meaning of being: what *is* is first and foremost what is *present*. To the extent that this solution will influence an entire philosophical tradition, if not the whole of Western thought, Heidegger argues that the metaphysics inherited from Aristotle is a metaphysics of presence. But presence, he adds, is not the ultimate or most fundamental meaning of being. It actually presupposes a more hidden meaning, which it cannot access, namely, time. The meaning of being as presence presupposes the present as the origin of time. But this privileging of the present is precisely what metaphysics cannot think. This unthought of metaphysics is precisely what fundamental ontology must think. In doing so, it reveals the fundamental structure and unity of metaphysics, as well as the origin of time itself. What metaphysics takes to be the origin of time, namely, the present, and the fundamental meaning of being, namely, presence, turns out to be a secondary and derivative mode of what Heidegger calls the essence, or the temporalizing of time. Time, in other words, is the key to solving the mystery of being or presence in general, the underlying and unifying phenomenon behind all the senses of being Aristotle sought (but failed) to discover in his *Metaphysics*. Whenever and wherever there is something, whenever something becomes manifest, whether as a source of practical concern, of theoretical investigation or as a human being, it becomes manifest on the basis of time. Time is the fundamental phenomenon, the primordial event: always and already 'there', everywhere and nowhere at the same time, always at work, yet never as an object, or as a thing. Needless to say, Heidegger's is a remarkable discovery, and one that revolutionized the way in which the history as well as the task of philosophy was to be perceived.

The access to the hidden phenomenon of time, which is to serve as the key to solving the mystery concerning the meaning of being, is provided by the being on which we have focused thus far, namely, Dasein. In order to interrogate being with respect to its meaning, and time with respect to its origin, it is necessary to observe and describe the way in which beings become manifest. Now we've already established that beings are disclosed on the basis of the being of existence itself. The being of the beings that surround us, and constitute our world, is illuminated on the basis of our own, 'ecstatic' being. The connection that now needs to be established is that between our own being – as the 'being-outside-itself-and-into-the-world' – and time. In what sense is our own being temporal? And in what sense is this temporal being irreducible to the dimension of the present, with which classical metaphysics identifies it?

Before I turn to the Heideggerian analysis of time, let me also ask about this other phenomenon, with which time is often associated, especially in modern physics, namely, space. In the context of *Being and Time*, and of the fundamental ontology this book seeks to establish, the phenomenon of space is ultimately understood in terms of time. As the title of the book indicates, it is time, not space, that constitutes what Heidegger calls the 'meaning' of being, or the transcendental horizon on the basis of which we 'understand' our own being as well as the being of other beings. In fact, Heidegger claims, it is of the utmost importance to distinguish between space and time, and to reverse the order of what he takes to be a metaphysical privileging of space over time: traditionally, time has been understood in terms of space, and specifically in terms of a line, whether circular (Ptoleme), rectilinear (Galileo) or curvilinear (Einstein); this spatialization of time is what has made the essence and true nature of time inaccessible to the tradition. Consequently, the spatial interpretation of time space must be neutralized. Does this mean that space has no place in Heidegger's thought? Or does it mean that space must be thought of differently, and on the basis of time? Can we ask about the spatiality of space, in a way equivalent to our asking about the temporality of time? In the previous chapter, we actually began to see how the being of Dasein involved a sort of spatiality. It is not as if the phenomenon of being-in-the-world were entirely devoid of spatiality. Far from it. It is just that space is now understood not geometrically, but existentially and ontologically.

In this chapter, I'll begin by examining the singular spatial nature of existence, and of the beings that it encounters in the world. In doing so, I'll reveal how the spatiality of existence can't be dissociated from that of the world itself. Then I'll show how this spatiality, and what it reveals about us, needs to be

analysed further in terms of time. I will show the extent to which time and
space are intertwined, and how they provide the key to understanding our own
being. These analyses will constitute the first part of this chapter. Following
the shift of direction I've sketched out in the previous chapter in relation to
truth, I'll be asking about the nature of time and space for Heidegger once we
no longer associate truth (or being) with existence alone, but when we try to
think of truth (or being) as 'older than', yet always in relation to, existence.
The second part of this chapter, then, will be devoted to tracing the evolution
of the question of time and space in Heidegger's later thought, and to asking
about the spatiality and temporality of a truth more primordial than that of
existence itself, and thus of a 'meaning' of being more fundamental than the
time of existence.

SPACE, TIME AND THE MEANING OF BEING

1. Space

We've already come across a number of features of existence that can help us
think of space anew in the context set out in *Being and Time*. It is now a question of making them explicit. There is, for example, the question of how we
need to understand the 'in' of being-in-the-world. I've already alluded to the
fact that Heidegger wants us to understand it in terms of a dwelling and not
in terms of spatial inclusion. Dwelling, then, is a mode of being that provides
us with a way of thinking through the spatial character of existence. Similarly,
I emphasized from the start Heidegger's insistence that we think of the world
(*Welt*) of existence as a world that surrounds us as a peripheral world or an environment (*Umwelt*) and not as a world that stands merely op-posed, as an object
would. Of course, whenever we think of the world as a matter to be investigated scientifically, we treat it as an object. But this is precisely Heidegger's
point: in doing so, we transform it, or, better said perhaps, we modify our originary attitude towards it. As it is, or unfolds, originally, and by that we need
to understand proximally and for the most part, in our everyday interaction
with it, the world is not an object: it is not there as something objectively
present, predisposed and pre-oriented towards our theoretical, scientific gaze.
We ourselves do not comport ourselves towards it as thinking things, as cognitive subjects. And yet, Heidegger insists, we understand it. But – and this
is one of Heidegger's most decisive insights – understanding and knowing are
two different modes of comportment. Our world is one that we understand
intuitively and pre-theoretically. It is a world we can operate in and navigate
and call our own without ever adopting a theoretical–scientific attitude
towards it. If we choose to do so, then the status of the world is somewhat modified: from a world that is essentially at hand, and the extension of our own
being, it becomes a world that is objectively present, there to be interrogated,
investigated, represented. Paradoxically, and thanks to the success of the
modern, metaphysical and scientific world-view, this objective world has come

to be seen as the real world – and sometimes the philosophically only valid one. Heidegger does not dispute that, objectively, the world *is* in the way in which it's been represented scientifically since Descartes and Galileo. He does claim, however, that beneath this theoretical attitude, with which we have come to identify our own being, and this objective conception of the world, and of truth, which we have come to privilege, lies a rich and decisive reality that we have forgotten and that we must now learn to 'see' again. Phenomenology is the philosophical method that will give us our eyes back in order to question and thematize this reality that we are, and from which we have grown estranged.

The nature of Heidegger's quarrel with Descartes and Cartesianism in general bears precisely on what he sees as the need to make philosophy concrete again. Specifically, Heidegger sees the dualisms of Cartesian thought as an inevitable offshoot of an abstract and somewhat artificial conception of the being of the world as well as our own. It is only with phenomenology, and its call to return philosophy to the world as it is there for us, in its immediate presence as it were, that philosophy is able to break with this abstraction, and move beyond the sphere of representation. Outside this commitment to 'the things themselves', philosophy shares its destiny with that of modern science, often providing it with its own metaphysical ground. How can we characterize this position that we could call 'theoretical' or 'metaphysical', and that Husserl qualified as 'natural'? It is a position for which the world exists as corporeal substance, or matter, and the human being as thinking substance. For Descartes, the world and the human being are both 'things' of a specific kind, namely, 'substances'. Substances are defined by the fact that they exist independently of anything other than themselves. As such, they each possess a distinct essence. The essence of matter, or bodily substance, is *extension*, and the essence of the human is *thought*. The *res extensa* and the *res cogitans*, the reality of extension and that of thought exhaust the *essential* reality of the world. The dualisms of mind and body, spirit and nature, subject and object, which are all so central to modern and contemporary philosophy, are derived from this initial division of reality. In this configuration, we notice that the only mention of space is restricted to material nature, and is identified with extension. This is precisely the space that Euclidean geometry is equipped to thematize, and that lies at the root of modern physics. Thus understood, the world can indeed be reduced to being this book written in geometrical characters at which Galileo marvelled, and the thinking power of the *cogito* is itself a power to represent the world mathematically. By orienting the world towards the objectively present, which mathematics is particularly well suited to grasp, Descartes sets philosophy on an entirely new course, one that lays the transcendental foundations of modern mathematical physics.[1] Whilst itself *also* material, and thus extended, the human being is defined not in terms of extension, but in terms of thought. Thought designates the essence of the substance 'human being'.

By contrast, Heidegger's 'definition' of the essence of the human being as existence is spatial through and through. But this spatiality differs radically from Cartesian extension. It cannot be mathematized, that is, represented through a set of coordinates. The spatiality of Dasein is not a matter of position, and Dasein's relation to space is not one of locomotion. Of course, Dasein can always be represented as a point moving across a flat space. In the process, however, Dasein is turned into a mathematical object, and is no longer the existent being that it is. Of what does the spatiality of Dasein consist, then? This is the point at which we need to return to the 'aroundness' (*das Umhafte*) of the environment (*Umwelt*) of Dasein, and to the in-ness of its being-*in*-the-world, which Heidegger understands as a relation of dwelling.

The 'dwelling' dimension of existence is explicitly brought forward and contained in the qualification of Dasein as 'being-in-the-world'. But if the world consists of the totality of beings, whether real or imaginary, which we encounter, do they not all have the structure of Dasein? Are they not also 'in' the world? They are indeed all encountered in the world; they emerge from within the world, and it is there that they find their place. And yet, Heidegger insists, they are not in any way 'in' the world in the way in which Dasein itself is in the world. Here, then, lies the difference between the purely immanent sense of 'in', characteristic of all things other than existence, and the 'in' of existence itself, which is transcendent. The difference between the two senses of being 'in' is precisely that between a relation of inclusion or enclosure and one of dwelling, one of mere being and one of understanding. For Dasein's way of being *in* the world is radically or qualitatively different from the way in which water is *in* the glass or the tree is *in* the forest. The world to which Dasein relates by in-habiting it is precisely not an empty container, pre-given and pre-constituted, awaiting to be filled up with things and events. Unlike the glass with respect to the water inside it, the world is not this neutral and indifferent enclosure within which existence finds itself. No more is the world of Dasein the natural environment of animal life. Rather, ex-sistence, as this standing-outside, or as this being which, already thrown into the world amidst things and their being, always pro-jects itself into a myriad of possibilities and projects, is nothing outside or in excess of this world. Dasein *is* its world. And this must be understood transitively: Dasein exists its world; its being is precisely its 'worlding'. Between Dasein and the world, then, there is a relation that is not one of indifference, but of concern (*Besorgen*) and care (*Sorge*): in the very way in which Dasein is, or exists its own existence, its own being is at issue for it. Existence *is* in such a way that, in its very being, the world as such and as a whole matters to it, is an issue for it. To be in something in such a way that we inhabit it or feel 'at home' in it thus presupposes this relation of familiarity born of an impossibility not to be concerned with, or to care for, that within which we find ourselves. Such is the reason why Heidegger insists that we understand the 'in' of Dasein's 'being-in' on the basis of the Old German verb *innan*, to inhabit, to dwell.

In thus dwelling amidst things, in relating to things in the world in such a way that one is from the start *there with* them, *near* and *alongside* them, and not op-posed to them, in what amounts to a derivative and abstract position that presupposes the identification of the human with a power of representation, a new sense of space also emerges. For the distinction between the relation of insideness that characterizes the water's relation to the glass, and the relation of *innan* or dwelling that characterizes Dasein's relation to its world, is one that is intrinsically spatial. More specifically, it is a distinction between two senses of space: whereas the former draws on a sense of space commonly accepted, as the physical enclosure within which things are contained or found, or as the set of coordinates according to which a material body or a dynamic system can be located, the latter corresponds to a more originary phenomenon and coincides with an *ontological* understanding of space.

But what is space understood 'originarily'? What does its pre-objective, pre-individuated dimension consist of? In the previous chapter, I alluded to the fact that objective space presupposes what I would call the event of space itself: not a given and already individuated thing or framework within which other things or events, and things of a different nature, would take place, but an ongoing process – a spacing. Space (*Raum*), Heidegger argues, as this dimension within which things can be located and contained, presupposes the more originary phenomenon of the spatiality of existence, which is nothing other than what he calls an *Einräumen*, a making room for things, the clearing of a horizon from within which things manifest themselves, with the closeness or distance, the urgency or obviousness, clarity and confusion, etc. with which they manifest themselves. The 'Da' of Da-sein itself, as a topological motif, alludes to the spatiality of existence, and points to it as to the proto-place from which things take place and find their place. This place (*Platz*), the proper place of things – and, in the everyday, practical context within which *Being and Time* situates itself, such things are first and foremost those readily available pieces of equipment with which we are surrounded – has nothing to do with their actual position in space–time, but has everything to do with the 'region' (*Gegend*) from out of which they emerge. What is primarily given or encountered, what constitutes the daily stuff of human existence, and which constitutes a positive phenomenon, is not 'a three-dimensional multiplicity of possible positions which gets filled up with things objectively present [*vorhandenen Dingen*]'.[2] This 'objective' dimensionality of space is itself derived from the spatiality of the *Vorhandene*. Our indicators, the ways in which we orient ourselves in this world and encounter things within it, the sense of space that we have is not a function of our ability to measure accurately positions in space–time. We orient ourselves from those things themselves, and it is in the contact with them that a space is being woven. For the most part, we find ourselves in situations in which

[t]he 'above' is what is 'on the ceiling'; the 'below' is what is 'on the floor'; the 'behind' is what is 'at the door'; all 'wheres' are discovered and circumspectively [*umsichtig*] interpreted as we go our ways in everyday dealings [*Umgangs*]; they are not ascertained and catalogued by the observational measurement of space.[3]

Because the world in which we find ourselves is not first and foremost the rep-resented world of mathematical physics that stands op-posed, but the world that is all around us (the *Um-welt*), because we do not first encounter points and positions, but things of use in everyday dealings (*Um-gang*), because the way in which we 'see' the world is from within the world, and is therefore circum-spective (it is an *Um-sicht*), the 'measure' of spatiality for us is pre-objective, existential–ontological and not physical–mathematical.

What determines the spatiality of a thing of use is not its actual distance or position, measured in either absolute or relative terms, but how it is oriented in relation to other things and to ourselves. Thus, there are many things that find themselves in the region of (*in der Gegend von*), say, the sun and its light and warmth. Its various 'places' throughout the day – sunrise, midday, sunset, midnight – are indicators of the regions that lie in them. There is, for example, the region 'house', or the region 'church':

> The house has its sunny side and its shady side; the way it is divided up into rooms [*Räume*] is oriented towards these, and so is the disposition [*Einrichtung*] within them, according to their character as equipment. Churches and graves, for instance, are laid out according to the rising and the setting of the sun – the regions of life and death, which are deter-minative for Dasein itself with regard to its ownmost possibilities of being in the world.[4]

And so, in the end, we orient ourselves in this world on the basis of those pre-established regions, those buildings and those places, those landscapes which we in-habit, and which provide us with our sense of space, our sense of belonging to a place, familiar or unfamiliar (when we travel, for example, and find ourselves 'out of place', amidst streets, buildings and landscapes to which our bodies are not accustomed and for which we lack a proper context), close or distant (which can happen even when and where we are actually and physically there, in those places that are unfamiliar, and which we encounter perhaps for the first time).[5]

Whilst pointing in the direction of the spatiality of Dasein itself, the spa-tiality of innerworldly, useful things does not circumscribe its specificity. The reason for that is that Dasein is essentially not an innerworldly thing, and this despite the fact that it is 'in' the world. The senses of 'in' in the case of inner-worldly things and in the case of Dasein's being-in-the-world differ funda-mentally. The two significant aspects of Dasein's spatiality are, according to Heidegger, *Ent-fernung*, which can be translated as de-severance, and *Ausrichtung*, directionality. These are traits we have already come across in con-nection with the question of truth in the previous chapter. *Entfernung* is not here taken in its usual sense of 'distance', but, playing on the privative prefix '*Ent-*', as what abolishes or cancels distance and remoteness, as what brings things close or nearby. As Heidegger himself emphasizes,[6] it should be under-stood not as a thing or a noun, but actively and transitively – in keeping with the way in which Da-sein itself is understood:

De-severing amounts to making the farness, and this means the remote-ness of something, vanish; it amounts to a bringing close or a nearing.[7]

Thus, things are encountered from out of the essentially de-severant comport-ment of existence, and from out of this comportment alone can things appear as 'far' or 'close', 'here' or 'there'. How far or close they are is a function not of some objective distance, and is not 'measured' in such objective terms, but is always the result of the manner and the urgency with which we relate to them: 'The objective distances of things that are merely present do not coincide with the remoteness and closeness of what is ready-to-hand within-the-world'.[8] When, in order to go to some place yonder, we say, for example, that it is 'a good walk', 'a stone's throw' or even 'half an hour', we intend not an exact measure, a quantitative stretch of time, but a 'duration', a qualitative dimen-sion that is imbued with the life and comportment of existence itself. For the most part, this comportment is practical and useful, and thus Dasein's relation to things is driven by a desire to have them nearby, to bring them closer.

The second character that serves to define the spatiality of existence is that of *directionality*. By that, Heidegger means that existence is always oriented towards things in a particular way, always engaged in this transitive activity of 'nearing' or 'bringing close' (*Näherung*), even if and when those things appear out of reach, too far or unattainable. In other words, existence is always directed at something, intrinsically directional: right, left, up, down, above, beneath, behind, in front are all according to some thing encountered there, and it is that very thing, in its relation to an embodied existence as proto-place, that provides Dasein with its sense of direction. These directions, which Dasein is said to always take along with it, are inscribed within its very body, as this *lived* body that it is. In an illuminating and unusual passage, which in some respect echoes Husserl's analyses of the constitution of bodily beings (*Leiblichkeit*) and prefigures subsequent developments in the phenomenology of the lived body, and of the flesh, Heidegger alludes to the way in which dwelling amidst things, and finding one's way in the world, presupposes the intrinsically 'bodily nature' of Dasein, whilst postponing (indefinitely) a detailed examination of this question:

> Dasein's spatialisation in its 'flesh' [*Leiblichkeit*] is also marked out in accordance with these directions. This 'flesh' hides a whole problematic of its own, though we shall not treat it here. . . .[9]

The body is itself the site of habits and of a constant exchange with familiar surroundings. It is it that 'remembers' places and orients itself accordingly. The body, as it evolves within specific surroundings, from which it cannot be abstracted, becomes familiar with them, and is itself constituted through a process of sedimentation, each region and local situation leaving its mark in the body, which by now has become the unconscious of existence, its ontolog-ical memory. And throughout, it approaches the world with the depth and the

thickness of these accumulated strata, the world thus becoming the continuation of its own body, its own body becoming world. This is the way in which
we in-habit the world: as existential bodies, and the world of existence is itself
a fabric made of bodily, carnal threads.

Ultimately, the spatiality of those things ready-to-hand we encounter
circumspectively is a function of the spatiality of Dasein itself. In other words,
'only because Dasein is spatial in the way of de-severance and directionality can
what is ready-to-hand within-the-world be encountered in its spatiality'.[10]
This is tantamount to saying that in letting things be encountered within the
world, we give them space. Dasein is spatial to the extent that it is space-giving
(*Raum-geben*), or room-making (*Einräumen*). In other words, Dasein frees or
clears a space for things to emerge, and frees the space or the place that is proper
to such things. The 'Da' of Da-sein is precisely to be understood as this clearing or this making room for things, and in such a way that those things are
freed for their own spatiality. The primordial phenomenon of space, which we
began by distinguishing from the physical–mathematical space of representation, is this active and transitive spacing, this ecstatic clearing whence the
world 'worlds'. Space, when properly understood, '*is not in the subject* [Kant]',
'*nor is the world in space* [Newton]'. It can become the homogeneous space of
nature only through a transformation of its essence, that is to say, only when
the phenomenon of space, in essence active and transitive, and coextensive
with existence itself, is abstracted from its existential–ontological soil and
re-presented as something objectively present. In and through this process,
which defines the theoretical–scientific attitude that characterizes modernity,

> [t]he world loses its specific aroundness; the environment becomes the
> world of Nature. The 'world,' as a totality of equipment ready-to-hand,
> becomes spatialised to a context of extended things that are just present-
> at-hand and no more. The homogeneous space of Nature shows itself
> only when the beings we encounter are discovered in such a way that the
> worldly character of the ready-to-hand gets specifically deprived of its
> worldhood.[11]

Only then can space be equated, as in Descartes, with extension, and only
then can it be envisaged as this abstract surface on which natural phenomena
take place, as in Newtonian space. Against such conceptions, or rather prior
to them, Heidegger attempts to retrieve an originary space that coincides with
the very *doing* of existence, with existence as spacing and clearing: as truth.[12]

2. Time

With time, we arrive at the question with which Heidegger's thought is most
associated. If he can be seen to have revived ontology at a time when the philosophical community at large no longer considered it a viable, philosophical
project, it is only to the extent that he identified time as the central issue and

mystery behind the question of being. It is only by understanding being *in terms of* time, and by transforming ontology into chronology, that Heidegger was able to revolutionize philosophy.

In order to show how time can surface as a – and indeed *the* – decisive philosophical issue, let me turn once again to a concrete experience – not that of my own dream, which was after all rather unusual, but that of boredom, which we have all experienced. Heidegger's claim is that certain experiences provide us with a distinct and indeed privileged way into the meaning of our own being as time. Certain experiences have this ability to bring ourselves face to face with our own temporal being. As such, they can be viewed as liminal experiences. For the most part, if time is indeed the fundamental and unifying phenomenon behind all our actions and relations, it is not one that we come across as such. If time is indeed implicated in everything we do – a hypothesis we need to verify – it is itself only very rarely present as such. It is not something we are aware of, or think about when we go about our daily dealings. This, Heidegger claims, is precisely due to the fact that we *are* it.

Let me begin by looking at various expressions we use ordinarily in relation to time. Often, they portray time as an object of possession: time is something we have more or less of. 'I haven't got time (to pick up your laundry)', 'I have plenty of time (before the departure of my flight)', 'I wish I had the time (to go to the theatre more often)' are all expressions that point to time as something we need in order to do this or that. Time is essentially *with a view to* . . . and is subordinated to a practical goal. In addition, it is as if time were itself spatial: we speak of it as if it were some kind of container given in advance and independent from us, which we could choose to fill in different ways, or which is filled by a number of constraints. In boredom, however, it would seem that time appears in a different light. For isn't boredom the point at which we have all the time in the world, the point at which we have too much time? Isn't boredom revealed in the fact that we wish we had less time, and perhaps no time at all? Isn't it the case that the frustration and unease of boredom is born of the fact that this surplus or excess of time that we have on our hands is actually not something that we possess, but something that we are? Are we not, each and every one of us, this temporal residue, this excess, that we all try to cover over and disguise by keeping ourselves busy? When I am bored, there is nothing other than myself, and there is time, pure time as it were: time I can't turn into anything, time I can't put to work. There is just too much time, and there is myself, torn apart by the sole presence of time. I am alone with myself and with time. Sartre famously wrote that hell is the other people. But we know that I can be my very own hell, that nothing has the ability to generate unease and anxiety like myself in the sole presence of myself – as the dream I began by evoking testifies to. But myself in the presence of myself is not what we generally call solitude. What we call solitude is a state of being on one's own. And one is never quite alone with oneself in solitude: we might be reading, or painting; in a prison cell, we might still have our dreams, our memories and our hopes. But there is nothing of the sort in boredom. There are no thoughts, no memories and no dreams. We do not day-dream when we are bored. Time is all there is. It is the very presence of time, and of time alone, which we find ourselves glued to and as it were condemned to, which generates the often unbearable feeling we call boredom.[13] The time of boredom is the time that possesses me, and not the time that I possess. What I feel and experience in boredom is this time that will not pass, that will not go away, that cannot be filled – not because there is, at that particular moment, nothing that can replace it, or occupy it, but because this time is the time that I am: genuine, originary time. It is the time of my being, or my being-time. Boredom reveals the fact that there is no difference between my being-in-the-world and my being-in-time, between my worldly being and my temporal being. Time appears as the horizon of the world itself: not as an innerworldly thing, or a thing *of* the world, but as the dimension from which the world itself unfolds.

Time is perhaps more immediately tangible in boredom than in the dream I began by evoking, and which testifies to what, elsewhere, Heidegger calls anxiety. But anxiety is itself the experience of coming face to face with oneself – and nothing else. In both instances, we experience a total withdrawal of the world. And the more the world withdraws, that is, the fewer things there are with which to engage and the fewer opportunities of immersing ourselves within the world, the more we find ourselves 'there', painfully present as it were, naked before our own worldliness. What boredom and anxiety have in common is our desire to escape its grip. We flee them by looking for some kind of distraction, such is their ability to unsettle. The question, though, is one of knowing whether there is some kind of experience that could reveal our tem-poral being and bear witness to the temporal meaning of being in general and that we would not want to flee, but to embrace and sustain. Furthermore, could this experience, this 'attunement' reveal more precisely the way in which time unfolds or temporalizes itself?

These questions bring us back to a phenomenon I introduced earlier in the second chapter, and which *Being and Time* describes as 'anticipatory, resolute disclosedness' (*vorlaufende Entschlossenheit*). This phenomenon, we recall, is the one that brought us before the primordial truth of existence. It reveals a dis-tinct possibility of existence, one in which existence is disclosed to itself *as* dis-closedness. In resolute disclosedness, existence becomes true to its own truth. Yet this phenomenon also provides the key to understanding the unity of Dasein's being as time. How? In resolute disclosedness, existence relates to itself and understands itself on the basis of itself, that is, on the basis of the fact that, as existence, it is always and essentially towards its own death. Death is the ultimate possibility for Dasein, the absolute limit that marks the point at which existence begins and ends. In existing, Dasein is always relating to its own end. This end is not the point at which existence ceases, but the closure on the basis of which disclosedness takes place, the defining horizon from which existence is born at every moment. In resolute disclosedness, Dasein does not flee its own mortality and finitude, but anticipates it, that is, brings it to bear on its comportment towards the world. What until then was only implicit is made explicit.

With this phenomenon, Heidegger believes, we can finally point to an existentiell, empirical attestation of Dasein's capacity for being a coherent whole, described earlier at the structural or existential level as 'care'. Care characterizes the various aspects of existence as involving three moments or dimensions (and not parts): a dimension of thrownness into the world (*Geworfenheit*), through which, each time, existence finds itself disposed towards or attuned to it in a certain way; one of self-projection towards a realm of possibilities (*Entwurf*), through which existence carries itself out as freedom; and one of being-alongside other beings in the world. With the phenomenon of anticipatory resoluteness, the fundamental existential phenomenon of care as Dasein's being is rooted ontically. Now that Heidegger has demonstrated the existentiell validity of care, he can ask the question to which the entire analytic of Dasein was subordinated: What is the ontological meaning of care? The answer is: time, or temporality (*Zeitlichkeit*). But this answer we find precisely in the phenomenon of anticipatory resoluteness, which most reveals Dasein's essentially temporal being. Why? Because anticipatory resoluteness reveals Dasein as an essentially *futural* (*zukünftig*) being: Dasein is essentially ahead of itself, yet always towards itself; it is, you will recall, ahead of itself as this being that is towards its own death. What we witness with Heidegger, then, is a decisive shift in the perception of where time originates: the centre of gravity of temporality is no longer the present, as was the case in the tradition, but the future (*die Zukunft*). The future is the source or the origin from which time flows. Traditionally, time was considered to originate in the present. The present was the primordial reality from which the rest of time flowed: the past was understood as what was no longer, and the future as what was not yet. The temporal horizon from which the being of our own being as well as that of other beings was interpreted was the present. As a result of this present-centrism, and as early as Plato and Aristotle, *presence* (*parousia*) defined the underlying meaning of being (*ousia*): to *be* always (implicitly) meant to be *present*. What Aristotle called *ousia* (a substantive forged after the present participle of the verb *einai*, to be, subsequently translated in Latin as *essentia*) was the fundamental, primordial meaning of being, from which all the other meanings (or 'categories') of being were derived. And *ousia* was itself interpreted further as *parousia*, or *praesens*. The task of exhibiting this basic presupposition of metaphysics, and of extracting its unthought, is what Heidegger called 'de(con)struction'.[14]

By thinking the being of the human being in terms of its directedness towards its own end, Heidegger reveals the *essence* of the human as futural: existence is essentially and always *to come*. Dasein is *always* coming towards itself, whether it understands itself 'properly' on the basis of its ownmost ability to be (*Seinkönnen*) in 'authentic' existence or whether it understands itself 'improperly' as a reality that is simply present in 'inauthentic' existence. This claim makes sense only to the extent that we think of Dasein's own death as its ultimate and ownmost possibility. It makes sense only to the extent that we think of existence primarily in terms of possibility and not actuality. By future, then, we need to understand not a 'now' that has not yet become actual, but the coming (*Kunft*) in which Dasein comes towards itself.[15] Death marks the possibility that is itself in excess of all actuality, the possibility that can never be actualized, and on the basis of which all other possibilities are defined and actuality itself is made possible. When we translate this temporally, we must come to the conclusion that there is a future for Dasein that can never be made present; further still, we must say that Dasein *is* this future that will never be present, this coming, this happening or this event that is not merely actual. The 'being' of existence is no longer equated with the presence of existence. 'Being' no longer means 'presence'. The implicit question that governs the history of metaphysics, namely, the question concerning the meaning of being, and to which metaphysics was never able to find an answer (for want of being able to pose it explicitly), is now finally solved.

To understand itself as being-towards-death 'authentic' Dasein must also take over its thrownness. Now to take over one's thrownness means nothing other than to be 'authentically' or 'properly' what one already was 'inauthentically' or 'improperly'. What Dasein *can* be is nothing other than what it already is, nothing other than its *having-been* (*Gewesen*). It is only in the anticipation of its end that Dasein can correspond to its original condition. Only insofar as Dasein ex-ists, that is, comes *towards* itself futurally, can it come *back* (*zurück-kommen*) to itself and what it already is: 'Anticipation of one's ownmost and uttermost possibility is coming back understandingly to one's ownmost 'been'. Only so far as it is futural can Dasein be authentically as having-been. The 'having been' [*die Gewesenheit*, and not *die Vergangenheit*, the past] arises, in a certain way, from the future'.[16] This is tantamount to saying that Dasein can *be* its past only insofar as it comes back to it on the basis of its own future. If the having-been arises from the future it is because there can be facticity only within the horizon of a can-be (*Seinkönnen*). So, once again: the future, properly understood, is not a now that is not yet actual, but Dasein's coming towards its ownmost can-be, which occurs in the anticipation of death. Likewise, because Dasein is not a pre-given entity, an entity present-at-hand, it is not, strictly speaking, 'past', but has always already been and *is* this very having-been: the 'having been' (*gewesen sein*) is the original phenomenon of what we call the past. Traditionally, the past is what is no longer. But the temporal dimension associated with Dasein's thrownness is not past in that sense. On the contrary: it is a dimension that persists and insists, although not as something present. Thrownness indicates that Dasein exists in the mode of having-been, a mode that is irreducible to a mere 'modification' or variation of the present. What we normally call the present is not the founding moment of time. In fact, it is a derivative mode of time. For presence always arises out of the futurity and pastness of existence. Anticipatory resoluteness, in which existentiality is disclosed as essentially futural, also discloses the present. Indeed, anticipatory resoluteness reveals what Heidegger calls a 'situation' by making present an entity. The present as a mode of temporality is originally a making present, or a presencing (*ein Gegenwärtigen*). The spacing and the clearing with which we already associated the operation of existence is at bottom a making *present*. The spatiality and the truth of Dasein are fundamentally a function of its temporal nature. Coming back to itself futurally, resoluteness makes present the beings that it encounters environmentally. This is the phenomenon Heidegger designates as temporality (*Zeitlichkeit*). It has the unity of a future that makes present in having-been (*gewesend-gewärtigende Zukunft*).

Let us now recapitulate: as the 'proper' or 'authentic' modality of existence, anticipatory resoluteness is made possible by temporality alone. This, in turn, implies that care in general is rooted in temporality and that temporality constitutes the ontological meaning of care. Thus, temporality alone makes possible the unity of existentiality, thrownness and fallenness as the fundamental *structures* of care. Temporality is the arch-structure, the phenomenon that lies at the root of all the aspects of existence.

But what about the present? Whilst we can say that the primary meaning of existentiality is the future, and the primary meaning of facticity is the having been, we lack such an indication for the third structural moment of care, namely, the fallen 'being-alongside'. Here, Heidegger equates the being-alongside with falling. Now, this should not mean that falling is not also grounded in temporality; rather, it should indicate that making-present, as the primary basis for falling into the ready-to-hand and present-at-hand with which we concern ourselves, remains included in the future and the having been.[17] What Heidegger is saying, then, is that the present is not a separate moment, an original mode of temporality *per se*, but a derivative one, one that is made possible on the basis of the future and the having been. The 'alongside' of the being-alongside, then, does not suggest immediately a temporal dimension, but a spatial one. It is presence, more than the present, which is here emphasized. And presence is made possible only on the basis of time, specifically, on the basis of Dasein's coming towards itself as a coming back to itself. Presence, then, or the present, is only a function of the way in which Dasein relates to its own temporalizing.

If, for the most part, the present is associated with fallenness and decline, is there a mode in which it is revealed authentically? Does the present manifest itself differently in resolute existence? The term that Heidegger reserves to designate the present of resolute Dasein is the 'moment'. Now, the present that is opened up in resolute disclosedness is radically different from that of this or that particular situation. It differs from the kind of present that is linked to a punctual and practical situation, in other words, from the mostly 'concerned' and 'absorbed' present of our everyday life, the present of needs and ordinary dealings with the world. Furthermore, it is also to be distinguished from the abstract present (the 'now') of the theoretical attitude, which we now unquestioningly consider to be the very form of the present, unaware of the spatial, and specifically linear understanding of time such an attitude presupposes, the ontological–existential ground of which we can trace back to the ordinary, fallen nature of our relation to the world in everyday life. Rather, the present that is at issue in the 'moment' is the present in which existence is present to itself as the very operation of disclosure, or as the very *there* of being. In the 'moment of vision', or the *Augen-blick*, Dasein 'brings itself before itself':[18] it *sees* itself for the first time for what it is, that is, the originary 'clearing' or the 'truth' of being. Thus, the 'moment' is not linked to the disclosure of a particular situation, but to the disclosure of situatedness as such. It is the present or the time of truth's disclosedness to itself as the originary event of being. As such, the *Augenblick* designates a different relation to time and to the present in general: it marks at once a rupture or a caesura (*Gebrochenheit*) in the continuum and the fascination of 'fallen' time, and a return to the essence of time as finite and ecstatic. This, then, does not mean that the 'moment' marks the possibility of a flight from time into eternity.[19] On the contrary: it means that existence becomes *all the more* open to the world and to the situation in the essential modification that takes place in resoluteness. For the situation is now disclosed from out of Dasein's disclosedness to itself as originary disclosure:

> When resolute, Dasein has brought itself back from falling, and has done so precisely in order to be 'there' in the moment all the more authentically for the situation that has been disclosed.[20]

Nothing occurs *in* the 'moment': no single thing, no concrete situation, but the sheer power of occurrence which Dasein itself is. In the 'moment', time itself occurs as the suspension of the impersonal, anonymous and objective dimension within which things, events and situations are believed to take place. For these, as things to be handled or as objects to be contemplated, are first encountered from out of the event of time itself, which presents itself in the 'moment'. Unlike the 'now', as the empty form within which events and facts take place, the 'moment' marks the very advent or gathering of time, the fold at which and within which past and future are folded into one another.

In resoluteness, existence liberates itself from its own entrapment in the absorbed life of everydayness. It frees itself for itself, as this ability to be or disclose being. Thus, the modification or conversion brought about by resolute disclosedness is also at the source of a renewed understanding of what it means to act, of the very possibility of action in the most essential sense, and, yes, of what I would be tempted to call, albeit under erasure perhaps, the very possibility and beginning of ethics: 'The moment of vision is nothing other than the *look of resolute disclosedness* [*Blick der Entschlossenheit*] in which the full situation of an action opens itself and keeps itself open'.[21] Thus, in the moment, Dasein has an eye for action in the most essential sense, insofar as the moment of vision is what makes Dasein possible as Da-sein. It is to this that the human *must* resolutely disclose itself. The human must first create 'for himself *once again* [my emphasis] a genuine knowing concerning that wherein whatever makes Dasein itself possible consists'. And this, Heidegger tells us, is the 'fact that the moment of vision in which Dasein brings itself before itself as that which is properly binding must time and again stand before Dasein as such'.[22] Thus, in the moment of vision, existence resolves itself to itself, to itself as Dasein, thus allowing it to become free for the first time – free not to *do* this or that, at least not primarily, but free to be its own being, free to be in the most intense and generous sense, that is, free to be for its own freedom or its own ability to be.

What have we established thus far? We've established that temporality makes possible the unity of the three fundamental structures of care. This means that temporality has itself a unity that does not consist of the piecing together of future, past and present. Temporality is itself a unitary phenomenon. But it is not a being at all. We cannot say that temporality *is*, but only that it *temporalizes* itself. So when Heidegger claims that temporality *is* the meaning of care, we need to understand that only in the self-temporalizing of temporality does Dasein exist according to its own possibilities of being. As Heidegger emphasizes at the beginning of § 65 of *Being and Time*, by 'meaning' we need to understand that wherein the understandability of something lies.[23] The meaning of something, therefore, is that which is necessarily presupposed in that thing for it to become understandable. In other words, it is the condition of possibility of that thing. In that respect, when we say that time is the meaning of care, we say that it is only on the basis of the temporalization of temporality that Dasein's being as care can come to be understood.

How are we to understand the temporalization of temporality? What does Heidegger mean by that? To say that time is essentially a temporalizing is tantamount to saying that time does not constitute the 'internal sense' or the 'interiority' of a 'subject', but that it is 'the *ekstatikon* pure and simple', 'the original outside-of-itself in and for itself'.[24] Heidegger borrows the term *ekstatikon* from Aristotle's *Physics*, where it designates the nature of change (*metabole*).[25] It is to be understood in its literal Greek sense as a coming out of oneself, and must hence be related to the notion of existence (or ek-sistence, as Heidegger will later begin to write).[26] By defining the future, the having been and the present as the *ecstasies* of temporality Heidegger emphasizes the temporalizing of temporality as a movement or an event, and not as the coming out of itself of a hitherto self-contained subject: 'Temporality is not, prior to this, a being that first emerges from itself; its essence is a process of temporalising in the unity of the ecstasies'.[27] Thus temporality needs to be understood as an ekstatic unfolding, and not, as thought by the 'ordinary understanding', as a pure sequence of 'nows', without beginning and without end. Ek-sistence, then, as the event of being, is entirely outside: it is not an interiority that externalizes itself, but the outside as such, pure exteriority, pure throwing (pro- and retro-ject). It has no inner life withdrawn from the world since, as the being that exists, it is nothing other than this being-in-the-world. Even its most intimate secrets, the riches of its so-called inner life, are a function of its being 'out there' from the very start, thrown into the world. It is only with the characterization of our being in terms of time that

Heidegger is able to understand fully the meaning of factical life as being-outside-itself-and-towards-something.

At this point of the analysis, Heidegger points to a difficulty concerning the relation between the three ecstases. All three ecstases are equiprimordial (*gleichursprünglich*). This means that the nature of temporalizing can be equally determined in terms of the different ecstases. Yet the future has a priority in the ecstatic unity of primordial and 'authentic' temporality. So, it is only with respect to 'authentic' temporality that the future is said to have a priority: 'Primordial and authentic temporality temporalises itself in terms of the authentic future and in such a way that in having been futurally, it first of all awakens the present'.[28] Once again: having revealed time as an *ekstatikon*, Heidegger does not then proceed to reintroduce a sequence within the three ecstases, one according to which the future would come first, the past second and the present third. It is precisely our 'fallen' understanding of time that forces us to think in this sequential way. The priority of the future with respect to authentic temporality became evident in the phenomenon of anticipatory resoluteness. Resolute disclosedness, in which Dasein's capacity-for-being-a-whole is made manifest, reveals the essential finitude of existence. Dasein ex-ists finitely. Temporality itself is originally finite, since the primordial and authentic future is the 'towards-oneself', in which Dasein exists as the possibility of its own nullity. It is only on the basis of this being-towards-one's-self as a being-towards-one's-end that we can understand the unfolding of time as a temporalizing.

This, of course, does not mean that time simply ceases with the no-longer-being-there. Time goes on in spite of my no longer being there. Many possibilities still lie in the future. But to think this time and this future, one still needs to presuppose the original time of existence. At issue in Heidegger's analysis is not so much the question of knowing what is contained within time as to analyse the way in which time temporalizes itself. Heidegger's thesis concerning the originary finitude of temporality is an attempt to grasp the originary character of temporality, which is revealed in the thrown projection of Dasein. Dasein exists as a possibility and a freedom whose future is ultimately closed off. And it is precisely to escape the finitude of originary temporality that the 'vulgar' conception of an in-finite time containing the multiple finite temporalities becomes necessary. Because the possibility of the finitude of time is *a priori* dismissed, we come to wonder how the infinite time of generation and corruption can become a finite temporality, when the problem, in Heidegger's terms, is 'that of how *in*authentic temporality arises out of finite authentic temporality, and how *in*authentic temporality, as *in*authentic, temporalises an *in*-finite time out of the finite'.[29]

By way of summary, we can bring Heidegger's analysis of originary temporality under four theses: 1. Insofar as time makes possible the constitution of the structure of care, time is the originary *temporalizing* of temporality. 2. This implies that temporality does not refer to the interiority of a subject, but that it is essentially *ekstatic*. 3. Temporality temporalizes itself primordially on the basis of a priority given to the *future*. 4. Such an ekstatic–existential temporality characterizes primordial time as *finite* time. Time, in short, is horizonal, finite, futural and ekstatic.

On this originary temporality Heidegger grounds the phenomenon of history (*Geschichte*). History needs to be distinguished from the mere chronological conception of time that underlies our ordinary sense of history and of historiography (*Historie*); the time of the event of being needs to be clearly distinguished from the essentially successive time of 'facts'. Yet this is a very delicate and complex question. Why? Because, first of all, Heidegger's concept of history, as developed initially in *Being and Time*, is itself subordinated to what he calls originary temporality. If being, or Dasein, is historical in the ordinary sense of the term, if, in other words, events seem to take place chronologically within history, and if history can be seen as the succession of events that occupy time conceived as present, it is only on the basis of an abstract or fallen understanding of an originary historicity of time, characterized first and foremost by its ecstatic and finite nature. Chronology, and the *Historie* that articulates it, Heidegger claims, is only the visible side of a primordial historicity that, whilst always operative, nonetheless remains in excess of its actualization. Thus, the event of being is never fully realized or exhausted in the worldly events that unfold in the present tense. If history is indeed conjugated in the present indicative, historicity, on the other hand, constitutes this present that cannot be located, the present that unfolds between an immemorial past and an absolute future and that resonates with echoes of a manifold of co-existing epochs. The time of being or of becoming is not that of presence, but of subterranean and transepochal correspondences, the time of echoes that bounce off one another, to the point, perhaps, of constituting a secret history.

Being and Time is the culmination of Heidegger's early thought, which sets out to construe a fundamental ontology by revealing the unifying meaning of being as time. It corresponds to Heidegger's first major effort to wrest being from inert substantiality and recover its forgotten origin as pure becoming. 'Being and Time' really reads: 'Being as Time'. But time itself, pure becoming, must be distinguished from the time of the world and of actuality, the fallen time, as Heidegger puts it, in which things and events seem to succeed one another in what amounts to a merely sequential order. Real time, on the other hand, is not the time of succession, or the linear, actual time in which events replace one another. Nor is it the time of eternity, of the absolute present, which events occupy for a while before vanishing into the past. And the past itself is not what's no-longer-present and held in reserve, waiting to be reactivated or brought back into the present. The present is only an *effect* of time, not its point of departure. When understood on the basis of the essence of time as rapturous or ecstatic time, the present appears in the 'moment' (*Augenblick*): unlike the present that is severed from its co-implication with the past and the future, or rather, with the future as that which is approaching from afar, that which is coming towards existence, and towards which existence is oriented, and the past that 'is' in the mode of what has been, the 'moment' designates the coming together of these raptures, the joint or the binding of past and future, the fold where past and future touch one another and reveal the site of the present. The 'moment' no longer has anything to do with a measurable now: it is at once less palpable, less graspable and infinitely more real than that. It is not quantitative, but qualitative, not extensive, but intensive. To think time from the present alone, then, is to think abstractly, for it amounts to taking the effect for the cause, even if no actual cause can be associated with the unfolding, or the temporalizing of time. It also amounts to constructing time as a sequence of instants, which, in turn, can be represented as a line made of points and segments. In doing so, time is spatialized, and denied its own temporal essence. Heidegger's concept of time, on the other hand, is precisely aimed at despatializing and dereifying time in order to uncover its eventful or ontological power. Time, he says, 'is' not, but temporalizes itself; there is no such *thing* as time, only a temporalizing, and from out of this primordial and ongoing event, everything takes place and finds its place, possibilities emerge and a world begins to take shape.

Despite this considerable achievement, *Being and Time* goes only so far in establishing time as the meaning of all beings (and not just that of the human being), and wresting philosophy from anthropology once and for all. We must bear in mind that the book only contains one of two parts initially planned, and only two of three divisions. This means that the third division of the first part, which was to reveal time as the meaning of the being of all beings, was never written, or at least not until 1962 (in a conference entitled 'Time and Being'). But by then the project had been transformed so radically that it was no longer possible to envisage the lecture as the missing third division of *Being and Time*. What *Being and Time* planned to do – this is clearly stated in the Introduction (§ 8) – was to reveal time as the transcendental horizon for the question of being. In a way, this programme is accomplished in the lecture course from 1927 that immediately followed the publication of *Being and Time*.[30] Yet what Heidegger does not manage to achieve, whether in *Being and Time* or in the lecture course, is to think the time or the temporality of being itself. He finds himself always drawn back into what Division Two of *Being and Time* had established, namely, 'the interpretation of Dasein in terms of temporality'. In order to carry out his initial intention, and fulfil the programme he had initially defined in the Introduction to *Being and Time*, namely, to reveal the meaning of being itself (as opposed to that of the human Dasein), Heidegger will have to transform his project radically, and abandon the project of a fundamental ontology rooted in human existence. Soon after the publication of *Being and Time*, Heidegger's thought began to shift from a transcendental–horizonal conception of the *meaning* of being, in which being temporalizes itself in the ekstatic temporality of Dasein, to what we could call an aletheic–ekstatic conception of the *truth* of being, in which Dasein finds its stance and to which it co-responds. This turning marks the point where being is no longer temporal because it constitutes the horizonal unity of Dasein's ekstatic temporality, but rather because it is historical in itself. There is a shift from historical time as rooted in the historicity of Dasein to history understood as a sending and a destiny that belongs to the truth of being itself. The conference 'Time and Being' concludes by saying that instead of 'being' and 'time' we should now speak of 'clearing' (*Lichtung*) and the presencing of 'presence' (*Anwesenheit*). It is this development I now wish to trace, albeit schematically.

SPACE, TIME AND THE TRUTH OF BEING

In the previous chapter, I sketched the transformation of the question of truth, and of its location, from the clearing of Dasein as the existent being to the clearing of being itself, in which ek-sistence finds itself drawn and implicated, but not as the main or decisive protagonist. I now wish to follow up the connection with time and space, and the way in which both are reconfigured in light of this shift. The main idea to retain is that space and time are being thought anew on the basis of the essence of truth I analysed in the previous chapter. Heidegger's analysis is complex, some would even say abstruse. The less inclined, or less patient, reader might want to move directly to the next chapter, and return to this one later.

The question, now, is one of knowing the extent to which the spatializing and the temporalizing identified with Dasein as existence in *Being and Time* are called into question, displaced or perhaps simply reinscribed in the light of the reworking of the question of being along the lines of the essential unfolding of truth. Indeed, having modified the nature of the link uniting truth and existence, the analysis of time and space that was complicit with the understanding of the truth of being as finite, ecstatic and horizonal temporality must now be reopened. In what does the operation of being consist, if no longer in the ecstatic making-room for things from out of a temporal horizon of finitude? The operation in question is still that of space and time. On this level, nothing has changed: in Heidegger's work after *Being and Time*, Da-sein (which Heidegger now often hyphenates, in order to emphasize that what's at issue in this word is the 'there' or the 'truth' of being) still refers to the operation of spatializing and temporalizing from out of which beings come into their own, come to be as the beings they are. Moreover, the different 'dimensions' of time are still referred to as ecstasies or, at times, as raptures (*Entrückungen*).[31] But the operation no longer coincides with the existing of existence. It no longer coincides with what Heidegger once considered to be originary time, namely, meta-physical time, or the time of the being whose being consisted in transcending beings towards their being.[32] Existence is now situated within this event that is 'older' than it, implicated in it in a way that is quite singular and which Heidegger characterizes as *Ereignis*. With this term, Heidegger hopes to designate the event of mutual and reciprocal ap-propriation between being and the human. In somewhat distancing the operation of time and space from existence, Heidegger does not bring it closer to traditional approaches. He does not have in mind, for example, the time of nature or of the cosmos, whether it be understood as the circular time of Ptolemaic and Aristotelian physics, the linear time of Newtonian physics and Kantian metaphysics or even the curved and finite space-time of generalized relativity. The time in question is neither that of existence, nor that of the cosmos, neither the time of metaphysics nor that of physics. With what does this operation coincide, then? And what, exactly, does this operation entail that was not contained in the analysis of temporality and of the temporalizing proper to existence? Two significant differences will need to be highlighted. First, time no longer stands in a privileged position with respect to space, but in absolute unity – which does not mean identity – with it. Second, the horizonality or finitude of time articulated in *Being and Time* is not so much abandoned as it is displaced and reinscribed as a trait of being itself. Time – in fact, time-space – is *of* being (or, as Heidegger begins to spell it in the 1930s, adopting an antiquated spelling so as to emphasize further the shift away from the metaphysical sense of being, still perhaps somewhat present in his own early thought, 'beyng', or *Seyn*). History itself is no longer rooted in the historicity of Dasein alone, but is now the history of beyng. Does this mean that, in the later work, Heidegger fulfils the programme announced, but never completed in *Being and Time*, namely, that of revealing time as the meaning not only of Dasein's being, but of being itself and as such?

1. The 'there' as time-space

We saw how, beginning with 'On the Essence of Truth', Heidegger discovers that the event of truth is not just an operation of clearing or disclosure. It is not a straightforward *aletheuein*. Rather, the operation of disclosure also coincides with a certain closure. A certain concealing always accompanies the operation of truth as clearing. In fact, truth properly understood is the co-originary event of clearing *and* concealing, and the 'there is' is the region that is held open by the tension between these two. Now this dimension of originary closure was already operative in the context of the analysis of Dasein in *Being and Time*, where death, as the possibility of the impossibility of existence, turned out to constitute the horizon of closedness on the basis of which the clearing of being took place. Death was the condition of possibility *and* impossibility of existence, the absolute limit and the impending end from out of which the world unfolded. Now, however, this horizon is displaced and reinscribed away from existence, as a trait of truth itself. Truth is, according to its full definition, 'clearing for the self-concealing', a clearing in and through the unfolding of which the originary concealing is sheltered. In other words, the advent of presence, in the sense of things present within presence, is at the same time the withdrawing of the movement of presencing as such. The event of presence is at once sheltered and concealed, inscribed and effaced in the phenomenal world onto which it opens. The German *Verbergung* (concealing), of which truth, as *Unverborgenheit* (unconcealment), is the negation, designates both directions at once, and in such a way that we can never simply decide in favour of one over the other (as we saw in the previous chapter, it is metaphysics that, according to Heidegger, equates truth with full presence and total transparency). Sheltering *and* concealing belong together in the very essence of truth. The economy of truth is equally and simultaneously one of in-scription and erasure, of the mark and the crypt, in short, of the trace. And it is as such that it escapes the economy of metaphysics, which, as we saw, is entirely located on the side of presence, and of truth's presence to itself. The 'there is', then, needs to be understood in terms of a twofold, antagonistic tendency in the strife of which a space is cleared and a time unfolds: the drive to presence and actuality on the one hand, the drive to withdrawal, erasure and refusal on the other.

Such is the reason why, when properly understood, the 'there' never refers to something that is *actually* there: insofar as it points to the 'there is' as such, it always implicates and retains what is never there *in* space and time, as a thing, but always withdraws and hides in the thing, as its very in-visibility. Such is the reason why the phenomenon, and indeed the event of world, when properly understood, cannot be reduced to those things that are present in it; as world, it always retains the trace of earth as its counter-force. The event of the world is itself nothing worldly. If the world worlds and roams and unleashes its forces, it is always, in the very moment in which it unfolds as world, called back into earth, as into its silent and forever withdrawn origin, as to this dimension in excess of presence and actuality. The artwork, as we shall see in Chapter 5, is itself an instance of truth in which the strife between world and earth is made visible as such, a peculiar type of 'thing' that presents or makes visible the *polemos* that exceeds presence, and accounts for it at the same time. If the human himself happens in the unfolding of the world, if he is brought out into the rapturous, ecstatic time of the world, thrown and pro-jected into its horizon, if he endures the world and with-stands it, he is also, at the same time, brought back into what Heidegger calls the 'captivating' refusal of earth, in the wake of which belongs the distant, delicate and discreet hinting (*Winken*) of the gods. Following indica- tions of Hölderlin's poetry, to which, beginning in 1934, he turns time and again, Heidegger locates the site of the sacred, and of the gods, on the side of the earth. This means that the gods are never simply present for Heidegger, but indicate the space of the sacred as the space in excess of presence to which we, as human beings, are destined. Insofar as we choose to dwell in the space of truth itself, in-between beyng and beings, we remain 'at the disposal of the gods'.[33] If Heidegger is inter- ested in rescuing a dimension of the sacred, and the possibility of a relation to the divine, it is not for religious purposes. The gods, he insists, are not to be thought 'from within "religion"', but 'from out of beyng'.[34] The space of the sacred does not follow from the presence and the transcendence of a god. It is the god itself that emerges from out of the dimension of truth that is held in reserve, and which we cannot access through beings and their familiar presence alone. To remain at the disposal of the gods means 'to stand far away and outside – outside the famil- iarity of "beings" and interpretations of them'.[35] It is to turn away from beings as the familiar beings and towards them from out of their unfamiliar origin, namely, the essence of truth. It is to engage with beings 'on the basis of' their hidden, self- effacing origin, on the basis of that which, of itself, does not grant itself.

As the 'there' (*Da*) of being, truth unfolds 'between' clearing and conceal-ing, world and earth, to which Heidegger associates the further concepts of 'rapture' (*Entrückung*) and 'captivation' (*Berückung*), 'granting' and 'refusal', to which I shall turn shortly. Truth itself, as the openness in which events and deeds take place, unfolds in the strife (*Streit*) between world and earth and in the en-counter (*Entgegnung*) between men and gods. As such, it is not so much a moment *in* time and a point *in* space as a region, a domain or a site prior to any objectification of space and time, prior to space and time having become the parameters for the representation and mathematization of nature. Heidegger calls this site the 'between' or the 'in-between' (*das Inzwischen*) where being unfolds, or, as he often says, 'turns'. It marks the very emergence of time and space before any representation and mathematization; it charac-terizes the unity of space and time, the joint that joins together the tenden-cies in their strifely encounter. 'Ereignis' is the word Heidegger now uses to designate the spatial and temporal unity of being and beings.[36] As such, mob-ilizing and somewhat reinterpreting a determination already thematized in *Being and Time*, Heidegger characterizes it further as 'the site of the moment' (*die Augenblicksstätte*): 'The site of the moment unfolds from within *Ereignis*, as the strife of world and earth'.[37] And if it coincides with the domain of deci-sion (*Entscheidung*), it is insofar as it marks the space in which the fate of the world and of the human is being decided: in other words, the space of history.[38]

Heidegger gathers the various determinations of the *Augenblicksstätte*, which we shall have to clarify one by one, in the following, arguably complex terms:

> The site of the moment: uniqueness and assault of the greatest rapture [*Entrückung*] in the domain of the hint, out of the gentle captivation [*Berückung*] of that which refuses itself and hesitates, proximity and dis-tance in the domain of decision, the 'where' and 'when' of the history of beyng, clearing and concealing itself from within the occurring of the fundamental attunement of reservedness – such is the fundamental expe-rience of the there and thus of time-space.[39]

'Rapture' and 'captivation', 'refusal' and 'hesitation', 'proximity' and 'dis-tance', 'decision', and 'reservedness' are all terms, or concepts, which need to be clarified. They all point to a certain transformation of Heidegger's thought. This, of course, is making things more difficult for us: in connection with his early thought, and the project of fundamental ontology in particular, we wit-nessed a remarkable production of new ideas and concepts. We now need to familiarize ourselves with a new set of concepts, and with a decisive rework-ing of the assumptions governing the early work. Only later will we be able to ascertain the *necessity* of this new direction.

Let me begin by noting the fact that, in the passage I've just quoted, time and space are thought from out of what emerges as their originary unity, from the 'and' itself. This unity is the very movement of *Ereignis*. If I choose to leave this world untranslated at this point, it is for the same reasons that forced us to leave the word Dasein untranslated. In fact, it's a word – a decisive and pivotal philosophical term – that's even harder to translate than the term 'Dasein'. On one level, Heidegger retains the ordinary meaning of the word, that of *event*. Since the beginning of our enterprise, we've seen how insistent Heidegger is that we think of being, *Sein*, and of Dasein itself, not as a thing, or a substance, but as a movement, and a verb. The same, you recall, went for truth, which, as a result of his early texts on Aristotle, Heidegger understood as an activity, an *aletheuein*. So, it is perhaps not surprising that he is now explicitly interpreting being (or, as he now calls it, beyng) as an event. Naturally, the event in question is no ordinary event. It is not just *an* event, that is, the irruption of something new in time, the happening of something in historical time. It is not one event along this chain of events we ordinarily refer to as 'history'. Rather, it is the irruption, or the coming about of time and space as such, the advent of history as the open realm in which world-events take place. It points not to historical events and facts, but to the origin of history itself, to what we could call historicity, or the eventfulness of events. It is, if you will, the founding event – except that, as we shall see, it is itself without foundation. As the founding event, it mustn't be mistaken for something like a creative act – whether that creation be the work of an omnipotent God or the result of physical forces that produced the laws of nature as we know them. The event in question is neither theological nor cosmological. It is not an event that took place once, and from which everything else unfolds, but the event that does not cease to take place, and in the taking place of which a world is opened up, and beings find their own place. It is the advent of presence, or the opening up of being. As such, Heidegger uses the term 'Ereignis' to designate the nature of the relation between being and beings, between being and the human and between being and time (as well as space). In each instance, what's at stake is what he began by calling the ontological difference, and to which philosophical thought was to turn as towards its primary subject-matter. In the thinking of Ereignis, there is a great continuity with respect to the early work. We should think of Ereignis – Heidegger's most significant philosophical term from the 1930s onwards – as a deepening and a reworking of the problematic of the ontological difference and the quest for the unifying sense of being with which he began.

In an effort to clarify the meaning of time and space, let me now return to the passage I began by quoting. When understood not just on the basis of world and nature, but on the basis of the full operation of truth as involving a twofold movement of clearing and concealing, time and space emerge as the 'where' and 'when', the 'site' and 'moment' of beyng in its historical unfolding. Needless to say, then, time-space is not something of which we can say *what* it is independently of the *way* in which it is, and this means of its specific historical configuration. There is simply no 'essence' or 'identity' of time-space outside its concrete spatial-temporal inscription. Time-space, as an event, always refers to a site – the site of a specific and concrete strife (*Streit*) between world and earth and en-counter (*Entgegnung*) between men and gods, the site of a singular historical configuration. These are the limits within which history unfolds. Time-space is as it were framed, its field of action delineated by this fourfold horizon, in the unfolding of which comes to be decided what is possible and what is not, what is valued and what is not, what is necessary and what is superficial, etc.

At this point, leaving aside the question of the god, I simply wish to note the fact that 'the human' is mentioned alongside world, earth and gods as one pole or strip (*Bahn*) constituting the fourfold historical configuration of truth, which Heidegger will later on designate as the 'fourfold' (*Geviert*). This raises the question of the meaning of such a gesture, and of the place attributed to the human in this reconfiguring of truth. For if, as was already the case in Heidegger's early work, truth is indeed no longer either objective or subjective, or indeed a combination of both subject (*mens*) and object (*res*), it is also no longer simply equated with the disclosedness (*Erschlossenheit*) of finite existence, as in *Being and Time*. We recall how, in § 44 in particular, Heidegger derived the concept of truth from the existing – and this meant, ultimately, from the temporalizing – of existence, essentially envisaged as the most originary mode of *aletheuein*. Yet the human is not simply absent from the operation of truth as reformulated in the 1930s, even if truth is now *of* being. Truth is no longer *of* the human, or even of Dasein, yet the human remains implicated in the operation of truth. In fact, he is the only being (*Seiende*) implicated in this operation (for neither earth nor world nor even gods are actual beings). Thus, in a way, the human continues to be privileged in the new assembling of truth, in the very moment in which truth moves away from the human, and in the direction of the pre-individual and the pre-human. For truth, as the truth of beyng, is essentially *for* the human. Such is the reason why, doubling the fourfold articulation of truth as it were, the very movement of Ereignis, as the turning or the oscillation born of the strifely essence of truth, is envisaged as the reciprocal appropriation and the co-respondence of beyng and the human. In its turning, Ereignis turns itself towards the human, in such a way that such a turning cannot take place without the human. The human and being 'need' one another, and call for one another. The human is called forth by being, and being is gathered, grounded, and sheltered in the human's actions, in art and thought especially (I shall turn to the question of art in Chapter 5). The human is by virtue of its exposedness to the clearing of being; being unfolds truly and genuinely to the extent that it is sheltered and preserved in the human. Ereignis designates this co-belonging of the human and being.

After the so-called 'turn' of Heidegger's thought, Da-sein no longer refers to the human and existence alone, but to the concrete, historical place or site opened up and held open by a configuration of truth, the scene of the eternal strife between two tendencies or forces that oppose one another and yet reciprocally implicate one another. This is the 'site of the moment' (*die Augenblicksstätte*). Not the occurrence of something *in* a measurable instant and identifiable place, not even the vision of the *essence* of time and space, but the occurrence or the event of time-space. The essence of time and space, in a way.

Except that, here, essence can only be understood as the happening or the unfolding not of some essence that would itself not be entirely implicated in the happening, but as the unfolding or the taking place of a configuration of time-space, a specific and singular time-space assemblage, jointure or articulation. The unity of time and space as the 'site of the moment' designates this taking place of place or this temporalizing of time as history. History does not so much take place in time as it is the happening of time-space, every time absolutely singular and unique. The event of time-space is the emergence of history as such, which is also always the emergence of a historical configuration, from out of a turning in Ereignis. Every turn of the screw or the pole of Ereignis marks a new epoch, and by that we should understand a decisive reorganization or a new deal between world and earth in their eternal strife, and gods and men in their en-counter:

> History is not the privilege of the human but rather the essence of beyng itself. History is at stake solely in the between of the en-counter between gods and the human as the ground for the strife of world and earth; history is nothing other than the happening [*Ereignung*] of this between.[40]

What Heidegger is telling us here is that history is *of* truth and being. There isn't a history of truth, and a history of being, which would be a subset of a broader, more universal history. Rather, history is itself born of the essence of truth, and of its inner conflict. History is the very way in which truth unfolds and comes about. What is so striking about our own history is its remarkable unity. It is a unity marked by the systematic and increasing erasure of one aspect of truth in favour of the other, an erasure and a forgottenness recorded in the metaphysical tradition, and carried out most forcefully in the birth of modern science, and subsequently the domination of planetary technology and techno-science.[41] Our history is dominated by the withdrawal and the forgetting of untruth (or concealment) as the essence of truth, and so by the domination of what is left in the wake of this forgetting, namely, presence, the objective world and the human as its master and possessor. From the start, and until the bitter end, Heidegger's struggle will have been to reawaken Western philosophy, Western culture and the Western consciousness in general to its forgotten and repressed origin. This is what, in *Contributions*, and in other texts of that period, he calls 'the other beginning' – a new beginning towards which his own thought is only a 'crossing'. Heidegger viewed his own effort as an attempt to prepare thought for this other beginning, and to open it onto this other, hidden history, or, better said perhaps, this other side of truth that is pregnant with a different future. Given the remarkable unity of our Western history, Heidegger contrasts this 'other beginning' with what he calls the 'first beginning', which stretches from the Greek origins of Western culture to the twenty-first century. Despite his talk of various epochs within that first beginning, and his attempt to distinguish between moments 'within' a history that sinks deeper and deeper into the forgetting of its own origin, we must bear in mind that this is a unified and unidirectional history. The other beginning alone would be a genuine alternative, and mark a real turning within history. It alone would herald something like a historical break, and a decisive rupture.

But is this rupture a matter of temporal succession? Does the other beginning need to come 'after' the first beginning? It would seem that, in Heidegger's notion of a 'turning' within Ereignis, it is not so much a change of direction or heading *within* history, that same and very history from which it would depart, which is in question. Rather, it would seem that an altogether different move is announced: an unfolding of time and space that is entirely heterogeneous to history understood as the history of the abandonment by and of being (*Seinsverlassenheit*), an event that is incommensurable with any occurrence taking place in space and time, an event the repetition of which would not be reducible to the succession of its chronological inscriptions. It would mark something like the beginning of history as such, given the fact that, for that time, history would unfold, a site would open up, on the basis of the essence of history itself – that is, truth – having explicitly come to the fore. In that respect, the other beginning would consist in taking up *again* and *anew* what was left behind and abandoned in the first beginning. It would amount to a repetition of history from the point of view of its forgotten origin. Nothing 'more' would take place in that repetition; history would not become the site of a 'new' event. Rather, what would take place and, in thus taking place, would constitute an event of an unequalled and incomparable nature, is the taking place of place itself (as *Augenblicksstätte*), the event of the event (of beyng). Would that be history, then, at least understood from this 'turning' in which everything is transformed? The temporality of repetition is intriguing and complex: if, in the other beginning, that beginning that is to open onto, not yet another epoch or moment in history, but an altogether different history, one does not turn away from the 'old', but turns to it as if for the first time, that is, turns to what is forgotten and abandoned in the first beginning, then, to a certain extent, that history of the first beginning can be said to linger on; to a certain extent, it remains intact, untouched. And yet, on another level, it is profoundly subverted – for it now relates to the world in such a way that the world speaks from its unspoken and hidden ground, from the abyss onto which it opens and which sustains it. In a way, then, I would like to suggest that the other beginning does not succeed the first beginning, and that the temporality that is at stake in the other beginning escapes chronology altogether. The 'first' and the 'other' beginning can coincide, for the simple reason that they respond to two entirely different temporalities: their relation is one of chronological coincidence *and* historical disjunction. The time of the other beginning is the time that turns back onto the time-space of being as the presupposed and forgotten ground of the first beginning. It is the time that at once makes possible and exceeds chronological time, and this means the time of things and of the world – it is the time that is otherwise than worldly, or the time of the earth.

2. *The abyss of time-space*

Earlier on, I suggested that we think of Ereignis as the founding event –
except, I added immediately, that it is an event without foundation. You will
also recall that, in connection with the unity of the time and space of Ereignis,
which Heidegger calls 'the site of the moment', he spoke of a certain 'refusal',
also referred to at times as a 'hesitation'. This refusal, or hesitation, will turn
out to be the dimension that Heidegger associates with the *spatiality* of truth.
It is also the key to understanding why truth is itself without foundation, or
why it is abyssal. From what we have said so far, we know that the essence
of truth is concealment. We know that a certain self-withdrawing and self-
concealment belongs to the very essence of truth. In *Contributions*, Heidegger
says that the essence of truth 'stays away'. This is its nature, as it were. This
means that the sphere of presence, onto which truth opens, or which it opens
up as such, is itself a function of the self-withdrawing of truth. Where does
truth withdraw? Not in some other, distant place, in some noumenal or intelligible reality, but *in* and *as* the world itself. In other words, it is the opening
up of the world as such, in the clearing of which beings become immediately
visible and accessible, present in this or that way, that truth withdraws. There
is, if you will, something like a self-effacement of truth in the very domain
that it opens up. And this is the reason why the essence of truth is so elusive,
why the reign of metaphysics, as the metaphysics of presence, and of representational, objective thought, is so difficult to unsettle. This is what Heidegger
means when he speaks of the abyssal grounding of truth. Truth stays 'away',
withdraws and, in this very withdrawing, grounds. It grounds precisely in
withdrawing. Its withdrawal or staying away is the uncovering of a ground, of
a world that opens up and in which beings emerge. Thus, it is a grounding
that always falls short – but, once again, this lack is an excess, this poverty a
wealth – of anything actually and simply 'there', of presence as such. And yet
it is not simply indifferent and unrelated to presence: it grounds it. This
ground stays away in self-concealment. It thus amounts to a certain *not* granting the ground, to a refusal of ground. But this refusal, this *not*-granting is
itself not nothing; it is a manner of letting *be*, of opening up, yet in such a way
that it is never exhausted in the process, that it always remains in excess of
what it discloses. It is therefore not pure refusal, but a *hesitating* refusal. And
from out of this hesitation *everything* takes place. *Ab-grund* is the 'hesitant
refusal' of ground. It is in this refusal that the clearing occurs, but in such a
way that the clearing is never quite completed, definitive. For to the clearing
belongs the hesitation of its counter-tendency; it bears the trace or the memory
of its origin, even when and where this origin has been 'forgotten', as is the
case in metaphysics and contemporary techno-science. In that respect, the *Ab-
grund* is also *Ur-grund*: the *originary* grounding of the essence of truth.

Now the difficulty of the analysis lies in the demand to think of this hesitation as marking the unity of the essence of truth, the belonging-together
of clearing and self-concealing. And, in developing or analysing one side of

the operation, we must always bear in mind the other, and see the two as ultimately coextensive and co-originary. We must ultimately come to understand the truth of beyng in terms of a hesitation, or an oscillation between two opposed tendencies, in the opposition of which presence unfolds. There is, if you will, a certain undecidability at the heart of truth itself. At the same time, however, this oscillation, this hesitation, this originary undecidability is the domain of the utmost decision, the domain in which history as such is being decided: whether truth will recede more and more into the open and the disclosed only, whether there will ultimately be only beings – whether metaphysics will ultimately triumph across the board – or whether a counter-movement will be initiated, in which the self-concealing itself will be brought to bear on thought, on culture in general; whether, in other words, philosophy will confirm itself as 'representation', 'calculation' and 'machination', or whether it will be in a position to experience the ungrounding at the heart of ground, the absence that traverses and sustains presence.[42] But one thing is certain for Heidegger: history, our own fate takes place and is played out in the space of this oscillation. Everything that really matters takes place in the space of this 'between', in-between clearing and self-concealing, and in the echo that resonates between both. Thus, this oscillation is not a default, but the historical in excess of actuality. And the temporality that is implicated in this oscillation is itself entirely in excess of the present of chronological time. It is the temporality of time–space, or of the *Augenblicksstätte*.

We need now to see how the operation of grounding as hesitant self-refusal implicates time and space; how, in other words, time and space unfold from out of this originary operation. Heidegger characterizes the relation as one of simultaneity and coincidence: the abyssal ground, he claims, grounds by temporalizing (*Zeitigung*) and spatializing (*Räumung*).[43] In other words, time and space are the manner in which the abyssal ground grounds. But time and space are themselves thought verbally, and not objectively, since they are the very modality of the event of beyng itself – and no longer, as was the case in *Being and Time*, of existence alone.[44] Thus, they are not objective and purely formal dimensions, given once and for all and *a priori*. Rather, they mark a specific operation, a doing that delineates a concrete locus or site. In other words, Heidegger, in these pages devoted to time-space, does not set out to think time and space, as if these were pre-given, objective dimensions that one could decide to think. Rather, he reveals how anything like an object, and like thought itself, is itself a function of a peculiar, forever reinscribed event – the event of time-space. And so, in the end, it would be a matter of asking how space and time as objective dimensions of nature themselves unfold from the originary unity of time-space as the 'between' whence everything surges forth. And so, as Heidegger points out, to shift the terrain from the objective analysis of time and space to that of time-space does not mean that the objective knowledge of time and space (one can think here of the space-time of generalized relativity) is simply 'false', and to be replaced with this 'other' conception of the unity of space and time as 'time-space'. Such a move would be utterly meaningless, if not altogether preposterous:

> The interpretation of space and time from within time-space does not intend to demonstrate as 'false' the heretofore knowledge of space and time. On the contrary, this knowledge will be above all relegated to the naturally limited sphere of its accuracy. . . .[45]

By 'naturally limited sphere of its accuracy', we need to understand the sphere of objectified nature, which operates on a level that is altogether different from the onto-phenomenological plane which Heidegger, in his own way and after his initial attempt at laying the ground for a 'fundamental ontology', shares with the phenomenological tradition and its demand that we recover the world as it is, in its primitive, pre-scientific and pre-predicative state. It is in that context that what Heidegger, in that respect in a sort of complicity with Husserl, is attempting to think under the reciprocal appropriation of 'world' and 'earth' cannot be assimilated with the modern, scientific concept of 'nature'. That said, it is also not as if these two planes were entirely heterogeneous. For, at least on Heidegger's reading, 'nature' is first and foremost a metaphysical concept – the implications of which can be felt right through its scientific interpretation – and one that is derived from a structural inability to let it speak from its non-metaphysical, foundationless ground.

Following Heidegger's own analysis, let us now decompose this unity of time and space in both its temporal and spatial dimensions, bearing in mind, however, from the start and throughout, that this unity is originary, and that the following decomposition thus amounts to a certain abstraction. Whilst it is virtually impossible not to clarify time and space for themselves, we must bear in mind that we can do so only from out of their originary co-unity. Ultimately, what we need to think is the reciprocal implication of time and space. Thus, we shall have to see how, in the very temporalizing of time, space itself is implicated and how, in the very spatializing of space, time itself is implicated. How, in other words, the temporalizing of time is the spatializing of time and how the spatializing of space is its temporalizing.

Remarkably, the operation of time is characterized in terms of a certain *emptiness* (*Leere*), an emptiness that is itself rooted in the emptiness of the self-refusal.[46] Time, therefore, and this means also the present onto which it opens, springs from a certain twofold absencing, the twofoldness of which nonetheless points to a single event: as hesitating self-refusal, the truth of being is at once this event that is forever withdrawing, thus opening up the past, and forever approaching, turned towards Da-sein from the start, thus opening up the future. In other words, this absencing or receding points simultaneously in the direction of what Heidegger calls a 'belongingness' to beyng and a 'call' onto beyng, it is at once a drawing into the past (a remembrance), and into the future (an awaiting). Insofar as the being of Dasein draws from, and is drawn into the withdrawal of truth, to which Dasein belongs from the start, this self-effacement of truth marks the origin and the past of Dasein. Dasein's authentic relation to it, therefore, will be one of remembrance. At the same time, this is the very dimension that signals the future of Dasein: the future and the destiny of Dasein lie in its being called upon by the truth of being. The essence of truth is what's always and already awaiting Dasein, and to which thought needs to turn if it is to conform to its own essence.

It is in the space opened up by this twofold orientation that the event of time-space occurs. Specifically, time-space is the very occurrence of this double event, the very happening of a certain emptiness. Now this emptiness should precisely not be mistaken for an empty *space*, that is, for a mere capacity to contain, a void waiting to be filled by things and events. For such is precisely the way in which space, and even time, have never ceased to be thought of throughout the history of metaphysics: as that *in* which things take place. Rather, what space and time themselves are can be thought of from out of an originary understanding of *that* emptiness only. Furthermore, this emptiness is not synonymous with the rule and reign of chaos over cosmos. For the clearing and lightening that occurs in the presencing of presence is not a 'mere gaping and yawning open',[47] but a certain ordering and configuring of presence. In other words, the fate of things and of the world at large is decided neither 'here' nor 'now', in the present, but over there, in the 'how' of a ground that recedes. This is tantamount to saying that the world is shot through with emptiness, that its fabric is woven with invisible and intangible threads, and yet 'there', giving it colour and tonality, depth and texture. It is tantamount to saying that this emptiness, far from being a lack or a default, is rather an excess, a reserve and thus also always to come ('the fullness of what is still undecided'[48]); it is the (virtual) plenitude of being, which must not be mistaken for the (actual) presence of beings. Finally, and closely related to the previous point, this emptiness is not a cause for lament and nostalgia, or even hope in the straightforward sense of the term. For sure, this emptiness, when brought into view, opens onto a certain form of distress; but this is the distress born of the experience of the abandonment by being, the distress of 'reservedness' (*Verhaltenheit*), and not neediness. It is the experience of a certain excess and a certain plenitude, yet one that is bound up with the experience of its unmasterability and reticence.[49]

Thus, in the end, the dimension that metaphysics perceives as providing the measure for all other dimensions, the ideal that regulates its own economy and the ultimate goal that drives it, namely, presence, is here identified, in what amounts to an extraordinary inversion, with the site of a certain emptiness. At the heart of presence, at the heart of the determination on which the metaphysical edifice is built, Heidegger identifies a gap that cannot be filled, an absence older than presence itself. For the present is now envisaged as the 'effect' of a certain withdrawal that is infinitely richer and fuller than those present things with which metaphysics concerns itself, of a certain twofold horizon in excess of presence itself, structurally very similar to the temporal ecstases of existence thematized in *Being and Time*.[50] The present is now entirely envisaged from out of the founding event, the event of being as Ereignis, which frames both past and future in terms of a belongingness to being, and of the call of being, as if time now stretched between these two horizons, at once retaining the trace of an event forever past and, *at the same time*, tending towards that event as always to come. We must resist interpreting this turn towards past and future in psychologistic, even subjectivistic terms: it is the abandonment, the present itself that is structurally oriented in that way, even if such an orientation implicates the human from the start and defines who he is; as a result, and insofar as grounding involves a turning towards that towards which one is always already turned, 'remembrance' and 'awaiting' must not be understood psychologically, as possibilities or faculties that would belong to the human, but as the very form of grounding itself, in which the human as such takes place for the first time. Any grounding, whether it is in the order of thought, poetizing, creation, leadership, etc. amounts to a remembering *and* an expecting. These determinations must be understood historically (*geschichtlich*) and not anthropologically. It is not that the present remembers and anticipates in an 'intentional' sense. Rather, the present comes to be constituted in this remembering-awaiting. The source of time is not so much the present as the twofold horizon of belongingness and call. As such, the present bears the trace of this event that is 'before' and 'after' it, and towards which it is ex-tended, in a rapturous gesture, of which it is thus the remembrance and the anticipation. Time is as it were stretched out on the frame of being, towards which it tends as towards this past and this future, as this withdrawal that marks an irreducible event, and of which it is itself the trait. Time comes and goes, it stretches and returns, as in a bow or a hairpin turn (*Kehre*). In a way, we are faced here with something like yet another reworking of the famous Husserlian analysis of temporality, and of the tension (retention of the past – protention towards the future) that characterizes it. With the significant difference that time is not constituted for and by a consciousness, or even by an ex-sistence, but temporalized from out of the twofold horizon of the event of being. It is there, in the between of this twofold event, that the fate of time, and this means the coming about of history, is played out. Such is the reason why Heidegger, reinscribing the determination that characterized the 'proper' mode of the present in *Being and Time*, prefers to designate the present as the 'moment' (*Augenblick*), that is, not as an abstract point along the line of time, but as the gathering of the raptures of time, their point of convergence or intersection – their critical point, if *krisis* does indeed involve a sense of decision, a point at which an incision is inserted into the fabric of being. The moment is thus more a zone of intensity than a mere instant, a field of presence and individuation more than a singular point, the site of decision and of history, and not a mere 'now' always about to vanish into the past.

It is this excess, this plenitude, that is never present that translates into the emptiness of the present. The event in question is no ordinary event, however. From the perspective of the present and the representational attitude to which it gives birth, the present alone is plenitude, and past and future lack, essentially negative, essentially *not* present. If the present is the site of an emptiness, it is insofar as its ground is essentially self-refusal, turning away from the present: both to come and past. Time as such is as it were framed by this self-refusal – at once always already past, always already having been, and, as such, always already to have been, always ahead, to come. But does this mean, then, that the present can only be the site of this absolute abandonment and desolation? In the words of Hölderlin, are the gods moving further away from the present, deserting it once and for all, moving deeper into withdrawal, fleeing into a past and a future of which we have no intimation, so that not even the slightest possibility of remembrance and awaiting exists? Has the ground withdrawn once and for all and definitively? Such would indeed be the case, were the self-refusal not also *hesitant*, were the withdrawing ground not also turned towards us, drawing us into its very withdrawal, allowing us to re-enter the present as the site, not of this initial mere emptiness, but of this emptiness shot through with the plenitude of the un-grounding that breaks it open. Such would be the case, were this most discreet of oscillations not to resound across the domain – the event of time-space – opened up by the unique en-counter between self-refusal and hesitation.[51]

Whereas the operation of time that characterizes self-refusal is indeed that of a rapture into futurity and having-been-ness, whereas time is indeed ecstatic, torn between these two lines of flight, constantly threatened with infinite dispersion or dissemination (*Zerstreuung*), driven towards endless withdrawal and receding, the operation of space, with which time is essentially bound, consists in the inverse movement: not dispersion, but estrangement or alienation (*Entfremdung*), not rapture, or ravishing, this sense of being pulled or torn away, but captivation (*Berückung*), this sense of being held back, drawn into closure. Space, here, as the *Berückung* that brings back into an enclosure (*Umhalt*), plays a role equivalent to the horizonality of death in the early existential analysis: it limits time, and secures the finitude of being. It holds the raptures of time back, brings them back from infinite dispersal into estrangement, inscribes them within a horizon of finitude, or closure. It is the force at the origin of the gathering of time into the moment, the counter-movement or counter-essence of dissemination. Here, time is once again envisaged as finite, but with the following twofold difference. First, time no longer coincides simply with a finite being, the being who ex-ists being, but with being itself; it is the very finitude of being itself that is uncovered. Not as mortality, but as horizonality. Second, this horizonality is not simply and not primarily that of the future, or even that of time in general, but that of space (in time): the horizon is now entirely circular, it is an *Umhalt*. As such, it is the delimiting and the spatializing of time, much in the same way in which time is the temporalizing, that is, the counter-, disseminating move of space. Both call for one another and need one another: every move (*Rück*) calls for a counter-move, so that each dis-placement (*Verrückung*), whether rapture (*Entrückung*) or captivation (*Berückung*), comes into its own and unfolds only on the basis of its being met by a counter-move. This counter-turning marks the originary unity of time and space: it is the movement that brings them together in holding them apart, that separates them by referring them to one another.

How does this take place? The counter-turning takes place within each 'dimension': rapture is first and foremost a tendency towards dispersion. Yet it is also gathering (in the moment). This is its counter-move or counter-turning. Similarly, captivation is essentially a tendency towards estrangement. Yet it is also enclosure. As such, enclosure is its counter-turning. But, in each case, the counter-turning could not occur were it not for the fact that time and space are not heterogeneous, were it not for the fact that, from the start, they are turned towards one another. Thus, gathering is the spatializing of time, the becoming-space of time, or space-in-time. Likewise, enclosure is the temporalizing of space, the becoming-time of space, or time-in-space. Such is the reason why, in the end, Heidegger can claim that 'time spatialises' and that 'space temporalises'. Each has always already begun to become its other, is always already caught up in its *becoming other*. Each becomes itself only in becoming other. Every movement of owning is a movement of othering, every propriation an ex-propriation. The unity, or intimacy (*Einigkeit*, *Innigkeit*) of time and space lies in this counter-turning, in the becoming other of each: 'This counter-turning is indeed what is essential and indicates the originary referral of both to each other, on the basis of their separatedness [*Geschiednis*]'.[52] And so, it is on the basis of their being two counter-tendencies, one oriented towards dispersal, the other one towards estrangement, that each comes into its own. It is in their very separatedness, their very counter-orientation, that each is brought into its own essence and proper unfolding. But at no stage is this opposition dialectical, for both unfold, as counter-tendencies, from the structure of Ereignis itself, torn between – and this being-torn-apart, this quartering is not the result of some indecision, some temporary state of hesitation, but designates Ereignis in its essence – belongingness and call. This primal and irreducible 'event' is the forever-renewed origin of time-space, the very source of the spatializing and the temporalizing that is world configuring.

But in the end, what matters most is that this temporalizing and this spacing be that of Ereignis, understood as the unity of belongingness and call, as this singular and unique event on which the fate of the human hinges. Ereignis, as the event of time-space, is thus the unity and co-originarity of this movement of ecstasy and captivation, dissemination and alienation, in and through which time is from the start brought back into the hold of space, and space itself from the start carried away in the breaking out of time. History is nothing other than the state of equilibrium reached at any given time by this spatio-temporal economy. History is *of* time-space. It is the mark or the inscription of a particular configuration of the tension opposing time and space.

Being and Time set out to reveal time as the ultimate horizon on the basis of which the world opens up for us, and so as the 'meaning' of being. Yet the project of fundamental ontology remained incomplete. The reason for that was primarily to do with Heidegger's realization that, so long as we take the human Dasein as our point of departure, we shall not be able to extract the meaning of the being of all beings, or the meaning of being itself. For that, a change of direction was required. This is what Heidegger set out to achieve in the 1930s. In doing so, he realized that Da-sein now needed to refer not to human existence (at least not primarily), but to the truth of being itself, to the way in which being unfolds. The unfolding of being itself, in which the human being finds itself implicated, is what Heidegger calls history. The question regarding the truth of being becomes the question regarding its history. The historicity of being implies a temporality of a very specific kind, one that, whilst in certain ways reminiscent of that of ek-sistence, reveals itself as time-space. In his effort to rethink history from out of the essence of truth, Heidegger understands it in terms of the specific assemblage, or equilibrium, between concealment and unconcealment, between truth and untruth, which characterizes every epoch of being. An 'epoch' is precisely a given configura-tion of time-space, a singular interaction between rapture and captivation, or between world and earth. Heidegger's conclusion is that there is a remarkable unity behind the various events and defining moments of our Western history. This is a history that is the effect of an abandonment and a forgottenness of being that characterizes the manner in which, in the West, and beginning in Ancient Greece, we have 'received' this share or this lot that defines our humanity. So far, Heidegger argues, it is as if Western history had gone in one direction, and one direction alone, namely, that of the fascination with, and the conquest of, beings in their presence. Another, altogether 'different' begin-ning would be one in which beings would be encountered, and engaged with, on the basis of their self-effacing and self-withdrawing origin – on the basis of the essence of truth. In that respect, there is a remarkable continuity with the early work: Heidegger's sole ambition is to reawaken us to our lost and forgot-ten essence, to reverse or deflect the course of history by turning to that which, from the start, has been abandoned, and the abandoning of which constitutes our own historical, cultural and epistemological identity. If the later work does constitute a reorientation of the earlier work, it does not break with it in any way. On the contrary: it extends it by radicalizing it.

NOTES

1 SZ, §§19–21.
2 SZ, 103.
3 SZ, 103.
4 SZ, 103–4.
5 See Appendix 5 'Philosophy and Architecture'.
6 SZ, 105.
7 SZ, 105.
8 SZ, 106.
9 SZ, 108.
10 SZ, 111.
11 SZ, 112.

12 On the connection between space and truth, see Chapter 2.
13 Bergson, whose critique of the metaphysics of nothingness I alluded to in the first chapter, was perhaps right after all: there is still 'something' in 'nothing', namely, time. But time is precisely not a 'thing', an object.
14 See Appendix 6 'Deconstruction'.
15 SZ, 325.
16 SZ, 326.
17 SZ, 328.
18 GA 29/30, 247/165.
19 This is where, despite Heidegger's acknowledgement of his indebtedness to Kierkegaard's concept of the moment, he departs from it (see SZ, 338, footnote/497).
20 SZ, 328.
21 GA 29/30, 224/148.
22 GA 29/30, 247/165.
23 SZ, 324.
24 SZ, 329.
25 Aristotle, *Physics*, 13, 222b16.
26 See GA 24, 377.
27 SZ, 329.
28 SZ, 329.
29 SZ, 331.
30 See GA 24, §§ 21 and 22.
31 Especially in GA 65, §§242–4.
32 This connection is made most explicit in two texts from 1929, 'What is Metaphysics?' and 'On the Essence of Ground', both published in *Wegmarken*. 'Holding itself out into the nothing, Dasein is in each case already beyond beings as a whole. This being beyond beings we call "transcendence".' 'Going beyond beings occurs in the essence of Dasein. But this going beyond is metaphysics itself . . . . Metaphysics is the basic occurrence of Dasein. It is Dasein itself' (*Wm*, 15 and 18).
33 GA 65, 18/14.
34 GA 65, 508/357.
35 GA 65, 18/14.
36 GA 65, 13/10.
37 GA 65, 30/22.
38 I shall attempt to provide a genuine understanding of history further on, once I have clarified the nature of time–space. This understanding of history will turn out to be not just different from, but entirely heterogeneous to history as chrono-logy.
39 GA 65, 375/261.
40 GA 65, 479/337.
41 I return to this question in detail in the next chapter.
42 This question is the inspiration behind the next two chapters of this book, which deal with the questions of technology and art. According to Heidegger, the age of technology designates the culmination of the metaphysics of presence, and so the consumation of the destiny of Western thought.
43 GA 65, 383/267.
44 In that respect, and on a first, preliminary reading, there is no real difference between what Heidegger is saying here and what *Being and Time* thought under the heading of the *Zeitlichkeit* of Dasein, for it too was thought of as *Zeitigung* and *Einräumung*.
45 GA 65, 378/264.
46 GA 65, 383/268.
47 GA 65, 381/226.
48 GA 65, 382/266.
49 Throughout the 1930s, and in *Contributions* in particular (§§13, 249), Heidegger identifies 'reservedness' as the fundamental attunement of 'the ones to come' (*die*

Zukünftigen). This is the disposition through which Da-sein finds himself attuned to the essential hesitation or tentativeness of beyng – this hesitation, once again, that is not merely negative, but that signals an intimation of another, non-metaphysical beginning. The 'other beginning' Heidegger talks about, and for which he tries to prepare thought, is one that would be dominated by the distinct attunement of 'reservedness'. This is tantamount to saying that it would be dominated by a lack of domination. For reservedness is the attunement born of the realization that we, as human beings, belong to the essence of truth as concealment and hesitation. In other words, it is the attunement that comports itself to the world as to the gift of some-thing that also refuses itself, that cannot be turned into a thing, and so represented, domesticated and dominated. Reservedness signals our belonging to the earth, and not just the world, and so our belongingness to something that resists our grip, and to which we must learn to surrender. In belonging to the earth, we are dispossessed of our own drive for possession and mastery of the world as nature. But in being so dispos-sessed, we are at the same time recovering from a form of alienation. Heidegger's thought is an invitation to let go of the world, to loosen our grip on it. Is this yet another form of asceticism, another departure from the world, and into the illusory spheres of a higher reality? Absolutely not. For the loosening of our grip on the world is a way back into the world, as a dwelling place informed and made possible by the withdrawing of earth. It amounts to a radically different experience of the world. Can thought be drawn into the withdrawing of truth, and thus returned to its own, proper place? Can it see beyond presence, and so overcome representation and metaphysics? Or is it set so firmly on the path of objective, technological thought that its destiny will be consumed in an ever increasingly subjugated world and techno-scientific world-view?

50 GA 65, 384/268.
51 GA 65, 384/268.
52 GA 65, 385/269.

4

The Grip of Technology

In what sense is technology a philosophical question? What is the connection between technology and Heidegger's guiding question, namely, that of being and truth?

When we speak of technology, we tend to think of certain types of things (tools and machines), and certain ways in which things are produced, or manufactured. Technology is something that helps us use things faster, produce them faster, more efficiently and on a larger scale. It allows us to get to places we couldn't reach before, or reach greater results in data and information gathering. Technology, we believe, is a matter for specialists, for technicians and engineers, in spite of the fact that we all use its products. Historically, we think of the technological age as the age of the machine. Historians and social scientists define 'modern technology' as the application of power machinery to production. They locate its beginnings in eighteenth-century England, where large coal deposits provided a source of energy for the production of steam, which in turn propelled machinery in textile and other mills. The machine of the industrial age is (at least in its initial stage) a *thermal* machine, and thermodynamics is the branch of physics that made it possible. More recently, in what amounts to a second revolution in the modern, industrial age, technology has come to designate the introduction and the triumph of automation and, more recently still, of self-organization, the basic principle of which derives from the science of regulation and guidance known as cybernetics. This revolution is often referred to as the information or digital revolution.[1] The machine itself has become 'intelligent', and its intelligence is essentially a function of its ability to process and communicate extremely large quantities of information at an almost unbelievable speed. Intelligence, in turn, whether natural or artificial, is understood as a 'system of internal states governed by a system of computational procedures, or an interactive set of such systems governed by a set of such procedures'.[2] The difference between the two types of intelligence resides solely, it is argued, in the fact that whereas the CPU (Central Processing Unit) of a computer can only process one computation at a time (albeit at the rather extraordinary speed of over a million transformations per second), brains have a structure that allows them to process billions of computations *simultaneously* (this ability is now known as *parallel processing*, and is distinguished from mere *serial processing*).[3] Technology seems to reduce the gap between the human and the machine, between what's natural and what's engineered.

Heidegger's contribution to the question regarding technology is to have examined this phenomenon in the light of a question that is itself not techno-logical, and apparently wholly unconnected to it. This is the question of its *essence*. If we are to understand this phenomenon, that is, isolate its origin and essence, Heidegger claims, we must move away from its historiographical and scientific interpretation. We need to identify and thematize a layer of reality beneath the one I have just evoked, and which we all assume to be the reality of technology. Technology, he claims, is in fact not at all, or at least not pri-marily, a matter for technicians. Rather, it is a historical phenomenon in the strong, onto-destinal sense he gives to that term, and which I began to sketch in Chapters 2 and 3: it is an event that characterizes our Western history at its very core, a certain way or manner in which we apprehend the whole of being, a mode of disclosedness of reality itself – in short, a distinct mode of truth. By 'truth', you will recall, Heidegger understands the manner in which the world is there for us at a given time, as a configuration of presence, born of the inner strife or tension between concealment and unconcealment. To claim that tech-nology is itself a mode of truth is tantamount to saying that it is the dominant and unquestioned horizon from which the real as a whole manifests itself to us. This is what makes it a complex phenomenon: it is linked to truth (the truth of being), and to history (the history of being), but its mode of manifes-tation, or expression, appears to be disconnected from both truth and destiny. It is precisely this lack of questioning, and its decisiveness, which Heidegger wants to reveal and to rectify.

THE ESSENCE OF TECHNOLOGY

Heidegger's views regarding technology (*Technik*), which he began by calling 'machination' (*Machenschaft*), were shaped in the years 1936–40. This we know from the series of texts from that period, published for the most part since 1997, from *Contributions to Philosophy* (in which the word does not yet appear as such), published in 1989, to *Meditation* (1997), *Metaphysics and Nihilism* (1999) and *The History of Beyng* (1998). This means that we now have a clear picture of the historical and philosophical context that led to the conception of Heidegger's famous essay from 1949, revised and expanded in 1953, and entitled 'The Question concerning Technology'. We are now in a position to trace the genesis of that question. The last three texts I mentioned all date from the years 1938–40, possibly Heidegger's most prolific period. The time frame is not incidental. They were written in the first years of the imperialist phase of the Third Reich, and against the background of the outbreak of World War II. This is the war that displayed the greatest power of devastation in history, as well as the mobilization of all economic and human resources. Rightly or wrongly, Heidegger cannot help understanding this moment of destruction and madness as consistent with his onto-historical diagnosis con-cerning being's abandonment of beings (and, as a result, man's forgottenness of being), and the completion of this metaphysical process in the unrestrained, global and violent domination of what, adopting Nietzsche's terminology, but interpreting it in a different sense, he calls the will to power.[4] Technology (*Technik*), he claims in *Meditation*, shares the same essential space as that of metaphysics, from which it grew. In fact, it is the completion of metaphysics, as well as its 'highest and most far reaching triumph'.[5] In what sense? In the sense that it constitutes the ultimate level of the forgottenness of being, or the total occlusion of the *essence* of truth itself (as untruth, or concealment). As such, it amounts to the 'devastation of beyng'. The devastation of Europe in war is itself, for Heidegger, an instance of a deeper and decisive devastation, that of being, which he also equates with the completion of European nihilism. It is this diagnosis that allows Heidegger to bring together phenomena and events as seemingly diverse as the destruction occasioned in war, the distortion of history and politics through propaganda in totalitarian regimes, labour camps and death camps, the threat under which the earth has come as a result of the systematic and orchestrated extraction of natural resources, the new 'horizons' opened up by contemporary scientific research, and the general commoditization of nature and culture. To this list, we could add those problems and crises that are a direct effect of post-industrial capitalism, often stigmatized under the (only partly satisfying) rubric of 'globalisation'. Whether in war or in peace, it is the same logic, the same demand that is at work. Heidegger has been much criticized for it, mainly because he refuses to see these issues as moral and ethical problems, and because he refuses to distinguish and decide between them. It is precisely this refusal that I think is worth considering. It is precisely the distinct light he throws on them that may prove to be philosophically valuable in the end.

Since the most relevant texts from the period when Heidegger forged his conception of technology have not yet been translated into English, I shall limit myself to drawing out those elements that allow us to better understand the lecture from 1949 entitled 'The Question Concerning Technology'.

Heidegger begins his essay with a few words of warning – words that seem to have been ignored by many. It is going to be a matter, he warns, of questioning technology, that is, of turning technology into a question. How? By raising the question concerning the *essence* of technology. The sense of essence is quite specific in Heidegger, as we've already seen in connection with the question of truth in Chapter 2 (we'll come back to this question regarding the sense of essence). By raising the question of the essence of technology, Heidegger goes on to say, we'll be able to develop a 'free' relation to technology. This free relation is the ultimate aim of the lecture – if not of Heidegger's later thought as a whole – and of the questioning it develops. The question of freedom is not one with which Heidegger's thought is normally associated.[6] I believe it to be crucial, though, as I've begun to show in connection with the questions of life and existence in Chapter 1. It is perhaps nowhere more important, and more visibly at stake, than in relation to the question concerning technology. Why? Because technology as it has developed and is experienced today constitutes the ultimate degree of *alienation* of the European man.

Naturally, when Heidegger makes such a claim, he finds himself on a terrain occupied mostly by the thought of Marx and his followers, for whom 'alienation' designated the state of contemporary society. This state of alienation, Marxism claims, is primarily a function of the fact that, unlike the artisan of the early modern period, the average worker of the nineteenth and twentieth centuries, who works in the factory, and no longer in the workshop, does not own his means of production. The possessing class is, according to Marxism, equally (although differently) alienated: it does indeed own the instruments of production, the machine, yet it has no direct relation to the process of production, that is, to labour itself. The solution, Marxism claims, is to transform the nature of the relation between labour and the means of production by reuniting labour and capital, and by collectivizing the means of production. The problem, according to Marxism, is a socio-economic one, and the solution consists in transforming the social organization of labour. For Heidegger, though, the problem is not primarily social, or economic. As a result, the solution cannot depend on our ability to decide between capitalism and socialism. Does this mean that the problem is essentially political? In Chapter 6, we shall see why Heidegger does not believe in the primacy or the autonomy of the political sphere, which is always subordinated to the historical, or onto-destinal situation. This means that the alienation of contemporary man is not in relation to labour, or in relation to other human beings, as typified in Hegel's dialectic of the master and the slave – a dialectic taken up and extended by Marx.[7] It is not even an alienation from the actual machine, from the technological object. Rather, it is an alienation from technology as such, from its *essence* and *provenance*. So long as we do not understand the significance and origin of technology, we will not be free in relation to it. A 'free relation' to technology, however, is not the same as its rejection: the phenomenon that this word designates is of such magnitude, and its roots go so deep, that it cannot be a question of opting out of it. Does a free relation to technology, then, amount to a mere embracing of technology? In no way. So long as we remain stuck at the level of a discussion for or against technology, we remain chained to technology, unable to grasp its true significance. What is this freedom that is not the freedom to reject it, or turn away from it? This is what we need to investigate.

By choosing to envisage technology from the point of view of its essence, it would seem that Heidegger is asking *what* or what sort of thing technology is. This would be a very traditional thing to do. It would seem natural and legitimate. And to that question, it would be equally natural and legitimate to answer by saying that technology is essentially two things, namely, a means to an end, and a human activity. This would amount to a definition of technology. Definitions point in the direction of essences, understood as designating something with respect to what it is (its 'whatness'). The double definition we've just provided points to the instrumental as well as the anthropological dimensions of technology. It is a very practical and all-encompassing definition, one that allows us to include the most rudimentary and primitive tool (such as a hammer made of stone) as well as the most sophisticated and complex machine (such as a particle accelerator, or a communication satellite) under the same, basic, human activity. In doing so, it seems that we are even coming close to defining the human itself in terms of its ability to fabricate tools (man as the *homo faber*, to use Bergson's terminology), that is, as the technological animal.

It is this very – seemingly obvious, correct and unassailable – 'definition' of technology that Heidegger sets out to challenge. Technology, at least when considered from the point of view of its essence, has nothing to do with our ability to fabricate tools. It does not designate a moment in the long history of man's relation to tools. If Heidegger challenges the traditional definition of technology, it is not in order to provide an alternative definition of technology. Rather, it is to provide another sense of *essence* after which technology can be evaluated and illuminated. In other words, he is asking whether our 'correct' definition of technology exhausts the 'truth' of the phenomenon in question, or whether it describes this phenomenon only very superficially. Given the clear distinction we've already established in Chapter 2 between truth as correctness and truth as disclosedness (or unconcealment), Heidegger's suggestion should not come as a surprise. The sense of essence that he is interested in pursuing will not lead to a definition of technology, but to its truth as a phenomenon. As a phenomenon, it is a manifestation. But of what? What does it reveal? A distinct ability of the human? An activity? Or is it the other way around: does technology disclose and dispose the human in a certain way? Is it not itself a specific mode of presence, a specific way of revealing the world, a singular instance of truth as *aletheia*? And if this is indeed the case, if 'technology' designates the manner in which the world as such and as a whole is disclosed to us, and we ourselves find ourselves disclosed in its midst, should we not conclude that technology is itself the meaning of being, at least in its modern, historical unfolding? This is the hypothesis Heidegger is inviting us to consider.

We have a first clue regarding this disclosive dimension of technology in the root-word *techne*, and the way it was used by the Greeks. This is a word we've already come across in connection with the question of Dasein's everyday, practical and pragmatic existence in Chapter 2, and one that we shall come across again in connection with the question of knowing and science in Chapter 6. It's a word we shall also return to in the next chapter, that is, in connection with the question of art as designating the other, hidden side of technology. By the end of our journey, the word *techne* will turn out to have been with us all along, and to have surfaced in a variety of contexts. This is an indication of the importance it has for Heidegger. But nowhere is it more important, and more decisive, than in relation to the question concerning technology. *Techne*, like *episteme*, designates knowing or science in the widest sense. Heidegger's claim is that, historically speaking, the meaning of science has undergone a progressive technologization. Science has become techno-science. At the other extreme of techno-science, however, stands art and genuine thought ('meditation'). They represent modalities of science, and ways of knowing, which are increasingly under threat, and constitute the one decisive alternative to the technologization of all areas of life. If technology is sustained and perpetuated by the will to power as the basic attitude of man, it is 'serenity', or 'letting-be' that characterizes the attitude of the non-technological mode of knowing.

TECHNO-SCIENCE

Allow me to explore this connection between technology and science, before returning to the question regarding the essence of technology as an instance of truth. The important point to remember is that the advent of modern science, and by that we need to understand the mathematical–physical revolution of the seventeenth and eighteenth centuries, whilst certainly making possible the extraordinary progress in the various technologies of the last two centuries, is not the phenomenon that accounts for the essence of technology. In fact, the decisive phenomenon is that of the technologization, and thus the transformation, of the meaning of science itself – a transformation that, according to Heidegger, did not happen overnight, but has its roots in metaphysical thought. By 'metaphysics', Heidegger understands the dominant form of thought in Western history, the origin of which lies in its inability to envisage beings from the point of view of being, and man from the point of view of his essential openness to the truth of being (*aletheia*). Technology, then, has its roots in metaphysics itself, which characterizes the singular nature of Western history. That which makes our history 'Western', according to Heidegger, is metaphysics, and metaphysics culminates in the age of technology. The truth of our Western conception of what it means to know is revealed in modern science, and is completed as techno-science. It is not modern science as such, therefore, that constitutes the decisive feature of our technological age. Rather, it is the technological world-view of Western man that made the scientific revolution, and the transformation of the scientific paradigm, possible. In a lecture from 1967,[8] following a clue he finds in Nietzsche, Heidegger suggests that it is not the victory of science as such that characterizes our time, but the victory of the scientific *method* over science.[9] What does 'method' mean in this context, asks Heidegger? 'Method' does not refer to the instrument with which scientific research elaborates its objective domain. Rather, it refers to the way in which, from the start, what in each instance constitutes the objective domain subjected to research is delimited in its objectivity. Method refers to the specific *project* that has taken hold of the world and secured its grip over it in advance, and established the extent to which the world can be subjected to scientific research. In what does this project consist? It consists in subjecting to measure, calculation and planning all that can be accessed through experimentation and controlled by it. The various special sciences remain subservient to this project. This is the sense in which method is a 'victory over science'. This method also reveals a decision regarding the real: only that which is scientifically verifiable, that is, calculable and measurable, is considered to be truly and genuinely real. Through calculability, the world is increasingly subjected to man's mastery. 'Method' designates the particular manner in which the world is provoked so as to be at the service of the human. This victory of method originated in Europe, and is exemplified in Descartes' *Discourse on Method* (especially the sixth discourse) and his *Regulae ad Directionem Ingenii* (especially the fourth rule), as well as in Galileo and Newton. The method of this new science, that is, modern science, consists of this: to secure the calculability of nature, ultimately with a view to controlling and dominating it. It is an essentially European phenomenon, albeit one that, today, has reached the most remote corners of the earth, and a paradigm that has come to dominate the planet as a whole. This, then, is Heidegger's point: the singularity of modern, Western science lies in its technological dimension. Control and domination is what science is now all about. Science is intrinsically technological: its questioning and research is oriented in advance towards mastery. Technology itself relies on science for its efficaciousness. Without technology, science is goalless; without science, technology is powerless.

Where is this alliance displayed? In every aspect of contemporary life. What form does it take? That of a systematic organization of this life, and of reality as a whole. Technology refers to the way in which the world as such and as a whole has been taken up, seized, mobilized, ordered, homogenized and used up so as to enhance man's will to hegemony. Often, the ordering takes the form of a total planning, or an equipping (*Rüstung*), which consists in the division of the whole of being into sectors and areas, and then in the systematic organization and exploitation of their resources. Each domain has its institute of research as well as its ministry, each area is controlled and evaluated with a view to assessing its potential. Eventually, they are calibrated for mass consumption. Resources are endlessly extracted, stocked, distributed and transformed, according to a logic that is not that of need, but that of inflated desires and fantasies of consumption artificially created by the marketing techniques of our post-industrial era. Nothing, Heidegger claims, falls outside this technological organization: neither science nor politics, neither economics nor culture. The hegemony of technology, which can take various forms according to the domains it regulates, seems to be limited only by the power of its own completion. It is, for technology, a question of organizing the conditions of its optimal performance and ultimate plan – whether these be the totalitarian politics of yesterday or the global economy and new world order of today. Yet behind this seemingly ultra-rational organization rules the most nihilistic horizon: the absence of goals. For why is such an ordering set up? What are all those plans, targets, aims and objectives for? For the sole sake of planning. For no other purpose than the artificial creation of needs and desires, which can be fulfilled only by way of an increase in production and further devastation of the earth. Man has become his own slave, a working animal that must carry on working in order to produce, and to produce in order to consume. His will, this very will that constitutes his pride and that he erects as an instrument of his domination over the whole of the earth, is nothing but the expression of what Heidegger calls the 'will to will'. Yet this man does not realize that his labour and his will spin in a vacuum, moving him ever more forcefully from his essence. Busy as he is at using up and consuming, at producing and manipulating, today's man no longer has the eyes to see what is essential. At best, he seeks and accumulates what he calls 'experiences' (*Erlebnisse*), which he flaunts as his 'truths', and which give him the feeling of being alive.

Nowhere, however, is this 'method', or this alliance of knowing and controlling more visible, and more efficacious, than in the relatively new science of cybernetics. Given the impact and the extraordinary fluidity of this science that developed during Heidegger's lifetime, given its ability to cut across and connect previously separated domains and boundaries, Heidegger does not hesitate to label it the new metaphysics or, better said perhaps, the completion of the metaphysical ideal of a universal language that can be applied to all spheres of life and knowledge. Cybernetics is Norbert Wiener's term for the study of control and communication in machines and living beings.[10] The cybernetic world-view reveals the characteristic that underlies all the calculable worldly processes as one of command and control. What makes possible the command of one process by another is the transmission of information: the behaviour of the automaton, explains Norbert Wiener, is controlled through a set of messages. And insofar as the process that receives the order has the ability to return information to the process that commands it, the process as a whole has the character of *feedback*. The exchange of information that characterizes this process is essentially circular. Circularity – and self-regulation – are the defining characteristics of the world that cybernetics projects. As such, it erases the difference between automatic machines and living beings (as Wiener himself emphasizes), and so between the human and machines (and it is only once this boundary has been lifted that the idea of a cyborg becomes possible).

In the *Zollikon Seminars* (6 July 1965) Heidegger quotes Wiener's definition of the human – a definition he naturally wants to explain historically and challenge philosophically – as an information device, whose singularity, namely, language, can be computed and controlled.[11] As we shall see, Heidegger's interpretation of the human being, and of its relation to language, is radically different, if not altogether opposed. According to Heidegger, the human being is human only to the extent that he 'understands' being (as presence), that is, only to the extent that he stands in the openness of being. Being human means to *be* this openness. Language is a singular and privileged mode in which the human Dasein can be this openness. It is not, as cybernetics argues, a mere instrument of information and communication, however sophisticated. What the cybernetic projection of the world makes possible is a universal calculation – and so a degree of control – that applies equally to the animate and the inanimate realms. From the start, its ambition was to be a new and universal science – and this ambition turned out to be widely successful: the concepts of information and communication are at the heart of many natural sciences – neurology, evolutionary and molecular biology, cognitive science – as well as social sciences – sociology, psychology, economics, linguistics, computer science and many aspects of philosophy. Its vocabulary (adaptation, feedback, organization, intelligence, control, etc.) has penetrated virtually every sphere of contemporary life, from business to politics, from the media to education, to say nothing, of course, of the virtual space we call cyberspace, and which in many ways has become a reality all of its own. Cybernetics is largely characterized by its extreme flexibility, adaptability and elasticity, and, consequently, by its capacity to blur the boundaries between domains hitherto clearly demarcated. It is in that respect that we can think of it as having established a new scientific, cultural, socio-economic and political *paradigm*. It is our relation to the world as such and to our fellow human beings that we now understand cybernetically, that is, as a global network made of a number of local networks, as the site of an ongoing and circular exchange of information: the modern representation of the human, which sees it as the subject who relates to the world as a world of objects, which it can manipulate and transform, and which, in return, provide it with a greater knowledge of the world, is reinterpreted in the light of the theory of information. In fact, and following Heidegger's own interpretation, we can go as far as to say that cybernetics has done away with the modern subject, and invented a new conception of subjectivity, perhaps best revealed in Gregory Bateson's work.[12] This is a conception according to which the human is no longer the origin or the term of a process of signification and communication, but is entirely contained within it, and defined by it. The human is no longer an autonomous, self-grounding substance (as initially defined by Descartes), but an 'effect' of a broader system or network of information that defines it. It is itself only a difference, a differential barrier traversed by flows of information. The only reality is the system, itself characterized, in its activity, by the differences it generates. The Batesonian, 'informational' subject is entirely devoid of interiority: his being is entirely a function of the cybernetic system within which he is inscribed. Instead of the old Cartesian ontological dualism of substance, we now have an informational (cybernetic) monism of the flow.

From sociology to biology and feminism, the impact of cybernetics is remarkable. This is how the cyber-feminist Donna Haraway describes its mode of operation and measures its impact in her *Cyborg Manifesto*:

> In each case, solution to the key questions rests on a theory of language and control; the key operation is determining the rates, directions, and probabilities of flow of a quantity called information. The world is subdivided by boundaries differentially permeable to information. Information is just that kind of quantifiable element (unit, basis of unity) which allows universal translation, and so unhindered instrumental power (called effective communication).[13]

The world has, in short, been translated into a problem of *coding*. As such, it cuts across previously rigorously defined boundaries. The French biologist and Nobel Prize winner François Jacob is very clear on the nature of this new phenomenon:

Every interaction between the members of an organisation can accordingly be considered as a problem of communication. This applies just as
much to a human society as to a living organism or an automatic device.
In each of these objects, cybernetics finds a model can be applied to
others. . . . In the end, any organised system can be analysed by means
of two concepts: message and feedback regulation.[14]

Jacob's comment illustrates and extends Wiener's earlier claim that the physical functioning of the living individual and the operation of the communication machines are alike in 'their analogous attempts to control entropy
through feedback'.[15]

Jacob's intervention is no coincidence. Nowhere, perhaps, has the impact of
cybernetics been greater than in the life sciences, and in biochemistry and bio-
physics in particular.[16] Biochemistry has discovered the 'map' or 'blue-print'
of life in genes. This is what's known today as the genome. Genes are seen as
the source of information, and the command post, from which organisms
develop, and replicate themselves. Still in the Athens lecture, and in what
turns out to be an accurate and surprisingly well-informed account of the biological research of the time, Heidegger alludes to the way in which this
research has allowed the scientific community to move beyond the idea of pre-
formism (according to which the gene contained a miniature form of the future
organism, germinally as it were) and adopt a more epigenetic stance (according to which the genes stock the necessary information for the development of
the organism). The genes, in other words, amount to an alphabet (the 'alphabet of nucleotides'), or a code, the sequence of which characterizes a given
organism. Accordingly, life is understood as a 'book', analogous to the geometrical book of nature Galileo celebrated at the dawn of modern physical science.
The difference is that this book has found the way to pass on information from
one system to the next, and so to evolve. It is a book written in a code of its
own, which allows it to replicate itself, and invent itself as it goes along.[17] The
genetic code of information, Heidegger goes on to say, echoing the most recent
genetic theory of the time, one indeed derived from cybernetics, amounts to
something like a computer 'programme'.[18] Whether we speak of a genetic programme or of a genetic code alone, Heidegger's point holds, in that it reveals
the extent to which, with the advent of molecular biology, our conception of
nature, in this case of life, has shifted from physical concepts, such as those of
energy, mass, force and even organism, to those of information, control, repli-
cation, translation and transmission, coding and decoding and feedback. In
other words, the nature of the problem can no longer be characterized in terms
of the *flow of energy* (and especially in terms of thermodynamic energetism, as
was predominantly the case in the nineteenth and early twentieth centuries),
but in terms of the *flow of information*, that is, in cybernetic terms. Information
has replaced energy as the vital principle. In addition, Heidegger's point concerns the fact that our knowledge of the basic system of information underlying all life processes, and that of the human in particular, in turn secures our

ability to interfere with their development, and so to alter, rectify and even (re)produce them through genetic engineering. The victory of method over science has extended into the realm of life, and with staggering results.[19] In a text written only a few years before the Athens lecture, Heidegger quotes the American chemist Stanley: 'The hour is near when life will be placed in the hands of the chemist who will be able to synthesise, split and change living substance at will'.[20] This hour has come, as we know. The extraordinary phenomenon, according to Heidegger, is not the degree of technological progress displayed in this kind of procedure. Far more extraordinary is our inability to take its full measure, to understand fully and reflect upon the 'attack' with technological means that is organized on the life and nature of man. In comparison, Heidegger adds, 'the explosion of the hydrogen bomb means little'.[21]

At the level of nature as a whole, Heidegger's claims regarding the elevation of cybernetics to the status of an undisputed and unquestioned paradigm are further confirmed. The concept of the ecosystem, so abundantly used today, would be a good case in point.[22] This concept, coined by Odum, a student of the influential ecologist Hutchinson, himself an active member of the Macy conferences already mentioned, has its roots in the naturalization of the cybernetic model on a planetary scale.[23] According to this model, it is nature as such and as a whole that becomes one vast cybernetic system. Driven by the technological optimism and the ideological progressivism of the forefathers of cybernetics, its advocates we see information technology and computers not only as effective ways of controlling and managing environmental interactions, but also as more ecological and less polluting than the modes of production born of the industrial revolution. This technology remains industrial, however. In fact, and following the words of one commentator, we should say that it is not post-, but hyper-industrial. As such, it perpetuates and extends the logic of the domination and exhaustion of nature that characterizes Western modernity.[24] It is essential to bear in mind that, halfway between science and technology, cybernetics is first and foremost 'the art of securing the efficaciousness of action' over nature. It constitutes the very matrix of technoscience in that it designates an epistemological project oriented towards operational control more than fundamental research aimed at understanding a given phenomenon. In virtually every respect, contemporary science has become *cyberscience*. By that, and in the words of the contemporary writer and urbanist Paul Virilio, we need to understand the 'product of the fatal confusion between the *operational instrument* and *exploratory research*'.[25]

From what we've seen so far of our modern conception of knowledge and science, which, following Nietzsche, we began by tracing back to the 'victory of method over science', and followed through its evolution in the last hundred years or so, all the way to its culmination in the (today omnipresent) cybernetic paradigm, we can speak of a techno-scientific paradigm as governing our conception of what it means to know and, more generally, our very relation to the world as such and as a whole. 'Method' points to the origin of our technological relation to the world, and cybernetics to its undisputed and unquestioned victory. This is precisely the meaning of science, and of our basic experience of reality, that Heidegger wishes to challenge and call into question by retrieving another, forgotten sense of knowing, inherited from the Greeks.

TECHNOLOGY AND TRUTH

Let us now return to our initial guiding thread, and to the connection between technology and truth, or between *techne* and *aletheia*. We recall how, in connection with the question concerning the essence of truth, Heidegger found a decisive clue in Aristotle's *Nicomachean Ethics*, and in the way in which, in that text, the human soul is said to be essentially engaged in a number of operations of truth, or *aletheuein*. Aristotle mentions *techne*, or technical know-how, manipulation and production, as one such modality of truth. Through *techne*, Aristotle claims, man discloses something, brings it into presence. Specifically, man discloses it through a process of production and manipulation. His relation to it is one of use. Now, recall how *Being and Time* transposes this Aristotelian legacy in the context of the analytic of Dasein. In fact, technical, practical existence turned out to be the primordial and average mode of disclosedness of existence. Heidegger's ambition to make philosophy concrete again meant a return to the way in which the world unfolds and makes sense for us in our everyday dealings, and so a way of appropriating conceptually that which we are and live on a daily basis. However, in light of the transformation of the question of truth, as we encountered it in the second half of Chapter 2, that is, as evolving from its rootedness in existence to its historical unfolding, the question now becomes one of knowing whether technology can be traced back to the disclosedness of existence, or whether existence itself finds itself disclosed in a specific way as a result of the event and unfolding of technology. Once truth is no longer the truth of Dasein, but of being, is *techne* itself still a possibility of existence, or a configuration of being in its historical unfolding? Is technology simply a modality of existence, or is it a historical and destinal event, in the wake of which existence finds itself drawn?

Technology (*techne*) is a mode of revealing (*aletheuein*). But how is the world revealed in technology? As something to be used and manipulated. Technology also refers to production, to a specific way in which something is brought into presence. Production too is a disclosing. There is a difference, however, between the technical object (say, the screwdriver), and the work of art. Both are produced, both disclose the world, yet in radically different ways – ways I shall return to in the next chapter. But isn't there also a significant difference, something like a difference in kind, between technical objects, between a watermill and an electric dam, or between a bow and arrow and a nuclear bomb? Are all technical objects an indication of the technological destination of man, or is there a distinct mode of revealing of technology, a distinct light thrown on those objects themselves, such that questioning about technology no longer has anything to do with discriminating between objects, with analysing the nature of instruments and tools throughout history? Can we ask about technology, about its orign and provenance, without reconstructing a history of technologies and following the evolution of technical objects? What, after all, is the difference between the watermill and the electric dam, or between traditional modes of agriculture, such as ploughing, and mechanized, intensive agriculture? So long as we focus on the objects themselves, we will not be in a position to identify their real difference. It is only when we look at the specific way in which they disclose the world and ourselves in relation to it, that we begin to understand where and how technology unfolds. A watermill, for example, uses the force of the river without altering the nature of the river. This is in contrast with the hydroelectric dam, which takes hold of the river by enclosing it within its own walls. The difference between the two is that between an act that follows the course of nature and one that takes hold of nature, seizes and captures it, and so constitutes an act of aggression towards it. It is the difference between a technique that extends the power of nature, that remains driven by it, and one that highjacks and deviates its course, and imposes its own power over it. Between the two, there is a fundamental difference – a difference of comportment towards nature, and so a different way of envisaging it. Whereas nature in the Greek (and perhaps poetic) sense of the term, namely, as *phusis*, refers to 'that which grows and lives', and thus to a process that is autonomous and that does not take place *for* the human, nature in the modern, technological sense of the modern term, secured in the science called physics, refers to what can be predicted and calculated in advance, and so domesticated and made endlessly available. The revealing that rules in modern technology is less akin to a *letting-be* of nature in its growth and general unfolding, and more akin to an insistent and relentless challenging (*Herausfordern*). It is a summoning that borders on harassment:

> The revealing that rules in modern technology is a challenging forth [Herausfordern], which puts to nature the unreasonable demand that it supply energy that can be extracted and stored as such. The earth now reveals itself as a coal mining district, the soil as a mineral deposit . . . even the cultivation of the field has come under the grip of another kind of setting-in-order, which sets upon nature. It sets upon it in the sense of challenging it. Agriculture is now the mechanised food industry. Air is now set up to yield nitrogen, the earth to yield ore, ore to yield uranium, for example; uranium is set upon to yield atomic energy, which can be released either for destruction or for peaceful use. . . .
>
> The hydroelectric plant is set into the current of the Rhine. It sets the Rhine to supplying its hydraulic pressure, which then sets the turbines turning. This turning sets those machines in motion whose thrust sets going the electric current for which the long distance power station and its network of cables are set up to dispatch electricity. . . . What the river is now, namely, a water-power supplier, derives from the essence of the power station.[26]

There is, Heidegger goes on to suggest, a certain 'monstrousness' in this process. Why 'monstrousness'? Because, in and through this process, the founding and primordial relation of man to beings, once understood as growth and opening up (*phusis*), is increasingly threatened. Because, with the technological world-view, man moves further and further away from his own essence, to which, from the very start, Heidegger was concerned to reawaken us.

Technology transforms the nature of our relation to beings, and to the world as a whole. As a result of this challenging that characterizes the specific mode of disclosure of technology, what is disclosed is there in a certain way. It stands there, always already available, in reserve. It is, in Heidegger's terminology, mere standing-reserve (*Bestand*). The German word normally means 'stock'. But here it means something more. It points to the way in which things are envisaged from the start, pre-viewed as it were. The *Bestand* is what stands by, awaiting to be called upon, released, transformed and distributed. It doesn't even have the appearance of an object any longer. 'Subject' and 'object' defined ways in which 'man' and 'world' stood with respect to one another. The 'object' defined the thing insofar as it stood opposite the subject (as a thinking thing). The German for object is *Gegenstand*, and means literally that which stands opposed. As such, it retains a (perhaps minimal) autonomy and self-subsistence. Now, the object has dissolved into the merely available, into the stockpile. It is entirely on hand. The subject–object dualism was a necessary stage on the way to the progressive technologization of the world. It amounted to a first moment of reification of man and of nature. But this dualism, and the world-view it projected, underwent its own dissolution. In technology, there is only one reality, which amounts to a further stage in the process of reification. The fact that, nowadays, the world is increasingly seen in terms of flow, whether of energy or information, does not contradict the idea of a progressive reification. For the flows in question are entirely derived from a mathematical, and often cybernetic *representation* (known as a modelling) of the world, through which differences between beings are annulled. As a result, we humans find ourselves equally challenged and summoned in this process we call technology. We are called upon as the being who can carry out this summoning of nature. We are part and parcel of the process itself, and not simply the being for whom it is activated. The human itself is measured and evaluated in terms of resources, energy, productivity and power. The human drives technology forward, and takes an active part in ordering as a way of revealing. But the unconcealment itself, within which this ordering unfolds, is itself not a function of the human. We ourselves have already been claimed by a way of revealing that challenges us to approach nature as standing-reserve. We find ourselves predisposed towards nature as what is there to be used, extracted and manipulated.

And so, we return to the question raised a little while ago, namely, who is the subject of the *aletheuein* that characterizes technology, if not man? Who or what reveals nature and man in this way? Heidegger's answer is gathered in one, relatively complex word: the *Ge-stell*. Allow me to spend a bit of time unpacking the meaning of this word, as it differs markedly from its ordinary usage. In ordinary German, the word refers to something like a stand, a shelf, a rack, a frame (for a bed, a table or a pair of glasses), a trestle, a chassis or even the landing gear of an airplane. In all instances, it designates that which supports and holds together whatever it is applied to. Heidegger retains this ordinary meaning. At the same time, however, by interpreting it literally, he adds another meaning to it. First, he says, we can understand the prefix '*Ge*' as signifying an operation of gathering, similar to the Greek *syn-*, or the Latin *cum-*: *Gebirge* is a mountain chain, and *Gebinde* refers to flowers arranged and tied together in a wreath, or a sheaf. What is gathered in this gathering? The real itself, as such and as a whole. The *Ge-stell* points to the way in which the real is gathered, or held together. As such, it signals a situation analogous – yet in a way fundamentally opposed – to the one Heidegger calls the *Ge-viert* (the 'fourfold'), and which I analysed in the chapter on space and time. Second, the word contains the root-verb *stellen*, to place, to stand. In a way, then, the *Ge-stell* refers to the frame or the armature on which the real as a whole – and this includes the human – is placed or stretched, and at the same time gathered together, assembled as a single reality. Translating the *Ge-stell* back into a Greek word that is familiar to all of us, we could understand it as the System designating the way in which things are assembled or held together in a coherent unity. The Greek *systema*, which designates an assemblage, a totality or a composition, is built from the prefix *syn-*, together, and the verb *istemi*, or *sistemi*, which means to stand, or to make to stand, as well as to set up, to raise, to be set or placed and even, in Homer especially, to *be* in a certain state or condition. The German *Ge-stell* is, quite literally, a translation of the Greek *systema*. Yet the kind of translation that is at issue here is not just linguistic. It is historical in the strongest sense of the term. For what Heidegger is after with this word is the precise *manner* in which things are held together for us today, and the manner in which we, as human beings, fit into this assemblage. And this manner is radically different from the one experienced in Greek antiquity, or in the Middle Ages: it is precisely as an increasingly violent challenging forth, and a relentless summoning, as well as an increasingly integrated system, also known as a network. The System designates the way in which things stand together at the end of metaphysics, in the technological, and especially technoscientific age. We speak today of physical, chemical and biological systems, of ecosystems and information systems. We speak of neural networks, research, media, commercial, political and terrorist networks. What do these have in common? The fact they are all considered from the point of view of their formal structure, held together by the flow of information and communication that runs through them.

Around the root-verb '*stellen*', Heidegger gathers a number of other verbs, which all converge in the *Ge-stell*:

- *vorstellen* to represent – a necessary stage in the taking hold of nature; the representation in question is that of modern physics as an exact science,

which sets nature up to exhibit itself as a coherent totality of forces calculable in advance;
- *herstellen* to produce, to make, to establish in the sense of bringing to stand
  within presence;
- *erstellen* to erect, to construct – a verb in fact very close to *herstellen*;
- *sicherstellen* to take possession of, to appropriate;
- *bestellen* to order, or summon, in this case nature (to appear as resourceful
  energy).

All these determinations speak in the *Ge-stell*. The 'System', Heidegger writes,
refers to the gathering together of that set-up (*Stellen*) that sets up the human
itself, that is, challenges it forth, to reveal the real as stockpile or standing-
reserve (*Bestand*).[27] Beings can be envisaged as reserve only to the extent that
they have been requisitioned in advance. The militaristic vocabulary I am
using and emphasizing here, and the way in which it is mixed with that of our
contemporary economy, is not incidental. It is our relation to the world itself
– and not just to war – that has become warlike, as the origins of cybernetics
reveal. It is the contemporary organization or the system of presence that has
become intrinsically violent, marked as it is by a well-oiled and executed chain
of control, command, mobilization, requisition and capture of energy,
resources and information. Nature now stands in reserve, awaiting to be
'mobilized'. The boundary between war and peace, or between the economy of
war and that of peace, has all but vanished. This is because we live under the
all-pervasive and all-encompassing demand of technology, which sets man
upon nature, and man against man.

   With this somewhat detailed investigation into the meaning of the *Ge-stell*,
we can see how the System designates the mode of revealing that unfolds in the
essence of modern technology, an essence that is itself nothing technological.
We have shown how technology – or rather the essence of technology – designates neither a human activity nor a mere means towards a human goal, but
the *systematic* organization of presence and, with it, the obliteration of the
moment of presencing that is intrinsic to – and decisive for – that organization.
Ultimately, the System designates the way in which things stand together at
the end of metaphysics, in the technological, and especially technoscientific (or
cybernetic) age: as part of a vast network regulated by feedback.

   As such, the System signals a supreme danger, one that reveals itself to us in
two ways. As soon as what is unconcealed no longer concerns man even as
object, but exclusively as standing-reserve, and man in the midst of objectless-
ness is nothing but the systematic organizer of the standing-reserve, then he
comes to the point when he himself will have to be taken as standing-reserve,
if not as disposal waste. This is the point at which he is denied his dignity. And
how many monstrous examples of this commoditization beyond objectification
have we had in the last 100 years, from the coalmines to the death camps, from
eugenics to ethnic cleansing? At the same time, however, whilst threatened in
this way, man comports himself as lord of the earth, as if the earth were there

for his own consumption and abuse, with the devastating ecological consequences we know. Yet in so comporting himself, man moves further away from
his own essence, from the possibility of encountering the essence of man. This
is where the greatest danger lies, perhaps: in the fact that man can no longer
intimate revealing as such, and so is in danger of becoming disconnected from
the essence of truth as such. The possibility of a mode of revealing other than
that of the System is under threat, as the revealing of the System is essentially
all encompassing. Revealing as such is in danger of being concealed. Truth as
revealing is about to become extinct in the total revealing of everything as
standing-reserve. The danger inherent in the revealing of nature as standing-
reserve lies in the fact that revealing as unconcealing is itself completely
covered over. The greatest danger lies in the total occlusion of concealment in
unreserved revealing. The greatest threat – greater, for more originary, than the
threat of total destruction of the earth, greater than the threat that comes from
the lethal machines and apparatus of technology – is the complete disconnec-
tion of the human from its essence, that is, from its openness and exposedness
to the essence of truth as (un)concealment. This, according to Heidegger,
signals the threat of a total *alienation* of man.

TECHNOLOGY AS DESTINY

So far, we've managed to shift the terrain of the question concerning technology, from technology itself to what Heidegger calls its essence, or its provenance. We now need to establish explicitly the connection between this
essence, or the System, according to which the real is revealed everywhere,
more or less distinctly, as standing-reserve, and its historical impact. Is the
essence of technology thus understood historically delimited? Is it an epoch of
history, one that began at a certain time, and may end at some other, or is it
historical in yet another sense? We saw how Heidegger disputes the idea that
the essence of technology emerged in the eighteenth century. He doesn't
dispute the fact that eighteenth-century England saw the emergence and
development of the application of power machinery to production, and that
this is what came to be known as the technological age. But he does dispute
the fact that the technological age – to which, today, we would need to
add the digital, or information, 'second' revolution – has its origin and essence
in the industrial revolution, or even in the scientific and epistemological break
of the seventeenth and eighteenth centuries. For him, this phenomenon was
announced long before. In fact, it began with the very dawn of Western
history. As I've already suggested, it is Western metaphysics itself that is
essentially technological. This, of course, is another provocative claim:
Heidegger is arguing that this relatively recent phenomenon we call the technological age, and which coincides with the industrial revolution, must be
traced back not just to the birth of modern physics in the seventeenth century,
not just, then, to the discovery of those laws of nature and those forces that
were subsequently applied to the production of machines, nor even to the birth

of capitalism in the late Middle Ages, nor even to a combination of the two, but to the very singular nature of our Western history. It is history as such – European history, which eventually became global through the conquest of the seas and the lands, through colonization and immigration – that is intrinsi- cally technological. In other words, the mode of revealing (the organization of truth) that characterizes our age, in which the world is revealed as standing- reserve, and man as the master and possessor of nature, is one that reaches as far back as the origin of Western history and culture. Naturally, this claim depends entirely on the way in which Heidegger understands the specificity of this history. It is to this understanding of history that we must now turn.

Our history, Heidegger argues, is marked by the fact that European man finds himself set upon a certain course, a certain way – the way of that very revealing through which, ultimately, the real becomes standing-reserve. European man is sent down that path. His history is defined by this course upon which he is set. This course is the share he inherits, his fate, or destiny, as it were. The German word for destiny is *Geschick*. It is made up of the prefix '*Ge*', which, once again, Heidegger understands as 'gathering', and of the root- verb *schiken*, which means 'to send'. Destiny is the sending that gathers men and beings in a definite manner. History (*Geschichte*) is essentially destiny. Is Heidegger saying that technology is our destiny, and that European history is essentially technological? In a way. The *Ge-stell* designates the way in which, today, men and beings are gathered together. Destiny, however, is not to be thought of as the product of the invisible hand of some higher agency, such as God (or the gods), Reason or Freedom, to name but a few ways in which destiny has traditionally been conceived. And history is not to be thought of as the stage on which a process oriented towards an ultimate goal unfolds. History is not teleological. Technology is not the ultimate aim of history. If there is any agency involved in the unfolding of history, it is that of truth itself, understood as the truth of being (see Chapter 2). Truth is not 'behind' history, directing its actors from behind the stage as it were. Rather, truth unfolds *as* history. The essence of truth, in the sense of its unfolding, is historical through and through. In claiming that European history is *essentially* technological, Heidegger is not saying that it is *necessarily* so. Destiny is not 'fate' (*Schicksal*) understood as 'the inevitableness of an unalterable course'.[28] On the contrary: there is a degree of contingency in our history. Another response to the essen- tial historicity of the human, that is, to the fact that, in our exposure to the truth of being, we respond to it by remaining open to it, or, conversely, by turning away from it and shutting it down, could have been conceivable. In fact, the 'other beginning' Heidegger attempted to prepare us for was linked to precisely the possibility of responding differently to our essential belong- ing to truth, and so with the possibility of initiating another history. It is also conceivable, as Heidegger always suggests, that what we often refer to as 'cul- tures' other than that of Europe – such as that of Mesoamerica, or India – may have revealed a different, non-technological destiny.

For Heidegger, history begins with, or, put differently, 'there is history', only because there is this calling, or this address that befalls us. If humanity is *essentially* historical, it is not because it takes place in history, alongside the history and evolution of the universe, the earth and living organisms. Rather, it is because it is made to respond to something that is singular, and in the response to which it finds itself set on a specific course. This something, to which man from the start finds himself directed, and in the directedness of which he becomes historical, as well as human, is what Heidegger calls 'being', or 'truth'. The history of man is played out in the manner and nature of his response to this exposure to the truth of being, which distinguishes him as human. And the nature of the response that characterizes the European man is what ultimately leads to the sense of nature as standing-reserve. We are accustomed to thinking of history (*Geschichte*) as what happens or takes place in time, and this taking place (*Geschehen*) we understand in terms of the unfolding of events that are historically (*historisch*) observable. In so doing, we fail to understand history in terms of its essence or its provenance: in terms of destiny (*Geschick*). Destiny, for Heidegger, is a sending (*Schickung*) of being. What characterizes this sending, though, is that it implicates a certain reserve, an opacity: in sending itself, it also holds itself back. This is what, following the Greek, Heidegger calls the *epoche* of truth. The various ways in which truth holds itself back determine the various 'epochs' of truth. In manifesting itself, truth also conceals itself. In each case, this sending gathers itself (*Ge-*) into a unified domain. This unity is that of an epoch. It is therefore still being, or truth, that is destined in the *Ge-stell*, even if, in this sending and this revealing, the *essence* of truth remains entirely concealed.

What have we established thus far? That the essence of technology is nothing technological: it is an essentially historical phenomenon. Yet history, for Heidegger, is destiny. What does destiny mean? That which is sent our way, that on the course of which we find ourselves set. Who, or what, accomplishes the sending? Being. History is the temporal unfolding of being, and one that manifests itself as a singular configuration of truth, a unique way in which the world and other human beings find themselves illuminated. As a configuration of truth, and as a sending of being, technology signals the most extreme concealing of the essence of truth as un-concealment. This is what's difficult to grasp. The most complex aspect of this conception of technology has to do with its ambiguous status. On the one hand, technology is a configuration of truth, or an epoch of being: it is a way in which beings unfold within presence, a way in which they manifest themselves. At the same time, it is the mode of presence in which the 'mystery' of presence, that is, its relation to concealment (or what Heidegger calls untruth) as the 'essence' of truth is most concealed, or least in a position of being grasped. The result is humanity's further and furthest alienation from the essence of truth, and so from its own essence. The result is that man is cut off from his own essence, cut off from himself. This is the distressing situation Heidegger sees us in. For him, it is the ultimate form of alienation. Genuine 'thought' (as opposed to philosophy as metaphysics, and to all the (techno)-discourses that are the corollary of technology as the defining

feature of our time), as well as art (see Chapter 5), are, according to Heidegger,
ways in which we can open ourselves to this distress, and initiate a turn within
history, such that we will once again be in tune with our essence, and disclosed
to the disclosedness of being. After his failure of the rectorship (see Chapter 6),
Heidegger sees a possible 'rescue' from this state of alienation no longer in political action, but in 'thinking', and its proximity to art, which alone can establish a free relation to technology.

To finish, I'd like to take this issue concerning the origin of technology as
the defining feature of our time, and of our history as a whole, yet further. The
'event' of technology, we recall, is not one that we can locate in time: it is not,
for example, to be found in the epoch of history normally associated with the
appearance of machine technology. It is not even to be found in the scientific
revolution of the seventeenth and eighteenth centuries. We've been able to
trace it back to what, in *Being and Time*, Heidegger had already identified as
the greatest obstacle to philosophical thought, namely, the forgottenness of
being (*die Seinsvergessenheit*). There is an essential link between technology as
the dominant and, today, unquestioned form of knowing and the forgottenness of being identified almost from the start as the one question to which philosophical thought was to direct itself. The question of being is the question
Heidegger set out to revive. Almost from the start, he saw it as the single most
decisive question (not just philosophically decisive, but also historically, politically and culturally decisive), and all the more decisive, and in need of its own
reawakening, because it had fallen into total forgottenness. Overcoming this
forgottenness was considered the highest demand and the greatest challenge.
Initially, though, Heidegger did not know exactly to what to attribute this
forgottenness. As a result, the retrieval of the question was itself made more
difficult, if not altogether impossible. This is why the project of fundamental
ontology, carried out in *Being and Time* and other texts and lecture courses of
that period, was only partly successful. It amounted to a preliminary stage on
the way to a more complete understanding and retrieval of the question. With
the discovery of the significance of the phenomena of 'machination' and 'technology', Heidegger was able to take his question further and provide a preliminary reason as to why the question concerning being had fallen into
forgottenness. In a way, we could say that the question concerning the forgottenness of being evolved into the question concerning technology. In a way,
the event and the advent of technology can be seen as the preliminary 'cause'
of the forgottenness of being, and its global and total spread the reason why
'thinking' in the essential sense of the term has become virtually impossible.

The question, however, is one of knowing whether technology allowed us
to arrive at the ultimate or fundamental cause of this forgottenness. Are we to
go no further, and ask: if the advent of technology (or the forgottenness of the
truth of being) cannot be dated historically with any great accuracy, if
Heidegger is indeed right in disputing that the essence of technology ante-
dates the historically traceable and definable phenomenon historians and social
scientists call technology, where can we situate its origin? Or is this the wrong

question? Should we not give up our attempt to situate it historically or
historiographically, that is, to date it as an intra-temporal event, and acknowledge the possibility of another, deeper sense of history, one that would not be
chrono-logical, but onto-logical? Should we not at least consider the possibility that we might interpret chronology in the light of history as the event of
time itself (as *Geschichte*), rather than the other way around? In our pursuit of
the ultimate cause and essence of this historical phenomenon we call technology, should we not understand 'cause', 'essence' and 'history' differently? This
is precisely what Heidegger suggests we do. And the answer he gives to the
question concerning the ultimate essence of technology, and this means to the
question concerning the forgottenness of being itself, is at once surprising and
compelling. Technology, he argues, is not a recent phenomenon. It is not even
an old phenomenon. Rather, it coincides with European history as such, that
is, with what is being decided and played out in our history. Our history is
technological through and through. It is the history of technology. The age of
machine technology is only the latest phase – and possibly the ultimate manifestation – of the essentially technological destination of our history. We
cannot date the advent of technology, we cannot argue as to when it really
began, for, Heidegger insists, it has always already begun. Our historical
beginning is marked by an essentially technological interpretation of being in
the sense of presence, and of coming into being. It is phenomenality itself, or
presence which, from the start as it were, is understood technologically. What
defines us historically, what characterizes us as Europeans, according to
Heidegger, is this technological interpretation of the burgeoning of the world
and our relation to it. But this (in a sense contingent, as I was suggesting
earlier on) interpretation is one that is inscribed *structurally* within the essence
of truth. The forgottenness of being, with which our history coincides, has its
roots in the essence of truth itself. The structural phenomenon that Heidegger
identifies as the ultimate source of our forgottenness (*Seinsvergessenheit*) of
being, and so as the essence of technology itself, is what he calls the abandonment *of* and *by* being (*Seinsverlassenheit*).

Heidegger develops the concept of *Seinsverlassenheit* in a number of texts
from 1936 to 1940.[29] Eventually, he will contrast that concept, which marks
the origin of the forgottenness of being, and so of the first beginning, with the
concept, inherited from the great German medieval mystic Meister Eckhart, of
Gelassenheit (letting-be, or releasement, and serenity). This origin is structural.
So, it is not as if the forgottenness of being were a matter of some failure of our
memory, of some accidental moment within history up until then marked by
a close proximity to the event of being. The reason for that is simple, and has
to do with the fact that the event of being is actually the event of an erasure
and a withdrawing constitutive of presence and history as such, the unfolding
of truth as that which turns away from presence within presence (recall, in that
respect, what was established in Chapter 2 regarding the 'essence' of truth as
untruth). 'Abandonment of being', Heidegger writes in *Contributions*, 'must be
experienced as the basic event [*Grundgeschehnis*] of our history'.[30]

Now, if this is indeed the case, we have to draw the conclusion that, in a way, what Heidegger calls the 'other beginning', or the 'overcoming of technological nihilism', is not directed against technology, but towards the retrieval of its hidden essence: the 'memory' or 'remembrance' of the lost and forgotten origin requires this forgottenness. This, in turn, implies that there is no pure, immediate access to the truth of being. Its only access is through what Heidegger calls its non-essence, or its counter-essence, which is nothing other than the history of the 'first' beginning, nothing other than the history of the self-erasure and oblivion of being in and through technology. Nowhere is this emphasis on the connection between thought and remembrance stressed with greater emphasis than in a text from 1953 entitled *What is called, and what calls for Thinking?* There, Heidegger simply equates the possibility of genuine thought itself with the ability to remember an event that never took place in the present, but which is constitutive of the present as such, an event which opens up the field of presence, and conceals itself in the process. It is, of course, a kind of remembrance that strikes us as strange, as we are used to thinking of remembrance as the re-enacting in the present of something that actually took place in the past. But, for Heidegger, the remembrance that is here at issue cannot be that of an intra-temporal event, as it signals the very advent or opening up of time and history. It is an ontological, or, better said still, an onto-destinal, remembrance, and not a psychological one. Thought as remembrance is intimately and irreducibly bound up with the possibility of turning to that which, in beings themselves, has always turned itself away from them, and this at the precise moment when it allows them to unfold in their very essence, as the very beings that they are. This essentially elusive essence of being, this ontological structure, is untruth in the sense of concealment. The paradox, in a way, is that originary concealment (or the essence of truth) conceals itself in unconcealment (or truth): 'That being abandons beings means: being *conceals itself* [*verbirgt sich*] in the openness [*Offenbarkeit*] of beings'.[31] This means that unconcealment is itself the non-essence of truth. It is at once the way in which concealment unfolds (this is one sense of *wesen*: essential unfolding), and the mode of unfolding in which the essence of truth is concealed. In other words, it is at once its non-*essence* and its *non*-essence.

This structure is repeated in *Contributions*, and elsewhere. Technology – or, as Heidegger began by designating it in the late 1930s, 'machination' – is said to designate the *Unwesen des Seyns*, the non-essence of being. Now, *Unwesen* can and must be understood in two different ways here, granted that those two ways belong together and ultimately cannot be thought of independently of one another. We can begin by stressing the 'non-' in non-essence. In that sense, machination is the covering over of the truth of being, or the self-effacement of the event of presence. Machination signifies the concealment of the essence of truth as concealment. It signifies the forgottenness of the essence of truth as involving a strife, or a tension, between concealment and unconcealment. As such, machination knows of unconcealment or presence alone, a presence that is further qualified as *beständige Anwesenheit*, both in the sense of constant, continual or permanent presence, and in the sense of stock, or readily available stuff. Here, *beständige Anwesenheit*, or readily available and permanent presence, can be seen as a translation of the Greek *ousia*. Whilst it is true that, with Plato and Aristotle, *ousia* came to mean being in the sense of presence and essence (or 'whatness'), its ordinary meaning in Greek was that of an endurable and permanent good, and land in particular, as the most significant form of material possession. Already in the late 1930s, then, Heidegger understood reality as it appeared in the light of technology, or machination, as 'standing reserve'. Machination, in which the fate of the self-erasure and forgetting of being is played out, is nothing other than the history of this *non*-essence. It is the history of how the *event* of presence is erased in favour of presence alone, how truth, as the process of unconcealment out of originary concealment is progressively forgotten in favour of the unconcealed. But, equally importantly – and one cannot emphasize this point enough, for it is too often ignored or forgotten, and is the source of much confusion and basic misinterpretations – *Un*-wesen is also Un-*wesen*. Yes, machination is the *non*-essence or the counter-essence of being. But it is also its non-*essence* or its counter-*essence*. What does this mean? It means that between the event of being, to which Heidegger's thought as a whole is directed, and its own forgottenness or erasure in technology, there is a *structural* unity. Not an accidental, random relation, linked to some historical contingency, but an essential or intimate relation, precisely, which amounts to nothing other than the necessity of history. History is history of this necessity: it is the unfolding or the happening of the becoming-presence (and present) of the event of presence. Machination, as the non-essence of being, is precisely the non-essence *of* being. With the decisive consequence, then, that this non-essence is our only access to its essence or its truth. We cannot even begin to think this essence – and, for Heidegger, this means simply to *think* – without thinking the way in which, structurally, this essence unfolds as its non- or counter-essence: as metaphysics, and its continuation in contemporary science and technology. In other words, to think the essence or the truth of being is to think the way in which this essence or this truth has always and already begun to unfold in and as its non-essence, or untruth. The essential unfolding of being is the unfolding of its non-essence. *Unwesen* is the 'echoing' (*Anklang*) of *Wesen*. Tuning into this echoing provides the only access to the event of being and the only possible broaching of a counter-history, or a history 'after' or, rather, perhaps simply parallel to the history of metaphysics – the 'other beginning'.[32] Far from needing to be avoided, or condemned, technology – if and when considered from the point of view of its 'essence' – is a genuine and unavoidable access to the question regarding the 'meaning' (or the 'truth') of being.

Following Heidegger's own avowed goal, we began by saying that our questioning about technology was pursued with a view to establishing a free relation to it. Have we become freer in relation to an event that seems more all encompassing than we initially thought? Insofar as the origin of this event has become clearer, yes. We have perhaps lost the illusion that technology is something we control, and that it is there for our own benefit and good. But we have gained an understanding of its provenance, and of the way in which we can engage with it, without being instrumentalized by it. Far from having gained what we ordinarily call a critical distance, we have gained a proximity to its own hidden origin. And this origin, we saw, is itself nothing technological. In the realization of this non-technological origin, a certain overturning of technology has begun to take place. Our relation to nature, and to the whole of being, has begun to undergo a certain transformation. Why does the turn to the essence of technology alone allow us to free ourselves from its grip? Because the essence of technology is the essence of truth itself, and because the question concerning technology is the question concerning the constellation in which truth, as the play of revealing (*Entbergung*) and concealing (*Verbergung*), happens. As such, it alone brings us to the source of history, the source at which another relation to the truth of being becomes possible. Any opposition to, rejection or thoughtless embracing of technology, any attempt to master it only confirms its grip, and amounts to a further turn of the (technological) screw. To open oneself to the essence of technology is fundamentally different from agreeing to it and promoting it. It is equally different, though, from criticizing it and rejecting it.

The gathering that characterizes our age is that of the System (the *Ge-stell*). The interpretation of knowing (*techne*) in which we find ourselves is that of technical, scientific knowing. In the light of the hidden essence of truth that lies at the heart of these phenomena, the question, now, is one of knowing whether a different kind of gathering, and a different sense of knowing, is thinkable. These are precisely the ones Heidegger devoted himself to imagining. A short while ago, I introduced the concept of *Gelassenheit* as marking a historical alternative to the *Ge-stell*. In *Ge-lassenheit*, it is a different kind of gathering, and of cohesion, that prevails: not that of the total capture and seizure of all things actual, but that of a letting-be and releasement of such things from out of their essence (the essence of truth). *Gelassenheit* signals an attitude and comportment towards the world that is altogether different from that of the *Ge-stell*. It is an attitude of releasement of beings *for* their being, of letting beings be in their being. In and through this attitude, a certain serenity or composure is acquired. For Heidegger, though, this comportment is not a mystic state. It is a form of knowing. Thought itself, as meditation (*Besinnung*), can partake of this comportment. Heidegger contrasts the thought that meditates with the thought that calculates. Whereas the latter is directed solely towards beings, and towards their quantification and measurement, the former directs itself towards that which, in every being, cannot be quantified – towards beings in their *being*. Starting towards the middle of the 1930s, and increasingly thereafter, Heidegger will see art, and poetry especially, as one such form of knowing, in which the essence of things is released. It is to Heidegger's conception of art, and its proximity to thought, that I want now to turn.

NOTES

1 A digital – as opposed to an analogue – machine 'represents all quantities by discrete states, for example, relays which are open or closed, a dial which can assume any one of ten positions, and so on, and then literally *counts* in order to get its results' (H. Dreyfus, *What Computers Can't Do: A Critique of Artificial Reason* [New York: Harper & Row, 1972], p. xix). Whereas analogue computers operate with continuous physical quantities, digital computers are discrete, state machines.

2 Paul M. Churchland, *Matter and Consciousness* (Cambridge, MA: MIT Press, 1988), p. 92.

3 See Paul M. Churchland, *Matter and Consciousness*, pp. 120–1.

4 In the years 1939–40, Heidegger was lecturing extensively on Nietzsche, and on two central issues of his thought in particular: the 'will to power' and 'European nihilism'. His analysis of the global and total nature of World War II, and of the economic as well as military struggle for world domination, can be found in GA 69, V. 'To Koinon', VII. 'The Accord. The Essence of Power. The Necessary', 'Koinon. From the History of Beyng'.

5 GA 66, 176.

6 There are significant exceptions, though, the most significant, in my view, being Jean-Luc Nancy's *The Experience of Freedom*, trans. Bridget McDonald (Stanford: Stanford University Press, 1993).

7 See A. V. Miller, *Hegel's Phenomenology of Spirit* (Oxford: Oxford University Press, 1977), B. 'Self-Consciousness', iv. 'The Truth of Self-Certainty', a. 'Independence and dependence of self-consciousness: Lordship and Bondage'. On Marx's interpretation of Hegel's dialectic in connection with labour, freedom and alienation, see E. Kamenka (ed.), *The Portable Karl Marx* (London and New York: Penguin Books, 1983), 131–46 (from the manuscripts of 1844).

8 Heidegger, 'The Provenance of Art and the Destination of Thought'. The lecture was delivered before the Athens Academy of Science and Art on 4 April 1967.

9 Nietzsche, *The Will to Power*, translated by W. Kaufmann and R. J. Hollingdale, edited by W. Kaufmann (New York: Vintage Books, 1968), § 466. For Heidegger, 'science' is a term that is not precise enough to characterize the epistemological paradigm that governs knowledge in this century, and makes technology possible. 'Science' is one way in which he translates the Greek *techne*, and designates *authentic* knowing.

10 N. Wiener, *Cybernetics or Control and Communication in the Animal and the Machine* (Cambridge, MA: MIT Press, 1948). Drawing on his experience with 'goal-oriented' and 'self-steering' devices designed to improve the accuracy of anti-aircraft artillery, Wiener and his associates envisioned the construction of purposive machines that would resemble living organisms in every way. The emphasis of the machine was in principle one of organization and – increasingly in the 1950s and 60s – on *self*-organisation. I cannot emphasize enough the significance of the military origins of cybernetics. It is entirely bound up with the possibility of creating an 'intelligent' weapon and turning combatants themselves into fighting machines (into cyborgs). The immediate move from World War II to the Cold War only made the control of such a technology more urgent, and more precious: information ('intelligence') was understood to be a decisive factor in the conflict. The cybernetic representation of the human has its origins in war, and especially in the need to control weapon 'systems' and to establish lines of communication between them, in order to inflict maximal damage and incur minimal loss. Another factor that cannot be underestimated is the fact that this science originated in the United States: Wiener himself saw his book *The Human Use of Human Beings. Cybernetics and Society* (Garden City, New York: Doubleday Anchor Books, 1950/1954) as meant primarily for Americans living in an American environment (p. 113).

11 N. Wiener, *The Human Use of Human Beings*, pp. 74ff.

12 Gregory Bateson, an anthropologist and an influential member of the Macy Foundation in the late 40s and 50s, the aim of which was to rethink psychology in the light of the theory of information, and led to the invention of the clinical category of 'mental health', is widely recognized as having introduced cybernetics in the social sciences. Following Wiener's principle, Bateson conceives of information as a negentropic principle that favours the organization and the development of social systems. Information is seen as the 'differential value', or as the qualitative principle of order and organization that neutralizes (albeit only ever temporarily) the second law of thermodynamics, which stipulates that any closed system will tend towards an equalization of its thermic differences, and so the progressive death of thermic activity. Such is the reason why Bateson characterizes information as the differentiating factor, or as a 'difference which makes a difference'. See Gregory Bateson, *Steps to an Ecology of Mind* (Chicago: University of Chicago Press, 2000), p. 459.

13 Donna J. Haraway, 'A Cyborg Manifesto,' *Simians, Cyborgs, and Women* (London: Free Association Books, 1991), p. 164.

14 François Jacob, *The Logic of Life. A History of Heredity* (1970), trans. Betty E. Spillmann (London: Penguin Books, 1989), p. 251.

15 N. Wiener, *The Human Use of Human Beings*, p. 26.

16 In the last few years, a sub-discipline of biology called computational biology has emerged, and its scientists are trained in biology as well as computer science. There is an ongoing exchange of ideas and a genuine collaboration between cybernetics and biology. Increasingly, biology is turning to 'integration' and 'system behaviour' to understand the cellular system. Our approach to computers and our understanding of organisms is becoming ever more entangled.

17 The idea of a 'genetic code' first appeared in 1943 in a seminal article by the quantum physicist and Nobel Prize winner Erwin Schrödinger, who was the first to advocate the relevance of microphysics for biology, and to situate the question of heredity in the context of thermodynamics (E. Schrödinger, *What is Life?* [Cambridge, Cambridge University Press, 2002]). It is with the English molecular biologist Francis Crick, who discovered the double helix structure of DNA in 1953, however, that the term was given a more solid definition. Crick's most explicit version of this idea can be found in 'The Genetic Code: III', *Scientific American*, 1966, pp. 52–63.

18 Crick spoke only of a genetic *code*. In that, he was following the work and vocabulary of Shannon (1948). The idea of a genetic *programme*, however, first formulated in 1961, is due to the German-born, evolutionary biologist Ernst Mayr, as well as the French, molecular biologists François Jacob and Jacques Monod (E. Mayr, 'Cause and Effect in Biology', *Science*, 154, 1961, p. 1504; F. Jacob and J. Monod, 'Genetic Regulatory Mechanisms in the Synthesis of Proteins', *The Journal of Molecular Biology*, 3, 1961, p. 354). Of the term 'genetic programme', Jacob notes that it 'is a model borrowed from electronic computers. It equates the genetic material of an egg with the magnetic tape of a computer' (*The Logic of Life*, p. 9). Like many notions stemming from cybernetics, the concept of genetic programme spread very quickly to other domains, eventually finding its way into popular culture and the mass media. It dominated the fields of molecular biology and the philosophy of science for twenty years. In a seminal article on protein synthesis from 1953, Crick reveals that 'the main function of the genetic material is to control (albeit indirectly) the protein synthesis' (F. Crick, 'On Protein Synthesis', *Symposium of the Society of Experimental Biology*, vol. 12, 1958, p. 138. The 'indirect' nature of the control refers to the role played by the RNA, which is to carry the information contained in the DNA over to the proteins). According to this cybernetic view of genetics, a term coined by William Bateson, a biologist and the father of Gregory, in 1906, the 'cause' of protein synthesis is not just a thing, an object or even a convergence of factors, but an operation of *control*. This means that the synthesis in question is triggered by a *message*, or a *command*. The cell receives a message from the RNA, and the synthesis is based on this message. According to this image, the DNA

would be less a molecule than an algorithmic structure. It is this structure that would be the decisive agent, and that would have the power to generate proteins. It is important to note, however, that the image of the genetic programme, and of its algorithmic structure, has come under serious questioning in the last few years, and is now used far more cautiously, and critically. See, for example, H. Atlan and M. Koppel, 'The Cellular Computer DNA: Program or Data?', *Bulletin of Mathematical Biology*, 52(3), pp. 335–48. Two problems at least seem to emerge from a total adequation of the genetic programme with that of the computer. First, the programme of the living machine is such that it increases in complexity as it unfolds: its unfolding is precisely an evolution. This means that the programme has the ability to reprogramme itself: it is programmed to reprogramme itself. As such, the programme is essentially *open*. Second, the genetic programme, and its algorithm, is one that is not there from the start, but one that *emerges*. In other words, there is something within matter (and matter alone) that allows it to organize itself and produce its own genetic algorithm, but this possibility is not itself a function of the genetic algorithm. Time is a decisive factor in the production of the algorithm, or the programme.

19 Cloning by nuclear transfer, and growing new organisms from zygotes (first cell of an organism) that have been formed by fusing an adult cell of one animal with, or transferring the nucleus of that cell into, an enucleated oöcyte (or oöplast) of another of the same species, constitute perhaps the best two examples of such results. For further information on the theoretical and practical aspects of cloning, see Karin Knorr Cetina, *Epistemic Cultures* (Cambridge, MA: Harvard University Press, 1999), pp. 144–9.

20 Quoted in M. Heidegger, *Gelassenheit*, 20/52.

21 G, 20/52.

22 On the connection between ecology and cybernetics, see S. J. Heims, *The Cybernetics Group, 1946–1953. Constructing a Social Science for Post-war America* (Cambridge, MA: MIT Press, 1991).

23 B. Bryant, 'Nature and Culture in the Age of Cybernetic Systems', *CyberNatures/CyberCultures: Redefining Natural and Cultural Borders*, American Studies Association Annual Meeting, Detroit, Michigan, 12–15 October 2000. Referenced in C. Lafontaine, *L'empire cybernétique. Des machines à penser à la pensée machine* (Paris: Seuil, 2004), p. 77.

24 J. Grinevald, 'Progrès et entropie, cinquante ans après', in J.-M. Besnier and D. Bourg (eds), *Peut-on encore croire au progrès?* (Paris: Presses Universitaires de France, 2000), p. 206.

25 P. Virilio, *The Information Bomb* (London: Verso, 2000), p. 1.

26 TK 14–15/296–7.

27 TK, 20/302.

28 TK, 25/307.

29 See GA 65 (especially the second 'panel' of the book, entitled 'Echo'), GA 67 (§§ 131–42, grouped under the title 'The Completion of Metaphysics – Abandonment of Being and Devastation'), GA 69 (§§ 33–6, also grouped under the title 'The Completion of Metaphysics – The Abandonment of Being').

30 GA 65, 112/78.

31 GA 65, 111/78.

32 GA 65, 111/78.

RECOMMENDED READING

Janicaud, Dominique, *Powers of the Rational: Science, Technology, and the Future of Thought*, trans. Peg Birmingham and Elizabeth Birmingham (Bloomington: Indiana University Press, 1994). This study, published in French in 1985, is at once an extension of Heidegger's critique of technology, and of techno-science in particular, as well as a critique of Heidegger's own position and an attempt to rescue modes of rationality beyond their technological deviation and excesses.

Zimmerman, Michael, *Heidegger's Confrontation with Modernity. Technology, Politics, Art* (Bloomington: Indiana University Press, 1990). This is an insightful discussion of the link between Heidegger's critique of technology as productionist metaphysics and his engagement with National Socialism.

5

The Saving Power of Art

'We look into the danger and see the growth of the saving power.'[1]

Given what we've just said in the previous chapter, we understand how there can be – indeed how there must be – a proximity between calculative thinking, as the thinking born of the forgottenness of being, and the meditative thinking that is directed towards that forgottenness itself. This is because calculative and meditative thought share a common essence – the essence of truth. Both are children of truth. But whereas the former constitutes the concealment (or the non-essence) of the essence of truth (as unconcealment), the latter directs itself back towards this essence. Only a very thin line separates the two. Yet this line is also an abyss. Calculative thought, Heidegger insists, is not to be supplanted by meditative thought. It has its own great usefulness, and remains indispensable: we cannot, and should not, do away with the type of thought that plans and investigates.[2] Similarly, it would be foolish to 'attack technology blindly', and short-sighted to 'condemn it as a work of the devil'.[3] We depend on technical devices, which make our lives more practical and easier. But we should not find ourselves 'so shackled to these devices that we fall into bondage with them'.[4] We must learn to leave them in their right place, to let go of them as something inessential, as something that does not affect us in any decisive manner. In letting go of them, we turn to the world, and to the beings in its midst, from a position that is not technological. The world is there, yet not in a way that provokes us to attack it. All of a sudden, we dwell in the world in a totally different way. What sort of dwelling is at issue here? The essence of technology, we recall, is the *Ge-stell*. In the System, we dwell in the world as the rulers of the world. Technology signals the contemporary hold of man over nature. Planetary domination is its logical outcome. Yet, throughout, Heidegger insists that this appropriation of the planet's resources, and the extent of our power, stems from a radical separation from our own essence. This, we recall, is what Heidegger calls the 'greatest danger'. It is one that takes the form of a radical homelessness and estrangement, despite the fact that technology gives us the false impression of being everywhere at home in the world. World domination and ever-increasing power (*Macht*) is the contemporary form of homelessness, born of the forgottenness and abandonment of being. Today, we are in danger of losing the world as a *dwelling* place. There is a crucial difference between occupying a space, and the planet as a whole, as technological man does, and dwelling authentically in the world.[5] The other relation to the world, in which we gain a free relation to technology, Heidegger calls *Ge-lassenheit*. It amounts to a letting-be of beings, to a form of relinquishing and releasement, in and through which we gain a certain serenity, or composure.[6] It signals a mode of dwelling that does not amount to a domination of nature, a proximity to the world that is not an appropriation of it. Similarly, we should be lucid regarding the origin of calculative thought, and the manner in which it has become the only recognized form of thought, or knowing (*techne*). We should take into consideration its peculiarity. This peculiarity, Heidegger claims, has to do with the fact that whenever we plan, research and delimit a domain, we always reckon with circumstances that are given. And the way in which we reckon with them, or take them into account, is by calculating the specific purposes they will serve. Thus we can predict or count on definite results. This is the calculation that is the mark of technological thought. It remains calculation even when it neither works with numbers nor uses computers. Calculative thought always computes. It computes ever new, ever more promising and at the same time ever more economical possibilities. Calculative thinking races from one prospect to the next. It never stops, never collects itself. As such, and whilst realizing an essential possibility of the metaphysical destiny of man, calculative thinking runs the risk of alienating man from his own essence. Meditative thought, by contrast, abstracts itself from calculation and directs thought back towards that which calculation covers over, back towards the origin of the forgottenness that reigns in calculation. It is the thought that stops, collects itself as well as the world in which we live and 'ponders'. It is the thought through which, once again, a free relation to technology, born of a reflection upon its provenance, becomes possible.

At about the time that Heidegger began to think of thought in terms of 'meditation' (*Besinnung*), as distinct from 'calculation' (*Rechnen*) and 'machination' (*Machenschaft*), he began to lecture and write on art. This is no coincidence. Art, for him, came to represent the possibility of a relation to the world, and of a dwelling on earth, that was not technological. At the same time, however, and as I have already begun to suggest, he saw art as stemming from the same origin as technology itself. This means that, between art and technology, like between meditation and calculation, there is a relation of absolute proximity (with respect to their essence) and absolute distance (with respect to their outcome). Increasingly, art came to be seen as the other, hidden side of the *techne* that developed into technology. It began to stand for a historical possibility that technology covered over, yet one that could unfold from the essence of technology itself. Such is the reason why, from 1933–4 onwards, Heidegger's thought focuses on art, technology, and their relation to truth. Like Nietzsche, who saw art (at least a *certain* art) as the counter-movement to European nihilism, Heidegger envisages it as the possibility, held in reserve in the essence of technology itself, through which technological nihilism can be overcome:

Because the essence of technology is nothing technological, essential reflection upon technology and decisive confrontation with it must happen in a realm that is, on the one hand, akin to the essence of technology and, on the other, fundamentally different from it.

Such a realm is art.[7]

Art is at once closest to, and farthest from, technology, inasmuch as it stems from a response to, and a greeting of, that which remains hidden and suppressed in technology. Art is the unnamed, unknown and unsurpassed 'other' of technology. The history it opens up is not so much outside that of technology, as folded into it. And the unfolding of this fold, in which something else takes place, is the realization of the hidden and preserved essence of technology. This, I believe, is the sense of the verse by Hölderlin that Heidegger likes to quote:

But where danger is, grows
The saving power also. . . .[8]

To save, Heidegger suggests in 'The Question Concerning Technology', is not to draw something or someone away from the danger they face. Rather, it is to fetch something home into its essence, in order to bring the essence for the first time into its genuine appearing. To rescue, or to save, means to undo, to frank, to free, to look after and protect, to shelter, to take under one's wing, to safekeep and safeguard.[9] As the saving power understood in this sense, art does not save us *from* technology, as if technology signified this ultimate danger to be avoided. Rather, art forces us deeper into technology by bringing us face to face with its essence. The essence of technology harbours the growth of the saving power *within itself*. This power does not come from outside, but from within technology. In a lecture from 1949 entitled 'The Turning' Heidegger goes as far as to say that it is the danger itself (the essence of the *Ge-stell*) that is the saving power. Between art and technology, there is something like a reciprocal belonging, like a dialectic without negativity. But art and technology belong together only to the extent that they belong to the essence of truth.

Unlike technology, art, and poetry especially, signals the site of a true dwelling on earth. Why? Precisely because art begins with the world as this unfamiliar, uncanny phenomenon, which it does not seek to reduce, but to deepen, to 'understand' in a way that is radically different from its rational—scientific conquest. Historically, Heidegger argues, it is true that what we call knowledge (*techne*) unfolded as technology, and knowing as positive science. This unfolding – which is that of European history and of its metaphysics – is completing itself as cybernetics. Cybernetics, or the triumph of the techno-scientific world-view and appropriation of the planet as a whole, signals the end of philosophy. This end, however, means the beginning of the world civilization based on Occidental thinking. Yet the Greeks themselves, as well as 'the few and the rare' throughout history, intimated art as the place or the site in which man could reconcile himself with his forgotten essence, as the place in which man's belongingness to the truth that, in the word of one commentator, is not of (techno-scientific) knowledge, can be experienced and exhibited.[10] There was a time, Heidegger claims, thus echoing Hegel's and Nietzsche's view of the role of art in Ancient Greece, when *techne* did not designate the mode of revealing that reigns in technology, but a different kind of bringing-forth, a different modality of truth. There was a time when the word *techne* referred to a kind of revealing that revealed the radiance and splendour of truth itself. What was called beauty, or the beautiful, was not merely the aesthetically pleasing, and was not a purely subjective matter. Rather, it was an instance, and indeed a shining of truth. The beautiful was envisaged as that which shines forth most purely (*to ekphanestaton*). The beauty of a thing was a function of its truth-character, of its ability to let truth shine forth in its very appearance. The work of art was one such thing, if not its exemplary instance, its 'truest' incarnation. Art in Ancient Greece was revered and brought to a height perhaps never experienced ever since, because of its intimate link with truth as *aletheia*. Today, we think of science as the domain in which truth is sought, established and verified. But for the early Greeks, because of their different relation to the essence of truth, it was art, not science, which brought us closer to truth. The fine arts spoke of the gods in their presence, and of the destiny of human beings in their dialogue with the divine. In doing so, the arts opened up and kept open the sky and the earth and the region between those two. They had a power to disclose the world, and to grant gods, humans and things their place. Much like technology today, art had the power to gather and hold things together (*legein*). Yet it did not do so in the same manner. Its *logos* was not that of techno-science, and its many techno-discourses, but that of a *poiesis*, or a poetic power, in which the power of revealing was brought forth as such, presented in the work. The reality it revealed was not that of the *Ge-stell*, but of the *Ge-viert*, in which world, earth, mortals and gods were gathered and held together as the space in which our fate is played out and decided. As such, the arts were not a sector of 'culture'. And because man himself found his place in and through the relation to the gods, the sky and the earth that was opened up in the work, the force of art was not rooted in aesthetic pleasure. No doubt, aesthetic pleasure was a decisive aspect of the experience of the work of art, even in its most terrifying aspects, such as in the tragic poem. Yet pleasure was not the primary motivation and soil from which the need for art grew.

Today, Heidegger claims, art has become a personal experience, and, for the most part, has become subordinated to, and engulfed in, the general framework, or the System, in which the world is held together. Art has become technologized. This does not mean that art always relies on technological media to express its world-view. It is the world-view itself that is technological through and through (with notable exceptions, as we shall see later on). Art no longer performs the role it once had. It is no longer at the centre of things. Technology is. And art gravitates around it. This means that, for the most part, art does not reveal a modality of truth, and a gathering of reality, that is fundamentally different from that of technology. Yet this is precisely the modality of art that Heidegger is concerned to reawaken. How can art *matter*? To what extent can it be made significant *today*? What must be its relation to technology as designating the contemporary mode of scientific, cultural, social and political organization?

OVERCOMING AESTHETICS

As a direct effect of the loss of the primacy of art, and of the rootedness of art in aesthetic pleasure, the philosophy of art has become 'aesthetics'. Aesthetics, and its history, are for Heidegger surface effects of the metaphysical destiny of man. If there is to be an overcoming (*Überwindung*) of metaphysics, or, more precisely, a return (*Verwindung*) of thought to what remains hidden and unthought in metaphysics; if a decisive confrontation with technology through a reflection on art is to take place, a confrontation with, and overcoming of, aesthetics is itself required. This is a task that Heidegger set out to achieve over a number of years and in numerous volumes and essays, most notably, perhaps, in his interpretation of Nietzsche.

The section from his *Nietzsche* entitled 'The Will to Power as Art' (§ 13) is the place where, arguably, Heidegger expresses his views most succinctly and economically. What does aesthetics mean, he asks? The term, he claims, is formed in the same manner as 'logic' and 'ethics'. As a science (*episteme*), logic is knowledge of thinking, of the forms and rules of thought. Ethics is knowledge of *ethos*, of the inner character of man and of the way it determines his behaviour. Aesthetics, for its part, is knowledge of human behaviour with respect to sense, sensation and feeling, and knowledge of how these are determined.

What determines thinking, hence logic, and what thinking comports itself towards, is the true. What determines the character and behaviour of man, hence ethics, and what human character and behaviour comport themselves towards, is the good. What determines man's feeling, hence aesthetics, and what feeling comports itself towards, is the beautiful. The true, the good and the beautiful are the objects of logic, ethics and aesthetics.

Accordingly, aesthetics is consideration of man's state of feeling in its relation to the beautiful; it is consideration of the beautiful to the extent that it stands in relation to man's state of feeling. The beautiful itself is nothing other than what in its self-showing brings forth that state. But the beautiful can pertain to either nature or art. Because art in its way brings forth the beautiful, inasmuch as it is 'fine' art, meditation on art becomes aesthetics. With relation to knowledge of art and inquiry into it, therefore, aesthetics is that kind of meditation on art in which man's affinity to the beautiful represented in art sets the standard for all definitions and explanations, man's state of feeling remaining the point of departure and the goal of the meditation. The relation of feeling towards art and its bringing-forth can be one of production or of reception and enjoyment.

Now, since the aesthetic consideration of the artwork is defined as the beautiful that has been brought forth in art, the work is represented as the bearer
and provoker of the beautiful with relation to our state of feeling. The artwork
is posited as the 'object' for a 'subject'; definitive for aesthetic consideration is
the subject–object relation, indeed as a relation of feeling. The work becomes
an object in terms of that surface which is accessible to 'lived experience'.

The name 'aesthetics', meaning meditation on art and the beautiful, is
recent. It arose in the eighteenth century. But the matter which the word so
aptly names, Heidegger argues, the manner of inquiry into art and the beautiful on the basis of the state of feeling in enjoyers and producers, is old, as old
as meditation on art and the beautiful in Western thought. Heidegger goes as
far as to say that philosophical meditation on the essence of art and the beautiful even *begins* as aesthetics. So, from his perspective, it matters little that the
word aesthetics came to designate the knowledge of art from the point of view
of feeling only recently; for this is how Western thought has understood art
ever since Plato and Aristotle.

When Heidegger claims that he wants to begin to think of art outside aesthetics, he is setting a difficult and ambitious task for himself. To think of art
outside aesthetics means to think of art outside metaphysics. How can one
think of art non-metaphysically? Before we can answer this question, we must
highlight the link between aesthetics and metaphysics. We already know why
Heidegger wants to drive thought away from metaphysics. This, we recall, is
because metaphysics fails to address the question concerning the essence of
truth, or ask about being in the mode of its unfolding (the 'grounding' question), focusing instead on the question 'What is a being?' (the 'guiding' question). But we do not yet know how 'aesthetics' stems from metaphysics. This
is what we need to establish. One thing is certain, though: if Heidegger is
right in claiming that there is an essential – albeit unthought – connection
between metaphysics and the question of truth, and if he is also right in claiming that aesthetics is concerned with the question of art from the point of view
of the beautiful, then there must be a crucial link between truth and art. This
link, which runs through virtually the whole of metaphysical aesthetics,
revolves almost exclusively around the question of imitation (*mimesis*).

Let me address this connection by referring to the first three of the 'six basic
developments', or the six stages in the history of aesthetics Heidegger lists in
§ 13 of 'The Will to Power as Art'.

The first stage is the one that precedes the birth of aesthetics. Oddly
enough, it corresponds with the greatest flourishing of art the West has
known, or with the advent of what Heidegger calls 'great' art. This age of
'magnificent art' is that of Ancient, classical Greece. This age is characterized
by a remarkable absence of reflection or meditation on art. This, Heidegger
claims, is because there was no need for it: art was knowledge itself. To know,
we recall from the previous chapters, refers to a specific manner in which we
relate to, and are at home in, the world. Art was the dominant and all perva-
sive form of knowledge. It was the way in which things were apprehended and

perceived, 'understood' and made familiar. There was simply no need for a further, more abstract or reflexive moment. This, in turn, means that the great philosophies of Anaximander, Parmenides and Heraclitus, which coincided with this first stage, were not about reflection and abstraction, but were somehow echoing the world of art. This is the extent to which art was great: not because it was more 'beautiful' (as we've already begun to see, the category of the beautiful is itself metaphysical, that is, born after the age of 'great art', and so in a sense a decadent category) than the art of the Italian Renaissance, or that of French classicism; not because it had reached some higher degree of 'aesthetic' (and the use of this word is, in this context, already anachronistic) perfection, then, but simply and exclusively because it was the manner in which things were 'known', the way in which nature and man, man and the divine were integrated into a unified and meaningful totality. The artwork manifested the way in which man was 'passionate' about the world, that is, in a state of wonder before its sheer presence and opening up. This is the sense in which, to use Hegel's own words, art 'is and remains for us, in its highest determination, a thing of the past'.[11]

This first stage is crucial, as it will remain the measure by which Heidegger will evaluate the place and significance of art in our own age, that is, in the age of consummated technology. It is equally crucial to note, however, that Heidegger is not proposing that we return to the Greeks (as if this were possible), or that we relate to the present only out of nostalgia for a bygone era. As paradoxical as it may seem, Heidegger is not interested in the past. Rather, he is interested in the past only in relation to the future, that is, only to the extent that the past is somehow still ahead of us, still orienting and shaping history, and so still alive, holding something in reserve, which not even the past was able to manifest. In fact, the status of this first 'phase' is most ambiguous, and problematic. We recall that from the early 1930s through the 1940s, Heidegger lectured and wrote extensively on the question of truth, and specifically on what he took to be the decisive feature of metaphysics, namely, an essential transformation of truth from 'unconcealment' to 'correctness'. Later on (1966), and in the face of the convincing objections formulated by the classicist Paul Friedländer, who argued that although *aletheia* may indeed have derived from *letho* (*lanthano*) and the alpha-privative, the sense of 'unconcealment' seems to have vanished even before Homer, Heidegger revised his position.[12] There was, he argues, no transformation of truth from unconcealment to correctness, at least not in classical philosophy. There is instead continuity in the history of 'truth', from the start understood as correctness. This revised position suggests that we should not understand Heidegger's talk regarding a pre-metaphysical stage in any actual, chronological sense. This is a phase that is still to come, and its prior dimension has to do with the priority of the question and the domain that metaphysics presupposes and yet is unable to access.

Aesthetics proper begins only in the second phase, only at that moment when the great art and the great philosophy of the Greeks come to an end. This age is that of Plato and Aristotle, and is normally considered the golden age of Greek philosophy. This is when the founding concepts of the history of philosophy are forged. Amongst them, that of the beautiful as the *ekphanestaton*, that is, as what properly shows itself and what is most radiant. The beautiful is first understood as what is most 'shining' – not literally, of course, as if the shining came from the surface of the beautiful thing, as if its beauty came from its shining materiality. Plato, especially, understands the shining in question as the shining of the 'true' face or nature of what is thus exhibited in the work. The true face or aspect of a thing is called its *eidos*. Consequently, the beautiful is taken to be a manifestation, indeed a shining, of the thing in its truth, that is, in its *eidos*. Most beautiful, then, is truth itself. Insofar as the *eidos* is what appears and radiates most brilliantly, every *eidos* in the Platonic sense of the term is beautiful. Beauty itself is nothing other than full, manifest presence, in short, truth. This is the origin of the essential connection between art and truth, and between aesthetics and metaphysics. Where the *eidos* is most 'visible', given in its purest state, however, is not in the work of art, but in its philosophical manifestation, that is, as a concept (an *idea*). The *idea* is not just one of a number of concepts, then: it is the concept of the concept, the standard by which all else is measured. Art can provide an *image* (*eikon*) of truth, but in doing so it allows the idea to show itself by appearing through something else. Art is indeed a manifestation of truth, a mode of presencing of the idea, but an incomplete one. It is essentially and irreducibly ambiguous, then, inasmuch as, whilst not merely producing phantoms that would mislead and corrupt, whilst opening disclosively upon things, and, in doing so, generating pleasure and delight, it fails to present them in their complete truth and their full presence. Philosophy alone can provide truth itself, truth as such. To put it differently, we could say that whereas art can only ever provide an imitation (*mimesis*), or a representation of truth (understood as the full manifestation and presence of a thing), philosophy can provide its (direct) presentation. Philosophy alone has the power to bring before one's eyes the thing in its full manifestation and presence, the *idea* in its pure form. Philosophy alone (and science later on) can claim to *know* the truth. Unlike the work of art, which is only an image, and so an imitation of truth, the philosophical concept (the *idea*) is truth proper. As such, art is exposed to the danger of deception and falsehood. This is the reason why, in his *Republic*, Plato allows art to assume a very modest position only in the hierarchy of modes of behaviour and forms of achievement, and a very limited role within the political community. Because of the utter seriousness of the matter at hand, namely, truth, and the deceiving and potentially corruptive nature of art with respect to truth, art is an activity that must be closely monitored and kept within strictly defined boundaries.[13] This, then, is how art, and the beautiful, came to be subordinated to philosophy, and philosophy to truth (becoming science, or knowledge – *episteme* – in the process). More still: the very category of the beautiful is a metaphysical one, and one that, from the start, flourished under the scrutiny, authority and authorization of philosophy. The discourse on art – on its place, function and significance – was a matter not for art, but for philosophy. The degree of beauty of a work became a function of its proximity and fidelity to the original, the truth of which was manifest as *idea*. This is how the birth of metaphysics, as the transformation of the sense of truth, from truth as *aletheia* to truth as correctness (*orthotes*) and correspondence (*homoiosis*), coincided with the subordination of the artwork to the concept.

Let me mark a pause in my review of the first two phases in Heidegger's short history of aesthetics, and extend his analysis by referring very briefly to Hegel's *Aesthetics*, 'the most comprehensive reflection on art that the West possesses'.[14] There, whilst rejecting what we could call a naturalistic conception of imitation in art, one according to which the purpose of art would be to imitate nature, Hegel reinscribes, ever more forcefully, ever more decisively, the Platonic conception of art as imitation of truth. The vocation of art, Hegel writes, 'is to unveil the truth in the form of sensuous artistic configuration and to present the reconciled opposition, and so to have its end in itself, in this very presentation and unveiling'.[15] As in Plato, art is, and remains, the sensuous presentation of the truth. Later on in the *Aesthetics*, Hegel defines beauty as 'the sensuous shining [*Schein*] of the idea'.[16] As such, though, beauty is the idea presented in a way that is not entirely adequate to truth. In art, there is an inadequacy between form (the sensuous) and content (the idea). The full and adequate (self-)presentation of truth, Hegel argues, is philosophy. It is with philosophy, and philosophy alone, that the Idea is present as such, and not as something else. It is with philosophy alone that we move beyond representation and into pure presentation, where form and content are one.

When, closer to us still, Nietzsche attempts to reverse this hierarchy, and so to overturn Platonism, declaring truth to be '*the kind of error* without which a certain kind of living being could not live',[17] and the sensuous, superficial and artificial nature of the work of art the only 'true' reality there is, he fails to modify the metaphysical structure of aesthetics. In simply reversing the hierarchy established in Platonism, he doesn't do away with it. In fact, he only confirms it, and brings the history of aesthetics to a close. By claiming that art is worth more than truth, and that truth is error, that truth is untruth, he fails to question the *essence* of truth (as *aletheia*), and see that there is a truth that is not of scientific knowledge.[18] As a result, he does not quite manage to wrest art from aesthetics, and from its fundamental tie to metaphysical truth.[19] Art may be worth more than truth, if we understand truth as correspondence and adequation between the sensuous and the supersensuous, or between a material copy and its ideal model. Art may be worth more than truth, if we do away with the supersensuous, intelligible realm on the basis of which it has been evaluated for so long, and recognize it as the only 'true' world, namely, as the world of appearances and surfaces, the manifold, plurivocal world that is the expression of the many perspectives constituting it. But if truth is understood differently, that is, as *aletheia*, then art does not find itself subordinated to it, nor reduced to the role of an imitator. Rather, it becomes one of its (indeed privileged) instances. This is the decisive feature of art we'll return to shortly.

A further, equally decisive concept for the birth of aesthetics was that of
techne. This is a concept we've already come across repeatedly. What we haven't
emphasized, though, is its truly metaphysical interpretation, or the way in
which it comes to be used as a concept by Plato and Aristotle, and is taken up
by an entire tradition. What is this interpretation? The one that understands
it in terms of *production*. When Plato and Aristotle understand art as *techne*,
they include it among a number of ways in which one can 'know'. *Techne*, for
Aristotle especially, is still a mode of knowing in the sense of winning a foot-
hold amidst beings, and establishing oneself in the world. It is still a mode of
truth, or of *aletheuein*, as I've already suggested. At the same time, however,
Aristotle himself, and after Plato, also develops a more restricted sense of
techne, which is the one the tradition will retain. This is *techne* in the sense of
production and manufacture. Whereas handicraft is the production of useful
things, art is the production of beautiful things. In his own thinking of art,
Heidegger questions the importance and privilege granted to production in
art. Naturally, he does not go as far as to suggest that art does not involve a
process of production (this would be absurd). But he does wonder to what
extent the work of art that is produced does not reveal more than its own
process of production, whether, in other words, the 'work' that the work of art
does is reducible to the process of production of the artist himself. In other
words, he wonders whether this 'revealing' of the work is not a matter of truth
in a different sense: not in the sense of *pro-ducere*, of bringing some thing (the
work) into being, but in the sense of *a-letheia*, of a revealing of revealing itself,
and of an instance or a happening of truth. Art 'works', Heidegger will insist,
to the extent that it brings truth to work, exhibits it as the play of concealment and unconcealment that it is. And this mode of revealing is not to be
confused with that of the process of production, which inevitably brings us
back to either the artist (and his 'genius', or his 'vision' – a phenomenon and
an emphasis characteristic of modern aesthetics) or the model (whether physical or ideal) as the *origin* of the work. As an occurrence of truth, art will turn
out to be the origin of both work and artist.

The third basic development in the origin and formation of aesthetics has
its roots in the decisive transformation of the place of the human being amidst
things in modern times. Previously, whether in Greek Antiquity or in the
Middle Ages, the being of the human was not located in the human itself, and
the position of man amidst beings was not one of centrality. In other words,
man was neither at the centre of himself nor of the world. He was neither his
own law (autonomy) nor ground (substance). With Descartes, and the discovery of the cogito, man becomes subject: a self-conscious thinking thing for
whom the sole criterion of truth has become certainty. Only that which is
certain is true, and only I, as a thinking thing, can establish the certainty of a
given matter. Consequently, only I am the guarantor and revealer of truth.
Truth is neither *aletheia* in the pre-metaphysical sense nor *idea* in the Platonic
sense. It is not even 'revealed' in the Christian sense. It has become certainty
– and certainty has itself become the criterion for a truth the veracity of which

is exemplified in, and also modelled after, physical science. In Heidegger's own words: 'I myself, and my states, are the primary and genuine beings. Everything else that may be said to be is measured against the standard of this quite certain being'.[20] The human is now the arena where the decision falls as to how things are to be experienced, defined and shaped. His position towards things, the way he finds and feels them to be, in short, his 'taste', has become the defining factor of appreciation. And this is how meditation on the beautiful in art slips markedly, even exclusively, into the realm of 'feelings' (*aisthesis*). Art becomes a matter of subjective (which does not mean merely personal), 'aesthetic' appreciation.

It should not come as a surprise, then, that Kant, arguably the most important modern philosopher, and the one to have set aesthetics on a course still vigorously debated today, chose to assess the question of beauty, and of aesthetic appreciation, within a 'critique of taste'. Taste, according to Kant, is our faculty of judging the beautiful. His philosophy of art, developed in the *Critique of Judgement*, takes place within the well-defined boundaries of what he calls aesthetic judgement. By 'aesthetic', Kant understands that of which the determining principle can only be subjective. By that, he means that in order to distinguish whether a thing is beautiful or not, we do not refer a representation (a concept) to the object through the understanding, and with a view to knowing it; rather, we refer the thing to the subject, and to its feeling of pleasure and pain, by way of the imagination (§ 1). What Kant is not saying, then, is that beauty is merely a matter of subjective, or personal, appreciation ('you may find this beautiful, but I don't'). In fact, he is very careful to distinguish beauty from the merely agreeable or pleasant (§ 7). What is the difference? Whereas the judgement regarding the agreeable is purely personal, and can be neither discussed nor disputed, the remarkable feature of the judgement of beauty is that, whilst subjective, it requires universal assent. We all agree, says Kant, that when I say, 'Wine from the Canary Islands is very pleasant', what I really mean is that it is pleasant *to me*. It is, as we say, a matter of taste. It would be absurd, and wrong, however, to claim that when I say that this landscape, or this work of art, is beautiful, it is beautiful only in my view. When I say that something is beautiful, I attribute this satisfaction to everyone else. I do not judge only for myself, but also for others, and speak of beauty *as if* it were a property of the thing. In saying that the thing is beautiful, I *demand* the assent of others. Whilst subjective and always singular, then, the judgement of aesthetic beauty is also (almost) objective, and universal. Whilst rooted in a subjective sensation of pleasure, it is expressed as a universal judgement. As such, it reveals and testifies to a common destination, if not a common destiny, amongst human beings – a destiny of agreement and harmony, a community of sense (*Gemeinsinn*), in the double sense of signification and direction, in which the faculties of knowing and desiring, hitherto kept apart, are finally reconciled (§ 20). The universal assent that is affirmed in the judgement of beauty is only ever postulated, however: it is an Idea, and not a fact. There is no rule after which someone could ever be forced to recognize the beauty of an object. And yet, in the presence of the thing we call beautiful, there is always the implicit demand that it be beautiful for all and as such. In the end, it is conceivable that the judgement of taste, with its demand for universal assent, reveal more than just taste. It is conceivable that it be a demand of reason, a demand to produce such a community of sense, and that this obligation, or the necessity of the unity of my feeling with that of everyone else, only signal the possibility – indeed the destiny – of a total accord and harmony (perhaps never to be realized) between men (§ 21). It is insofar as, in aesthetic judgement, and by means of a pleasurable sensation, the subject is elevated beyond this sensation, and so beyond its own, sensible self, and brought into a sort of community with his fellow human beings, a community of sense (and not sensation), of the intelligible (and not the sensible), that Kant famously declares beauty 'the symbol of the moral good' (§ 59). What aesthetic judgement reveals is the supersensuous destination of man.

As for art itself, Kant follows Aristotle's definition of it as a skill or disposition for producing things. In line with his immediate predecessors, Kant sees the fine arts as a particularly thought-provoking and singular species of art in the general sense of the term. Throughout his treatment of art in *The Critique of Judgement*, the emphasis is on skills and practices and not primarily on objects.

What can we conclude from this? That, following an ancient tradition, Kant continues to consider art from the point of view of production, be it that of a singular being (the genius), and, despite his critical, Copernican turn, continues to couch art in terms of a distinction between the sensuous and the supersensuous, between the sensible and the intelligible. The intrinsic value of beauty, or of our appreciation of it, lies in its ability to point beyond itself in the direction of the good. Despite the turn to feeling, and to aesthetic judgement, as the site in which to locate a philosophical appreciation of beauty and art, a form of Platonism remains at play in Kant. It is not that art imitates nature or the intelligible in any straightforward way. Through his detailed discussion of the problem of presentation and representation, of what he calls schematism and symbolism, Kant has problematized, and to a certain extent neutralized, the question of imitation. It remains that art, whilst not imitating the intelligible in any straightforward sense, opens disclosively onto it, and so remains decisively bound up with it.

It is feeling – especially *rapture* – that is still emphasized in Nietzsche, despite his opposition to Kant and Schopenhauer on the question of art, and despite his wish to overturn the whole of philosophy understood as Platonism. In a section of *Twilight of the Idols* entitled 'Physiology of the Artist' (VIII, 122–3), Nietzsche writes: 'If there is to be art, if there is to be any aesthetic doing and observing, one physiological precondition is indispensable: rapture'. And what is essential in rapture is defined as 'the *feeling* of enhancement of force and plenitude' (123). Art is worth something only to the extent that it is in the service of life. Life, in turn, is understood in terms of energy and power, and especially of 'will to power'. As such, art is an expression of life, and great art is an affirmation of great desires and strong affects. Its rapture is akin to that of sexual arousal, feast, contest, victory, destruction and cruelty. Art, for Nietzsche, is and must be a celebration of such strong feelings, which testify to the vitality of the will. In the same way in which he will wrest the problematic of art from taste, Heidegger will wrest it from vital forces and feelings. As we've already seen in Chapter 3 in connection with time, 'rapture' is an essential concept in Heidegger, and one that he probably inherits from Nietzsche. Furthermore, it is a concept that he uses to describe an aspect of art. Yet it is in no way connected to either artist or viewer, either producer or enjoyer. Rather, it is a trait of time (as opposed to space) and world (as opposed to earth). Rapture, in Heidegger, is always introduced alongside its opposite, namely, captivation, which signals the force of withdrawal and self-seclusion of truth.

ART AND TRUTH

Having revealed the metaphysical unity of aesthetics – especially regarding its commitment to the concepts of production and imitation – and established the need to overcome it, we now need to show the relevance of art for Heidegger's attempt to initiate another beginning for thought and provide an alternative to the technological project that is governing our scientific, social and cultural world. To do so, we need to address the 'non-metaphysical' connection Heidegger establishes between art and truth. It is this connection, really, that characterizes the singularity and originality of his approach to art.

To begin with, let me recall that, in his work on Aristotle from the 1920s, Heidegger had already marked such a connection.[21] *Techne*, Aristotle claims, is one of five ways – and possibly the least significant one – in which the soul can disclose (*aletheuein*) beings, or bring them into being.[22] It is a mode of 'truth' (*aletheia*), albeit one that Aristotle, and Heidegger himself at first, do not take to be of the same importance as, say, wisdom (*sophia*), or ethical prudence (*phronesis*). *Techne* means know-how (and as such includes craftsmanship as well as the fine arts) and refers to the activity of production.

In a famous lecture from 1936 entitled 'The Origin of the Work of Art', Heidegger returns to this connection, which he had simply left aside in his early work. Yet he does so from an altogether different perspective. The perspective has changed in at least two ways. First, the meaning of truth itself has changed, as we saw in Chapter 2: truth no longer refers to existence (Dasein) only, but to being itself. Truth is now *of* being, and not just of existence. So long as truth was rooted in Dasein itself, so long as the uncoveredness of things was a function of the *aletheuein* of the human soul, art itself could be considered only as an activity, comparable to other activities, such as the very practical and ordinary activities Heidegger describes in Division One of *Being and Time*.[23] And insofar as it is an activity oriented towards the production of a thing that is exterior to it, Heidegger agreed with Aristotle that it is not even as disclosive of the ownmost possibilities of existence as, say, praxis (or ethics). As for the thing produced, once produced, everything happened as if it fell outside the sphere of truth proper. Insofar as the work marks the end of the activity itself, the yardstick by which truth is measured, it falls outside the sphere of truth. This is where the second, decisive transformation takes place. Heidegger is now asking the following: If the thing produced marks the end of a certain process (the process of production), does it not also mark the beginning of something else, namely, of the work's ability to disclose, to make things manifest in and from itself? And wouldn't this ability designate the very difference between the thing of use and the work of art, or between production (whether pre- or post-industrial, whether understood as labour or as work) and the mode of disclosing that belongs to art? Is the work of art itself not also a site or an instance of truth? Is it not also a way in which being is there (*Da-sein*)? The connection between art and truth is the one we need to focus on. It is established most explicitly in all three versions of 'The Origin of the Work of Art'.[24] In revealing this connection, Heidegger also breaks with the twofold problematic of production (*poiesis*) and imitation (*mimesis*) that is so central to traditional aesthetics. It is this double move I now wish to trace, albeit schematically.

Let me turn to the first move, that is, the move from the product, to the artwork. What sort of thing is the artwork? I have already alluded to the peculiar ontological status of the work, which marks the end of a process or an activity, that of production, and the beginning of something else, altogether disconnected from that initial activity. Heidegger is most explicit about this twofold status of the work. In the early, so-called Freiburg version of 'The Origin of the Work of Art', he writes:

> The singular artwork is always also the production of an artist, yet this being-produced of the work does not constitute its work-character [*Werksein*].

So, although we cannot deny that the artwork is actually produced by an artist, what characterizes the artwork *qua work*, the *being* of the work (as opposed to its sheer *existence*) is entirely disconnected from the activity that governed the coming into existence of the work. In both versions of the lecture, Heidegger even goes as far as to suggest that 'the artist remains inconsequential as compared with the work, almost like a passageway that destroys itself in the creative process for the work to emerge'.[25] Thus, everything happens as if the birth of the work as work meant the death of the artist, as if the very being of the work was simultaneously the sacrifice of the artist. The artist is of course the cause or, Aristotle would say, at least one of the causes of the artwork. But the specificity of the artwork is to point beyond its thingly, produced nature, to something that from the very start exceeds the language of causality, something that allows us to see the work as a work of *art*. This something is the origin, the *Ursprung*, which Heidegger is careful to distinguish from the cause (*Ursache*). If the artist is indeed the cause and only the cause of the artwork, the work also has an origin, one that does not lie with the artist. But where does it lie? And how does origin differ from cause? Origin differs from cause in that whilst it does point to the thing in the sense of its existence, or of its coming-into-existence, it also points to the thing from the perspective of its being and its essence, that is, from the perspective of that which allows it to *work* and to continue to work as the work it is. Thus, the origin of the artwork is to be found not outside the work, but in the very way in which the work works, in the work-character of the work (*Werksein des Werkes*).

What takes place in this first move, then, amounts to a decisive break with the previous (Aristotelian), essentially poietic conception of art. The artwork is no longer primarily envisaged as the outcome or the result of a productive process governed by the producer's ability to mould matter after an *eidos*, a 'look' that is also an 'end'. Rather, it is now envisaged from the work itself, from what Heidegger designates as the unfolding (or the being) proper to the work, or its work-character. And the being of the work, Heidegger claims, consists in its ability to work, that is, in the work's ability to put something to work and bring it to work into the work. The work that belongs to the work is precisely the *origin* of the work. In the face of the artwork, the question is now: What does it do, what sort of work does it do? What does the work bring to work into the work? This question brings me to the second move and to the twisting free it introduces, namely, the move to another sense of truth, and the twisting free from *mimesis*.

So far, we've been able to establish that what distinguishes the artwork from a mere artefact is that something actually takes place in the work itself. Something takes *place*, something happens. As work, the work is nothing outside this *taking* place or this happening. Thus the work is not just a thing; it is also an *event*. What sort of event is it? An event of truth. But what is truth? Is it the *aletheuein* of human existence, this very operation of truth we find in Aristotle, and which Heidegger himself began by endorsing? If this were the case, we would be thrown back into a problematic of *techne* and *poiesis*, back into the very productivist aesthetics Heidegger is seeking to avoid. We would be moving away from the work itself, and from the possibility of questioning the way in which it works. In order for the work to be envisaged *qua* work, and not as the end product of a process of production understood in terms of truth, the work needs to develop its own relation to truth, it must itself be a site for the happening of truth. Only to that extent, only to the extent that it can function as the very space in which truth takes place, can it be seen as an event. And it is only as such an event that the work is indeed a work of *art*, and not merely a thing. The decisive move, then, consists in raising the question of truth with a view to the work *qua* work.

In what, then, does this new sense of truth consist? And what is the essence of the artwork, such that it can display a happening of truth? The sense of truth other than that of metaphysics is the one I exposed in detail in Chapter 2. By the time of 'The Origin of the Work of Art', truth is the play, or rather, in Heidegger's own words, the 'strife' (*Streit*) between its two constitutive opposed tendencies, between clearing (*Lichtung*) and concealing (*Verbergung*), between that which of itself is drawn towards the Open, the Visible, light, and that which is drawn towards concealment, withdrawal and shelter, the Invisible. Truth, Heidegger tells us, is indeed a process: not a thing, not a fact, but the eternal struggle between clearing and concealing, the primitive scene of an irreducible *chiaroscuro*. It is this very scene that the Ancient Greeks captured with the word *aletheia*, before truth came to be associated with a human capacity, with judgement and reason. This primitive scene stages the encounter between World, as the drive towards the Open, towards the manifest and the phenomenal, and Earth, as the drive towards sheltering and concealing, as the other side of the phenomenal. And from this en-counter, from this strifely assemblage, actual historical configurations are born, and what we generally call the world opens up:

> World and earth are essentially different from one another and yet are never separated. The world grounds itself on the earth, and earth juts through world. But the relation between world and earth does not wither away into the empty unity of opposites unconcerned with one another. The world, in resting upon the earth, strives to surmount it. As self-opening it cannot endure anything closed. The earth, however, as sheltering and concealing, tends always to draw the world into itself and keep it there.[26]

Now the artwork provides a place for this primordial strife. It does not represent it in any way. Rather it itself happens *as*, and is born *of* this strife. It is a mode – and only one mode, albeit a remarkable one – in which the essential strife of truth finds a place, takes place. It is a happening of truth. As such, the artwork brings the essential strife to work: it sets it to work into the work, quite literally brings it to *work*. The artwork is the work of truth: it is a work of truth as well as truth's own setting-to-work into the work. This happening of truth is perhaps best expressed in the following passage from the Freiburg version of the lecture:

> In the work, a happening of truth is set to work. And this setting-to-work of truth into the work is the essence of art. Art is therefore a mode in which truth happens; it is the opening up of the There [*Da*] in the work.[27]

In the work, then, it is the very 'Da' that is freed up – not the actual, physical contours of the work, its presence here and now, but the scene of presence itself, the 'there is' in excess of everything that actually is, including the artwork itself. 'There' is here to be understood as the unfolding of truth itself in its primordial strife, the very *being* of truth: Da-sein. In this context, the artwork, whilst coinciding with the event once reserved to designate the being of the existent being (the human Dasein), does not so much ex-sist or stand out into the Open as it in-sists, or lets the Open itself stand in the work. It is a mode in which truth comes to *stand*, an in-*stance* of truth.

But how, exactly, does truth happen in the artwork? How does the artwork set truth to work in the work? The work, Heidegger tells us, 'is' or unfolds to the extent that, 'installing [*aufstellend*] the world and bringing-forth [*herstellend*] the earth', it releases their essential strife, accomplishes it.[28] It is therefore the specific double operation of 'setting up' (*Aufstellen*) a world and 'setting forth' (*Herstellen*) the earth that characterizes the work. It is through this twofold operation that the work brings truth to stand in the work. Allow me to follow Heidegger's complex and subtle analysis as economically as possible.

The setting up of world is not to be understood here in the ordinary (German and English) sense of placing, as when a work is displayed in a collection or at an exhibition (*Ausstellung*). The setting up that is in question here is rather an erecting (*erstellen*), a bringing to stand (*errichten*), as in the case of a building (a church, a temple) or even a poem, a tragedy, for example, that one would present (*darstellen*) at a festival.[29] In all such cases, the work itself sets up, opens up something that is not reducible to the purely material aspect of the work: the building, the work commemorates, dedicates, consecrates or simply presents. It gives something to see. Yet what it gives to see is precisely what would otherwise remain invisible, what is never seen as such: the world. We dwell in the world; it is all around us, yet precisely to that extent the world is never present to us as such. In the work, the world itself comes to be gathered, and our experience of it is precisely the experience of this gathering, as when, faced with an Ancient Greek temple, we cannot help notice the way in which the Greek world, a world of mortals and gods, unfolding between sky and earth, between the political community and the forces of nature, comes together in the temple. In the temple, the world is allowed to 'world', it is brought to presence without being represented. Room is made, a space is freed for the unfolding of the world, and for its peculiar spaciousness, which we, as beings-in-the-world, inhabit.

And yet, whilst allowing the world to unfold and to deploy its own spatiality, whilst providing a place for the Open, the work also provides a place for that which resists being drawn into the Open, for that which, by its very nature, withdraws in the very drawing forth of the world. In a strange and surprising way, the work is said to set forth precisely that which of itself sets itself back, withdraws from the setting up of world. This aspect of the work is what is often referred to as the material, and which is perhaps best described here, borrowing the term from John Sallis, as the 'elemental'.[30] For the work is indeed made of some material: stone, steel, words, colour, etc. But, contrary to what happens in the production of equipment, in which the material is used up, disappearing into the very function of the product, into its serviceability and usability, the artwork is such as to allow the very material of which it is made, and into which it sets itself back, to come forth and shine as such. Matter, far from receding into usefulness, is brought forth as if for the first time, for it is brought forth precisely as the horizon or the origin whence worldly things and the world itself unfold. To be sure, the sculptor uses stone just as the mason uses it, but he does not use it up. Similarly, the painter uses paint, but in such a way that colour is not merely used up in the process. On the contrary: in the artwork, stone, colours are made to shine forth, and this shining forth is the very shining of earth itself. In literature even, and perhaps poetry in particular, language is not so much used up as brought forth as language, as the language in excess of sense and communication, with which we have come to associate it in our everyday use of it. In and through the work, our belonging to earth is at once remembered and affirmed. But this belonging to earth is precisely the belonging to that which, from within the world, resists the logic of world, namely, the logic of disclosure and accessibility, of availability and appropriation. Whenever we turn to earth in an attempt to grasp it, as if it were a part of the world, it withdraws as earth. Such is the paradox of earth, that it can be broken open only by being lost. The work of art alone retains earth as the impenetrable and the unbreakable. Let us take the example of the stone, on which the temple rests, and of which it is made. If we attempt to penetrate it by breaking it open,

> it still does not display in its fragments anything internal or disclosed. The stone has instantly withdrawn again into the same dull pressure and bulk of its fragments.[31]

Similarly, the colours of a canvas shine. That is all they do. If we approach them with a view to analysing them, their physical being as it were, measuring their wavelengths, they are instantly gone. Colours, like all earthy materials, show themselves and shine amidst the visible, only to the extent that they remain undisclosed. And how many times have we experienced the recess of poetic language into ever more distant and withdrawn horizons when attempting to break it open? 'Earth thus shatters every attempt to penetrate it'.[32]

With the transformation of the essence of truth comes also a decisive break with the interpretation of art as *mimesis*. This should no longer come as a surprise. Indeed, from what we have seen thus far, art can no longer be seen as an imitation of truth, and the work as an image or representation of truth. The work is indeed perhaps an image, but precisely in the sense of a shining, and not of a copy. Truth is not a model, something given in advance and outside the work, but what takes place in the work, whose work-character consists in making room for truth, in clearing a space for the unfolding of truth. And if the work is beautiful, it is not because it resembles an original, not because it reproduces a model faithfully, thus allowing us to intimate its truth as Idea, but because in and through it truth itself shines forth. In art, we have a putting-itself to work of truth into the work, a bringing of truth itself into the work. In this process, truth as such happens. This, in turn, means that under no circumstance can truth be distinguished from the very way in which it puts itself to work into the work. Under no circumstance can the work itself be envisaged outside of the strife that takes place within it, as if for the first time. Every artwork is an original.

With this double move, from the product to the work, and from imitation to instantiation, Heidegger has shifted the focus of art away from traditional aesthetics. In its place, he suggests we envisage the work as an instance or an event of truth, as a place or a site in which the essence of truth can actually be exhibited and experienced. This experience is getting increasingly unlikely, as the technological and techno-scientific perspective advances. Truth, space and art itself are increasingly defined and delimited by the techno-scientific project. On this point, Heidegger is in agreement with another great twentieth-century thinker of art and literature, Walter Benjamin. The reason why so very few of us read poetry is that the experience required to enter its domain is no longer with us. Similarly, Heidegger is suggesting that the sense of art itself has changed to such an extent that another word would be required to characterize the phenomenon we call contemporary art. The work is no longer this pivotal instance of truth, this grounding of the eternal strife of clearing and concealing, around which a people, a nation would be gathered. It is itself caught up in a gigantic, indeed global network, through which it is circulated, valued, advertised and exchanged. It is a commodity and an image booster, a thing no longer clearly distinguished from the many products available on the market. So yes, in a way, despite the mass production of artworks – and of those works that reflect the mass market and the context of reproducibility in which they operate (see Warhol) – Heidegger believes that art has come to an end. Yet he also believes that there are, and perhaps always will be, solitary and isolated voices that will sing to a different tune, and find the origin of their art in a different experience, one that is buried deep in the essence of truth, almost entirely forgotten, yet still to come. The poetry of Hölderlin was for him the most significant event of that kind. His voice speaks from a different place and a different time – from beyond metaphysics and its consummation in contemporary techno-science? For that very reason, Heidegger always wondered whether we were ready to hear it, collectively as well as individually. We, in turn, need to ask whether, closer to us, contemporary works and artists also facilitate a relation to the world, to nature, to presence and to things that testify to a reality other than the actuality of techno-science.

ART TODAY

In his lecture 'The Provenance of Art and the Destination of Thought', delivered in Athens in 1967, Heidegger asks whether today, after two and a half thousand years, art is still held under the demand that once ruled in Ancient Greece. His answer to that question is negative: art no longer stems from within the national boundaries of a people; it no longer enjoys the onto-historical role it once had, and which consisted in grounding and instituting a clearing of being.[33] This does not mean that art has disappeared from contemporary culture. On the contrary: our age is inundated with art, and today's works of art belong to the universality of world-civilization. Art, Heidegger claimed already in 1938, is part and parcel of the vast equipmental reality that characterizes our age, and that has transformed nature and our relation to it.

It has become an *Anlage* (construction/installation). *Anlagen* are forms of the general *Einrichtung* (Heidegger's early and first word for the *Ge-stell*), that is, the plan, scheme or frame, in which things are enclosed and set up. For the most part, the composition and the organization of today's works of art belong to the horizon projected and produced by contemporary techno-science, which has decided in advance the mode and the possibilities of man's sojourn on earth.[34] What, he asks, of art within our industrial society, whose world has become cybernetic? 'Man's relation to the world, and the totality of his social existence, are contained within the domain where cybernetics exercises its mastery.' We live in a scientific world, and the mathematical, physical sense of 'science' is one that goes unquestioned, even by art, which was once *techne* in the highest sense. As a result, and for the most part, art in the age of technology has become art in the service of technology. Often, the work itself is conceived as the image and the doubling, if not the instrument of the cybernetic world-view: 'The arts become regulated-regulating instruments of information'.[35] Its underlying conception of itself as 'language' is not fundamentally different from that of cybernetics, and its 'discourse' not fundamentally different from all the techno-discourses that surround us.

Let me refer to just a few examples of what we could call techno-art, and cyber-art in particular.

In the late 1960s and early 70s, a movement known as Art and Technology emerged in the United States. The movement attracted the energies of artists (such as Rauschenberg and Cage), scientists and technicians, and resulted in a series of innovations and collaborations. At the time, some even spoke of a 'marriage' between art and technology.[36] The interest in technology coming from art was not born in the 1960s: the Futurists, with their fascination with the machine and speed, some Cubists, such as F. Léger, who painted a world of valves, conduits and steel structures that posited the rhythm of the machine as analogous to everyday, human activity, the Constructivists, with their concern for the broader implications of industrial technologies for society and the future role and function of art, all testified to a strong awareness of the impact of technology on art, and a desire to engage with it.

Closer to us, and still by way of example, we can mention the trend that follows from the possibilities opened up by genetics and biotechnology. It is known as 'transgenic art'. One of its representatives, the artist Eduardo Kac, engineered a completely green rabbit with the help of the French National Institute for Agronomic Research (INRA). It was displayed at an art fair in Nantes in 2003 entitled Biotech Art.

Similar to the transgenic art of Kac, although different with respect to the technology it involves, is the 'carnal' art of the French multimedia and performance artist Orlan, whose performances over the last decade have consisted of cosmetic surgery. In 1990 she took the term 'operating theatre' literally and embarked on a project entitled 'The Reincarnation of Saint Orlan', which has consisted of performing – remaining conscious throughout, photographing, filming and broadcasting – a series of operations to remodel her face and body, and thus her identity, entirely. Carnal art signals a new alliance between art and contemporary medicine. One commentator of Orlan's work suggests that whereas the main achievement of body artists of the 1960s and 1970s was to discover the body as material for representation, carnal art of the 1990s (and that of Orlan in particular) relies very much on science and technological advance.[37] Although Orlan's cosmetic surgery cannot strictly be said to be modifying her genetic code (unlike Kac's rabbit), the radical and ongoing reconfiguration of her facial features, modelled after a computerized design, is consistent with the status of DNA as a modifiable, reprogrammable code. Central to the entire project is the possibility of contributing to the creation of a post-human, aesthetic era inspired by cybernetics' ability to blur the boundaries separating the human from the non-human (and the machine in particular), and the male from the female. If feminism sees cybernetics as a liberating tool, it is because of its ability to produce a quasi-infinite number of hybrid identities (cyborgs), which allows one to do away with any definition of essence and substance of womanhood. Orlan's work with electronic and digital media, Ince points out, conforms to the first of the two main types of cyborg identity, according to which information about the body is encoded into a cybernetic system. An interface between body and computer upsets the dualism of organism and machine by opening up a channel of communication between them. Digitally encoded information traverses the conventional bodily limit of the skin, and extends 'the body' to wherever the information is retrieved.

Stelarc, the Australian body artist who performs with a robotic 'third arm', is undoubtedly the performer who has most fully investigated the permeability of boundaries between the physical and the virtual body, thus creating a truly cybernetized human body. In recent performances, he has connected his body up to the Internet, in order to give live demonstrations of how the material body can be affected, and indeed controlled, by communication technologies. Advocating the need for the material body to shed its skin, once considered the beginning of the world and the boundary of the self, he recounts his experience of his 'own' body becoming a host for technology and remote agents: 'Imagine one side of your body being remotely guided whilst the other side could collaborate with a local agency. You watch a part of your body move but you have neither initiated it nor are you contracting your muscles to produce it.'[38] If anything, the process amounts to a disowning, in which the movements of 'my' body are no longer mine, and this body not even any longer my *own*. This experience, Stelarc argues, does not reflect a sadomasochistic impulse, but a purely cybernetic, post-human 'feedback loop of alternate awareness'. What it reveals is no longer a psycho-body, or a unity of body and mind, but a cybernetic system linking various 'machines' through a self-regulated exchange of information.

Beyond the modernist fascination with the industrial age of the thermodynamic machine – from F. Léger to Le Corbusier – and the post-modern infatuation with the second industrial revolution, best expressed in the cyber-art I have just briefly alluded to, we need to ask whether, in the margins of cybernetics, aspects of contemporary art reveal something like the 'free' relation to technology Heidegger is advocating for thought. Would such an art necessarily be anti-technological and 'reactionary'? Would it have to use traditional materials and techniques? Would it signal a return of the kitsch and the *gemütlich*, of the corny and the pastoral, and would it be fuelled by nostalgia for the pre-industrial age? Not necessarily. In fact, I would like to suggest that aspects of contemporary art reveal a conception of art, and of nature, that is free of the technological stronghold, whilst often resorting to the materials and the techniques inherited from the industrial and information revolutions, thus exemplifying the *Gelassenheit* Heidegger promotes. Here, we need to distinguish between technology as an instance of truth, and as the historical–destinal horizon within which we find ourselves, and technology as a means of artistic production. It is not because an artist uses video, or steel and concrete, that he or she is bowing to the techno-scientific mode of dwelling. Similarly, it would be naive to believe that by simply sculpting wood and stone an artist would escape the grip of technology.

It is true that, for a philosopher who is granting art with such a historical power, Heidegger does not say very much about the art of his time, about the many forms and movements that sprang in the twentieth century, from Cubism to abstract Expressionism through Surrealism, German Expressionism and Minimalism, to name but a few. We should beware, however, of the haste with which art critics – and sometimes artists themselves – coin 'isms' and labels, identify schools and filiations. We should wonder whether anything thoughtful was ever achieved by labelling a work 'expressionist', or a philosophy 'realist', for example, and whether, in doing so, we don't close off the very possibility of thinking through what's at issue in these works, instead of opening them up, and opening ourselves to them.

We know that, besides his interest in Van Gogh, revealed in his analysis of the so-called 'peasant shoes' in 'The Origin of the Work of Art', Heidegger greatly admired the work of Cézanne – the artist who claimed to have sought 'truth in painting' – and the way in which it inspired that of Braque and Picasso. We also know that he expressed a very strong interest in – and in fact a real fascination for – the work of P. Klee.[39] Yet, in the end, it is perhaps his relation to the Basque 'abstract' artist and sculptor Eduardo Chillida that is most significant. Petztet, a former occasional student of Heidegger and a life-long friend, introduced Heidegger to the work of Chillida in the mid-1960s. The artist and the thinker met in 1968. In 1969, Heidegger published a very short essay entitled 'Art and Space', which he dedicated to the artist who, in turn, produced seven litho-collages for the publication of Heidegger's text by the Erker Press in Saint-Gallen, Switzerland. In his essay, Heidegger does not mention Chillida's work. And yet, his thoughts are largely inspired by the sculptor's work, and by his relation to space – or, better said, perhaps, place – and the natural elements in particular.[40] It is as if, between the thinker and the artist, something like a genuine encounter, or a dialogue, had taken place. Let me turn to this remarkable essay.

The essay is remarkable in more ways than one. First of all, its very title,

'Art and Space', indicates that the focus of the essay is going to be the relation between works of art and space. Heidegger's early work, we saw, focused on time as the horizon of intelligibility and signification of the world of existence. Time, we recall, was the meaning of being. The spatiality (or spacing) of existence was itself ultimately understood in terms of time. Later on, in *Contributions to Philosophy* especially, we saw how Heidegger no longer subordinates space to time, but thinks them together as 'time-space'. This term pointed to the way in which, from the perspective of the truth (or essence) of being, time and space called for, and complemented one another, albeit by way of strife. The 'meaning' – now 'truth' – of being was not so much 'time' as 'time-space'. The difference is significant. What the title of Heidegger's short essay indicates is a further development. For the first time, he discusses space independently of time. That he does so in connection with art, and sculpture in particular, is no coincidence. Should we conclude from our observations that Heidegger's thought evolved from a focus on time to one on space? It would be a rather foolish conclusion, given his emphasis on history as the mode of unfolding of truth itself. Still, the fact that he can now isolate space as it were, and think it for itself, independently of considerations on time, is significant. The fact that he does so in the context of his many remarks and analyses, developed elsewhere, regarding the consummation of metaphysics, and of aesthetics, in cybernetics, is also significant. Should we conclude that he envisages the work of art, and especially that of Chillida, as opening up and onto *another* space, or another *sense* of space – other than the homogeneous, physical space of Galileo and Newton, equivalent in all directions, inaccessible to the senses, and which we now take to be the only *true* space? Should we be led to believe that, under certain circumstances, the work of art remains a *work* (and not just a product), and continues to work, or unfold, as a distinct site or place, in which what is most concealed in our cybernetic modes of representation, becomes visible for the first time? Does Heidegger's meditation on art as a site of truth move thought away from fundamental ontology, and towards something like a topology of being and truth? The sculpture, or the plastic body (*der plastische Körper*), Heidegger writes, embodies (*verkörpert*) space. But what is the space that is here at issue, and which the sculpture embodies?

The second, remarkable feature of Heidegger's short essay, itself related to the first, is its focus on sculpture, about which, thus far, he had said virtually nothing. The first and most obvious feature of sculpture is its three-dimensionality. Depth, it is generally thought, is what sets it apart from the other fine arts, and from painting in particular. But what is the nature of this depth? What makes the depth of a sculpture? Is it its geometrical aspect? Can we account for the depth, and the spacing that is proper to sculpture, by referring it back to a mathematical, Euclidean representation of space? Can we account for how the work 'works', and for what it presents, by subordinating it from the start to its mathematical representation? Or must we set the spacing of the work apart from any such mathematization? Is there a sense of depth, and, more generally, of space itself, that is not geometrical, but truly artistic, and that would apply equally (albeit perhaps differently) to painting? Depth, Chillida suggests in a series of sculptures, is the air.[41] Ordinarily, air is associated with the void and with emptiness, and is not considered a geometrical object. How can a sculpture – a three-dimensional object – present air and, what is more, as depth itself? How can it present air as that from which things come to presence, and obtain their own depth? Surely not by representing it. What is ordinarily referred to as 'abstraction' was a formidable invention of art, which freed it from the fetters – and the misunderstanding – of representation. Art never represented anything. Representation is theoretical, and especially mathematical. Chemistry can represent air, but art cannot. Yet, somehow, Chillida allows air to become manifest. In and through his sculpture, he provides a space for air, he allows air to come to the fore as one element that breathes through everything, and through the stone sculpture in particular. But most of all, he allows us to 'see' air as the origin of space itself, as what grants things their own spatiality. He reminds us that we are all *of* the air, and that, as such, it is not the third, but the first dimension.[42] It is a dimension that is remarkably absent, invisible shall we say. Yet from it all things become visible. It is the ultimate background, the origin or horizon. It takes a work of art to make it visible, or perhaps palpable, at least present in a way that is unlike all other things present. For even in the work, it is not visible, or palpable as such. It is not given to any of the senses. What is present and given to the senses is the work, but the work presents itself as that which comes from the air, and belongs to it. It is not the work that 'frames' the air, but the air that opens up the work. Another work, 'Wind Comb', installed against a cliff of the Basque coastline, is simply there to let the wind pass through, and to allow us to expose ourselves to its force. In and through the work, nature is made doubly present. But this doubling of nature is not its representation: at no point can we say that the 'comb' represents the wind. Yet it makes it more 'visible', more present or perhaps present in a different way, by simply allowing it to blow and sing through it, to be the first thing that it touches when coming from the rough, often ominous ocean. In and through the work, nature, and the Western wind in particular, which, in the Basque country, blows with a distinct force, is made more present, revealed or disclosed, not in the way in which it is revealed in the windmill, that is, as energy, but as a primal, undomesticated force (and the world 'force', which is so tied up in the vocabulary of Galilean and Newtonian physics, is perhaps not the right term to use in this context), which determines the orientation of the farms and their architecture, which brings about the rain that breaks against the mountains nearby and, with it, the growth of the earth, the trees, the grass and the necessary food for the sheep and the horses. The sculpture reminds the Basque country of its belongingness to the earth – to the sky and the sea, the wind and the mountain.

When it works, the artwork 'spaces'. Its work is a spacing (*Räumen*). It is not an object, then, or a representation, but an event. To space, Heidegger writes, means to clear, to free. This vocabulary, and this sense of space, is precisely the one *Being and Time* used to characterize the spatiality of existence. But what, exactly, does the work clear and free? The Free, in the sense of the

Open. The work spaces and, in doing so, opens up – and onto – the Open. This is the Open where man finds his dwelling. To dwell is not the same as to occupy. One occupies a territory, a country or even a planet. To occupy is to fill and dominate a space. Whether military or not, occupation is always techno-logical, that is, based on a geometrical projection of space, and oriented towards control and domination, whether of a people or of resources (and most often of both). But to dwell is something altogether different. It is to stand amidst things, the world and others in such a way as to shelter their essence, and relate to them from the point of view of their presencing. To dwell is always to dwell on earth, inasmuch as the earth is what cannot be occupied, appropriated or mastered. As self-secluding, self-sheltering matter, the earth opens itself only to those for whom reality is composed of more than just pres-ence, and space more than just actual, physical space. The earth does not belong to us. We belong to it. As we try to appropriate it, it withdraws. Where? In itself, of course, but also in certain works, and in Chillida's in par-ticular, where it is sheltered. The elemental (the air, the wind, the horizon, light, stone), as self-sheltering and self-harbouring, finds a shelter in the works of Chillida, and especially in Zabalaga, the park where many of them today are gathered, and gathered around a house, a shelter that shelters nature itself as much as from it.[43] It is also sheltered in 'In Praise of the Horizon', a monu-mental, semi-circular structure made of concrete, and also set on the coastline. The piece 'works' in a way similar to 'Depth of Air': the earth, the sea and the sky come together through the work. The work gathers them together, and lets them unfold from the horizon. The horizon appears not as a mere line, which can of course be accounted for physically, but as the fold of the elemen-tal itself, from which earth, sea and sky are gathered together. The gathering of earth, sky and sea in the work point to the priority of art over science, to the ancestral and immemorial dwelling on earth it facilitates. It reveals the extent to which, even in the age of techno-culture, there remains the possibility of artistic dwelling on earth.

The work spaces by letting what is otherwise closed off and concealed come forth, present itself *as* withdrawn. Whenever and wherever the things them-selves – in the case of Chillida, the elements – are freed for their own self-manifestation, they do not appear 'in' space – in the abstract, mathematical space of physics, homogeneous and common to all things. Rather, they dis-close their own, singular spatiality. They are themselves a space, or, better said perhaps, a place.[44] This means that they draw and gather together, shelter and harbour something that is in excess of their mere physical contours, or their objective spatiality. This is the exact opposite of the seizure of nature that char-acterizes the Occidental, technological approach. Here lies the difference between the *Ge-stell* and genuine sheltering, or between control and *Gelassenheit*. 'In Praise of the Horizon' might look like a gigantic frame made of concrete, through which earth, sea and sky are framed. In fact, this frame, far from en-framing nature, shelters it, and opens the viewer onto its own enduring, yet self-secluded presence. In doing so, it also establishes a relation between the viewer and the earth, which is one of mutual and reciprocal belongingness. Like any work of art, it gives us to see whatever it shows as if for the first time. In sheltering the earth, the work discloses the human to the site of its own dwelling, and its own essence.

Allow me to bring these considerations on art to an end by turning to language and to the way in which, it more than the visual arts perhaps, is in danger of a total cybernetization. Cybernetics, Heidegger argues, 'transforms language into an exchange of news'.[45] Cybernetics, we saw, is first and foremost a language, a set of messages between machines and organisms regulated by feedback. At the heart of it all is the assumption that language is information, or code. 'Language, in fact, is in one sense another name for communication itself, as well as a word used to describe the codes through which communication takes place.'[46] That language is a matter of communication, that what is communicated (its content) is information, that information is constituted of a series of encoded messages to be decoded could be described as the current *doxa* regarding language. Still according to this *doxa*, what characterizes human language is (a) the delicacy and complexity of the code used, and (b) the high degree of arbitrariness of his code.[47] Human language is essentially the same as computer language and the code through which organisms 'communicate' with the outside world and themselves. This *doxa* does not stem from popular wisdom, however. Its origin is technological. It presupposes an *instrumental* interpretation of language.

It is precisely this cybernetic, purely instrumental interpretation of language that Heidegger wishes to challenge. And it is in the context of this challenge that poetic language comes to play a crucial role in his thought, analogous to that of art. Poetry – at least a certain kind of poetry, and in principle – testifies to a different relation to language, and to things and nature as a whole.

Poetry, he claims, does not distinguish itself from the ordinary, instrumental interpretation and practice of language in that it communicates more effectively, and more beautifully. If anything, and were it to be reducible to its actual information content, poetry communicates less effectively, and the energetic cost to the reader is unreasonably high. The truth is poetry communicates much less well than instrumental language because it doesn't communicate at all. It does not have an information content that can be translated into a different and 'clearer' idiom. Whenever we attempt such a translation, we realize that we have missed what is decisive about the poem, namely, the fact that, in a way, there is a deficiency of signification in the poem, and an excess of language itself. We realize that the poem presents us with an excess of the materiality of language over its ideality, of its brute being over its meaning: we experience its own earthly origin and, with it, our own belonging to the earth. The poem confronts us with the fact of language (*that there is language*), and with our belongingness to this excess. In and through the poem, we open ourselves to language in a way that our instrumental use of language made simply impossible. And in doing so, we open ourselves to ourselves, and this means to our relation to the world, to things and to others, in a way that is not instrumental. We realize that, like the work of art we spoke of a while ago, language has this extraordinary ability to open onto, and open up, our very essence, as the being disclosed to the disclosed itself, or destined to the Open (to truth). We come to see language as the site of a dwelling, and not just as a tool. Here again, Hölderlin's voice resonates with all its force: 'Poetically man dwells . . .'. On the other side of technology, then, and of its obliteration of truth, stands poetry, and the historical destiny it holds in reserve for us.

In this chapter, I hope to have shown the philosophical, and by that I mean the historical, or onto-destinal significance of art for Heidegger. If art is such a decisive and recurrent theme in Heidegger, it is because of its power to reveal the world, the earth and our belonging to world and earth in a way that is radically different from that of technology. In the *Ge-stell*, things appear as immediately available, manipulable, transformable, in short, as standing by and in reserve. In genuine art, things acquire a different quality: they appear as the place or the site of an encounter between world and earth, between men and gods; they themselves reveal the essence of the real as the unfolding of truth, that is, as the forever renewed tension or struggle between concealment and unconcealment, between presence and the event of presence that withdraws within it. Heidegger found in art a place in which the rule of technology was not yet fully consummated, yet one that shared the same origin as technology. Similarly, poetry for him designated this relation to language that was not purely economical or cybernetic, but sacrificial: in the excess of language over sense and information, like in the excess of earth over world, it is the facticity of truth that is presented. With it, comes the remembrance of our belongingness to something in excess of the world and its forces, whether natural, socioeconomic, cultural or religious – our belongingness to the essence of truth.

NOTES

1 TK, 33/315.
2 G, 12/46.
3 G, 22/53.
4 G, 22/53–4.
5 As we shall see, and following Hölderlin's intuition, it is only *poetically* that man dwells on earth: 'Full of acquirements, but poetically, man dwells on this earth' ('In lovely blueness . . .', *Poems and Fragments*, trans. Michael Hamburger [Cambridge: Cambridge University Press, 1980], p. 601).
6 The way Heideger uses this word encompasses those various meanings: it does not refer to the way in which the world is set up into a System, and in which man comports himself as will to power, but the way in which the world is allowed to unfold from out of a releasement of its origin, through which thought gains a form of serenity.
7 TK, 35/317.
8 Hölderlin, 'Patmos'.
9 TK, 41.

10 J. Sallis, 'The Truth that is not of Knowledge,' *Double Truth* (Bloomington: Indiana University Press, 1995), pp. 57–70.

11 G. W. F. Hegel, *Ästhetik*, (ed.) Friedrich Bassenge (West Berlin: Verlag das Europäische Buch, 1985), vol. 1, p. 22. English translation by T. M. Knox, *Hegel's Aesthetics: Lectures on Fine Art* (Oxford: Oxford University Press, 1975), vol. 1, p. 11. A few lines up, Hegel had also declared that '[t]he magnificent days of Greek art, like the golden era of the later Middle Ages, are gone'.

12 See 'The End of Philosophy and the Task of Thinking' in SD, 77–8/BW, 390.

13 The most detailed discussion of art in relation to mimesis and truth in Plato is in *Republic*, Book X, 595a–608b.

14 'The Origin of the Work of Art', in Hw, 66/51.

15 G. W. F. Hegel, *Ästhetik*, 64/55.

16 *Hegel's Aesthetics*, 117/111.

17 Nietzsche, *The Will to Power*, § 493.

18 GA 6. 1, 163/160–1.

19 He does come very close, though, as Heidegger makes very clear in the last two sections of 'The Will to Power as Art'. Heidegger is quite concerned to emphasize the ambiguous situation of Nietzsche at the end of philosophy, as that of Plato at the beginning. Both beginning and end, Heidegger suggests, point beyond – or perhaps simply before or below – the history they institute and bring to a close. Plato and Nietzsche are both, to use the latter's own vocabulary, figures of dusk and dawn.

20 GA 6. 1, 81–2/83.

21 GA 19, 21/15.

22 Aristotle, *Nicomachean Ethics*, 1139b15ff.

23 See SZ, §§15–18.

24 The 'definitive' version, published in 1950 in *Holzwege* with the addition of an epilogue, is based on a series of three lectures delivered at the *Freie Deutsche Hochstift* in Frankfurt in November and December 1936. I shall refer to it as the Frankfurt version. Two earlier versions of the lecture have now been made available. In 1987 an unauthorized edition of the original lecture was published in France (OA). This is the version Heidegger delivered at the *Kunstwissenschaftliche Gesellschaf* in Freiburg on 13 November 1935. Heidegger repeated it in Zurich in January 1936. I shall refer to it as the Freiburg version. More recently still (1989), the editors of the *Gesamtausgabe* released an undated, but clearly earlier, 'first' version under the title 'Vom Ursprung des Kunstwerkes. Erste Ausarbeitung' (UK). I shall refer to it as the 'first' version.

25 Hw, 25.

26 Hw, 37.

27 OA, 34.

28 OA, 34.

29 In passing, let me emphasize the remarkable proximity with the vocabulary Heidegger uses to describe the *Ge-stell*, and which we analysed in the previous chapter. This proximity, I believe, testifies to the essence technology shares with art, whilst also emphasizing the two radically opposed directions they reveal: whereas the work of art is directed towards the essence of truth, as the play of concealment and unconcealment, and sets up the work as the place in which this strife is exhibited, the *Ge-stell* is directed towards presence and actuality alone, which it turns into an object of representation and control.

30 See John Sallis, *Force of Imagination* (Bloomington: Indiana University Press, 2000), Chapter 6 ('The Elemental').

31 Hw, 35/25.

32 Hw, 36/25.

33 See also GA 66, § 11 ('Art in the Age of the Completion of Modernity').

34 GA 66, § 11.

35 SD, 64/BW, 376.

36 See Marga Bijvoet, 'How intimate can art and technology really be? A survey of the Art and Technology movement of the Sixties', in *Culture, Technology and Creativity in the Late Twentieth Century*, edited by Philip Hayward (London: John Libbey and Company, 1990), p. 15.

37 Kate Ince, *Orlan. Millennial Female* (Oxford: Berg, 2000), p. 54.

38 Stelarc, 'Parasite Visions: Alternate, Intimate, and Involuntary Experiences', in T. Druckrey (ed.), *Ars Electronica: Facing the Future* (Cambridge, MA: MIT Press, 1999), p. 412.

39 In *Encounters and Dialogues with Martin Heidegger, 1929–1976* (Chicago: University of Chicago Press, 1993), Heinrich Wiegand Petzet, an occasional student and close friend of Heidegger's, recounts how Heidegger began to develop a deep interest in the work of Klee in the 1950s (pp. 146ff.). He visited the so-called 'Klee House' on several occasions. The house in question was in fact the vacant home of an aristocrat in the outskirts of Basel, where the art collector Ernst Beyeler, who had recently acquired from the American industrialist David Thompson one of the most important collections in the world of works by Klee, decided to make it available to his wide circle of friends: artists and lovers of art, scholars and writers. The impact of Klee's work on Heidegger was such that he thought he should now write a second part to 'The Origin of the Work of Art'. In a letter addressed to Petzet, and dated 21 February 1959, he went as far as to write that 'In Klee something has happened that none of us grasps as yet' (p. 150). Unfortunately, Heidegger never wrote an essay on Klee, nor indeed the 'second part' to 'The Origin of the Work of Art'.

40 One of Chillida's sculptures is entitled 'Topos', which is the Greek word for place. Heidegger always insists that the Greeks did not have a word for physical space in the modern sense of the term (as extended, measurable matter), yet had a very strong sense of place (*topos*).

41 The title of the sculpture is '*Lo profundo es el aire*', which, literally, means 'the air is what's deep' ('Depth of Air').

42 In this context, how could we avoid mentioning *The Forgetting of Air* (London: Athlone, 1999), a seminal book by the French-Basque feminist philosopher Luce Irigaray, whose work draws on that of Heidegger, yet also criticizes it. In the following passage, which echoes the sculpture of Chillida, she weaves together considerations of the elemental, of place and of dwelling:

> Is not air the whole of our habitation as mortals? Is there a dwelling more vast, more spacious, or even more generally peaceful than that of air? Can man live elsewhere than in air? Neither in earth, nor in fire, nor in water is there any habitation possible for him. No other element can for him take the place of place. No other element carries with it – or lets itself be passed through by – light and shadow, voice or silence. No other element is to this extent the Open itself – to one who would not have forgotten its nature there is no need for it to open or re-open. No other element is as light, as free, and as much in the 'fundamental' mode of a permanent, available, 'there is.'
>
> No other element is in this way space prior to all localization, and a substratum both immobile and mobile, permanent and flowing, where multiple temporal divisions remain forever possible. Doubtless, no other element is as originarily constitutive of the whole of the world, without this generativity ever coming to completion in a primordial time, in a single primacy, in an autarchy, in an autonomy, in a unique or exclusive property. . . . (p. 8)

Yet, Irigaray goes on to suggest, this element, which is irreducibly constitutive of the whole, compels neither the faculty of perception nor that of knowledge to recognize it. It is always there, from the start, and for that very reason allows itself to be forgotten. Taking our clue from Chillida's work, we could suggest that art brings this 'there is' of air into the open, that it brings the open into the open, presents it, in a way irreducible to any ideal or theoretical representation. We could suggest that art has the power to bring about air, and the elemental, as the archaic dimension, from which things and the world themselves begin to take shape.

43 In addition to 'Wind Comb', 'Deep is the Air', 'In Praise of the Horizon', we should mention 'In Praise of Light' and 'Listening to Stone'.

44 It is perhaps no coincidence if one of Chillida's sculptures is entitled *'Topos'*, which is the Greek word for place. Today, topology refers to a branch of mathematics, and topography to a branch of geography. But Chillida and Heidegger both develop a different topology, one that is not concerned with a representation of space, but with a presentation of place. In fact, Heidegger's own later thought can be seen as evolving towards a topology of truth.

45 SD, 64/BW, 376.

46 N. Wiener, *The Human Use of Human Beings*, p. 74.

47 Ibid.

6

Politically Adrift: The Affair with National Socialism

No aspect of Heidegger's life and work is more controversial than his engagement in favour of National Socialism, and his tenure as the first Nazi rector of the University of Freiburg from May 1933 to April 1934. And rightly so. The Heidegger controversy began immediately after the war, and has undergone various phases. In the last 15 years or so, however, and beginning with the publication of Victor Farias' controversial *Heidegger and Nazism* (1987),[1] it has gained in intensity, and ferocity. A considerable amount of books and articles have been devoted to the subject. Some are invaluable from the point of view of historical research, as they have enabled us to reconstruct the events, declarations and intrigues that marked Heidegger's life as an active and zealous member of the NSDAP. Others are invaluable from the point of view of their careful, scholarly and insightful analyses regarding the nature of the connection between Heidegger's political engagement and his philosophy. Others, unfortunately, are simply partisan and polemical. Few 'Heideggerians' or careful interpreters of his thought have escaped the debate. What, exactly, lies at the root of Heidegger's tumultuous and complex affair with National Socialism, and what brought it to its relatively sudden end? What I propose to do here is present the facts (which, as facts generally do, take us only so far), and then give a sense of what Heidegger saw in the National Socialist revolution and what he hoped it would achieve. I wish neither to exonerate nor condemn him for his infatuation with the revolution, but to draw some lessons from what he himself once called 'the biggest stupidity of my life'.

My grandmother – a highly educated, and politically sensitive woman born in France in the First World War – once asked me how Heidegger, who had been a Nazi, could have befriended and gained the admiration of the great French poet René Char, who had been a very active *résistant* in World War II, and whom my grandmother knew well. By asking this question, she was putting her finger on the paradoxical nature of Heidegger's case. René Char was not the only figure to have recognized the extraordinary, in fact unique, significance of Heidegger's thought, whilst opposing, sometimes in arms, the politics the German master stood for. Despite his deep disgust for Heidegger's association with the Nazis, Paul Celan, another major poet, and a Jew who by mere chance escaped the death camps where his parents were murdered, was also convinced of the greatness of Heidegger's thought, and of his contribution to thinking the essence of poetic language. Closer to us, another Jew, and

a remarkably educated and fine mind, the literary critic and philosopher
George Steiner became singularly angry when asked on French public radio
how he, as a Jew, could recognize Heidegger as a formidable thinker, and
encourage the reading of his work. There are many more examples of major
Jewish philosophers, and left-wing thinkers, who recognize an explicit debt
towards Heidegger's thought: Hannah Arendt (who was Heidegger's lover,
'the passion of his life', as he confessed to his own wife, and his life-long ally,
despite her flight to the US, and her opposition to all forms of totalitarianism),
Leo Strauss, Herbert Marcuse, Emmanuel Levinas and Jacques Derrida, to
name but a few, and despite their often critical stance, all held Heidegger's
work in the greatest esteem.[2]

THE FACTS

Heidegger's pettiness, his boisterous nature, his impatience and dismissive
attitude towards colleagues, his ingratitude towards Husserl, all of that is well
documented, in the years preceding his rectorship as well as during it.

According to one commentator and biographer of Heidegger, Rüdiger
Safranski, the first record of Heidegger's sympathies for National Socialism
date back to the early 1930s. In 1931–32, his support for the Nazi party was
no more than a political opinion. Like many Germans, he regarded the party
as a force of order amid the hardships of the economic slump and the chaos of
the collapsing of the Weimar Republic, and above all as a bulwark against the
danger of a Communist revolution. Still, these political sympathies were met
with utter surprise from his friends and students, as his philosophy and his
classes had remained entirely apolitical until then. This was to change a year
later. Following Plato, he seized what he saw as a historical opportunity to take
the philosopher out of his ivory tower and into the public arena, and play an
active role in the total transformation of the 'German Dasein' at a time of need
and destitution. Like Plato, he believed in philosophy's ability to guide and
show the way. Like Plato, and for a short while at least, he envisaged himself
as the philosopher-king.

What did Heidegger see in the National Socialist seizure of power?
Nothing short of a revolution, and by that we need to understand the beginning of a new epoch, a new relation to history. Was he alone in believing
this? Far from it. The vast majority of Germans experienced the rise to
power of National Socialism as a liberation from democracy. The democracy
of the Weimar Republic had come to be associated with ruin, massive un-
employment, social inequality, political paralysis and national humiliation.
Multipartism was relinquished with enthusiasm, as were basic civil liberties,
two pillars of democracy perceived to be tearing the nation apart.
Relinquished for what? For a genuine sense of hope, and the promise of a
Germany that would once again stand on its feet, and stand up to the rest of
the world (and I will show how the vocabulary of the stance and of erection
finds its specifically philosophical formulation in Heidegger's (aptly named)

rectorship address). The general impression was that Germany had finally returned to herself. By and large, the German people willed National Socialism. It is extraordinary what we are willing to give up and sacrifice in the name of order, security and pride. Even among the Jewish population, Safranski reveals, and despite the boycott of Jewish businesses and the dismissal of Jewish public employees as early as April 1933, there was considerable support for the 'national revolution'.[3]

Heidegger's support for the 'revolution' certainly matched that of the average German.[4] More enthusiastic still was his support of Hitler. Safranski goes as far as to say that, during that first year, Heidegger was 'bewitched' by Hitler. 'How can such an uneducated man as Hitler govern Germany?' Jaspers asked Heidegger on his last visit in June 1933. Heidegger replied, 'Education is quite irrelevant . . . just look at his wonderful hands!'[5]

What emerges from the work of reliable historians such as Hugo Ott and Bernd Martin is a Heidegger far more eager to play an active role in the new Germany underway than he himself ever acknowledged.[6] It appears that, in agreement with Heidegger, a group of Nazi professors and assistant professors had been actively working for his appointment as rector since March of 1933.[7] This, in part, explains why, when Wilhelm von Möllendorf, a Social Democrat and a close friend of Heidegger who was elected rector at the end of 1932 to replace Josef Sauer, expressed misgivings about assuming the office of rector and was subjected to great pressure from the Nazis to step aside, Heidegger became the natural candidate to succeed him. Paradoxically, he became the candidate of Möllendorf as well as of the Nazi members of staff. He was elected with virtual unanimity. The remarkable burst of activity he displayed immediately after his election also testifies to the fact that he had been thinking about the possibility of assuming the highest responsibility of the university for some time.

In what did these activities consist?

First of all, he made a series of speeches and declarations that all testify to his utter commitment to the 'revolution' and his enthusiasm in taking part actively in the reshaping of the 'motherland'. In his rectorial address of 27 May he proclaimed the Führer principle and the general alignment (*Gleichschaltung*) of the university, called for by the Nazis (he himself had joined the party officially – and demonstratively – a few days earlier). He congratulated the appointment of Reich Commissioner Wagner – a notorious hardliner who was responsible for the transportation of opponents to the Heuberg concentration camp – to *Reichsstatthalter* (governor) in early May with the following words: 'Delighted by your appointment as *Reichsstatthalter*, the Rector of the University of Freiburg im Breisgau greets the Führer of our native borderland with a 'Sieg Heil' from a brother-in-arms. Heidegger'.[8] The military tone of this note was reflected in his general attitude and vocabulary, thus showing the extent to which he saw the early months of the new regime as a struggle and a combat. For what? We shall see later. On 26 May, he made his first public speech at a memorial ceremony for Leo Schlageter, celebrating enthusiastically

the memory of the Free Corps fighter who, having performed bombing out-
rages against the French occupying forces in the Ruhr in 1923, was court-
martialled and executed. Among German nationalists, Safranski is right to
point out, he was regarded as a martyr for the national cause. Heidegger obviously identified with this hero, although only vicariously, as he had never
carried out any such 'heroic' attack, nor had any direct experience of World
War I (he was posted as a weatherman and never saw combat). This speech was
followed by a series of public declarations as rector: the rectorial address, of
course, in which he sets out his vision of the university in the new Reich, and
to which I shall return, his speech supporting Hitler's decision to withdraw
from the League of Nations (November 1933), his political tracts, published
in the Freiburg student newspaper (*Freiburger Studentenzeitung*), by then the
official student Nazi organ, in which he calls for a general mobilization of students in favour of the labour service and promotes the 'purifying effect' of the
work camp (20 June 1933), the purification of the university from its Christian
and liberal ideals, as well as the need to introduce martial sports in its midst
(?!) (30 June 1933). In another appeal to the students of the university (3
November 1993), in which he exhorts them to go to the polls in order to pleb-
iscite (*ex post*) Hitler's decision to withdraw from the League of Nations, he
concludes his exhortation with the following, rather extraordinary words:

> 'Let not propositions and 'ideas' be the rules of your being [*Sein*].
> The Führer alone is the present and future German reality and its
>   law . . .
>
>   Heil Hitler!'

This astonishing request was followed by two further appeals (10 and 11
November), addressed to 'German Men and Women' and 'German Teachers
and Comrades', to support Hitler and the National Socialist State. There are a
few more speeches and declarations, all in the same spirit.[9] They need not be
all recorded here.

So much for Heidegger's words, then. What about his actions? Do they
reveal a different sort of Nazi? In fact, they too testify to his commitment and
zeal.

First of all, immediately after his election to the rectorship, he introduced
the Führer principle in Freiburg, even before it was officially established by
the Baden university reform. According to the *Führerprinzip* the rector would
no longer be elected by the academic senate but would be appointed by the
Nazi minister of education. He would be the virtual dictator of the university,
with authority to impose his own deans on the departments. Heidegger knew
where he wanted to go as rector, and was quick to turn himself into such a dictator. For months on end he failed to call the academic senate. His memoran-
dums and circulars to the faculty bodies and departments were drafted in a
shrill tone of command. He wished to put an end to all haggling for increases
in salary, funding of chairs and the like. The spirit of the marketplace and eco-

nomic competition was to be replaced by that of the military, which he introduced to the teaching staff. This was made manifest in his instruction to Professor Stieler, a former naval commander, to draft a code of honour for the university staff, to be based on the relevant regulations for the officer corps.[10]

Heidegger sought to extend his Führer principle beyond Freiburg, and assume a leading position in the area of university politics. Following the available records, Safranski notes how, at the meeting of the Academics' Association in June 1933, the group of Nazi university teachers, in which Heidegger claimed a leading position, succeeded in getting the association's old board members to resign. At the rector's conference that followed, Heidegger called for the dissolution of the association. Moreover, Freiburg was to be declared an 'advance post' of the National Socialist transformation of the universities, in which event Heidegger would truly become a kind of Führer of the German universities. He had the necessary ambition. But he failed to prevail against the other rectors. The Nazi faction thereupon walked out in protest. As his activities on the national level did not yield the success he had hoped for, Heidegger lowered his ambition and set out to become a role model at the regional level. Today, Safranski concludes, there is no doubt that during the summer of 1933 he collaborated in the drafting of the Baden university reform that came into force in August 1933. Baden thus became the first Land, or province, where the alignment of the university according to the Führer principle was accomplished.

Another project Heidegger was keen to implement was the abolition of the division between manual and brain work, or between labour and science. This is an idea we've already come across in the context of his speeches and tracts. It was the direct effect of the total politicization of life: both labour and education were now in the service of the people and the motherland, understood in a nationalist–racist (*völkisch*) sense. You will recall how, in his early years, and in *Being and Time* in particular, Heidegger rejected the idea of a philosophy subordinated to ethical values and political world-views. In the year of his rectorship, however, he had no difficulty in subordinating philosophy, and science in general, to the 'higher' and 'nobler' task of bringing about a total transformation of the 'German Dasein'. His most extreme – and in many ways risible – initiative in that regard was the creation of the *Wissenschaftslager*, or the scholar's camp. The idea behind this initiative was simple, and consisted of living together, working together, thinking together – for a limited period of time and in open nature. As Safranski puts it, it was intended to be a mixture of scout camp and Platonic academy. The project was realized for a week in October 1933, in a place below Heidegger's cabin in Todtnauberg. The 'scholars' departed from the university in closed marching order. Heidegger had drawn up the stage directions: 'The company will proceed to the destination on foot. . . . SA or SS service uniform will be worn; the uniform of the *Stahlhelm* (with armband) may also be worn'.[11] Although the working parties and classes had themes prescribed by Heidegger, the ultimate goal of these gatherings was 'to create the appropriate ambience and attitude' to the ongoing revolution.[12] To this day, I cannot reconcile the fact that this harmless, yet grotesque initiative, emanated from the author of some of the most profound and original pages ever written in philosophy.

Far more serious, and ultimately damning, was Heidegger's attitude towards Professor Hermann Staudinger, a Freiburg chemist of international reputation, and a future Nobel Prize winner, suspected by the authorities because of his pacifist stance during the war and his request for Swiss citizenship in 1917 when working at the Technical University of Zurich. At the time, Staudinger also faced allegations of espionage, which turned out to be entirely unfounded, and which the Germans themselves could not use. As rector, Heidegger was asked to produce a report on Staudinger, and express an opinion as to whether he should be sanctioned. Heidegger's report – which he typed himself in total secrecy – was damning: by emphasizing Staudinger's opposition to the war and his anti-German stance during those years, and retaining the charge of espionage, he felt justified in calling not for Staudinger's retirement, but for his dismissal. We don't know why the report was so harsh (subsequently, and in the light of Staudinger's own defence, as well as that of Freiburg's Nazi mayor, Heidegger recommended that Staudinger be sent into early retirement). A clue, perhaps, lies in the fact that, by 1933, Staudinger had changed his attitude completely, and had endorsed the National Socialist cause, thus becoming a potential rival to Heidegger. The animosity displayed towards Staudinger was, I believe, personal, and reveals one of Heidegger's darker sides as a human being – opportunistic, ruthless and, at times, indifferent to the human cost of his actions.

It is the same side, only in circumstances more gruesome still, that Heidegger revealed in connection with the treatment of some of his Jewish colleagues. In an historical context marked by the early persecution, and ultimately the genocide, of the Jewish people carried out by a regime Heidegger endorsed unreservedly, there is no accusation more serious than that of anti-Semitism. Was Heidegger an anti-Semite? This is a crucial and complex issue that has received considerable attention, and one that is still much debated today. In the light of the evidence available, and having spent the last 15 years of my life reading Heidegger, I can say that I believe there is nothing in his *thinking* that suggests any anti-Semitic tendencies (were this to be the case, taking his thought seriously, teaching it and writing about it would amount to nothing less than a complicity in what ought to be characterized outright as an immoral and criminal endeavour). There is, in other words, nothing in his thought that suggests he ever believed in the inferiority of the Jewish race, its threat to the German nation and European culture in general, its concerted effort to weaken the spirit of the German people or its collective guilt (whether in the death of Christ or the lamentable state of Germany under the Weimar Republic).[13] There is nothing in common between the hatred, nastiness and sheer brutality of the anti-Semitism that ran – and, unfortunately, continues to run – deep in our Western culture, and the depth and brilliance of Heidegger's thought. In fact, soon after his resignation from the rectorship,

Heidegger began to attack systematically what he called the 'biologistic' attitude of Nazi ideology and its widespread anti-Semitism.[14]

What, then, is at the source of this most controversial aspect of the Heidegger controversy? What has led to the charge of anti-Semitism? A series of episodes that, when looked at closely, reveal his special stance towards Nazi anti-Semitism, perhaps best captured in Safranski's own opinion that, whilst unsupportive of its actions, he accepted them nonetheless.[15] When told that *Being and Time* could be reprinted only if its dedication to Husserl 'in friendship and admiration' were left out, Heidegger bowed to this anti-Semitic policy. Yet he insisted that the 'true' homage paid to Husserl's *Logical Investigations* on page 38 be left in. And if it is the case that he failed to contact Husserl's widow after the death of his friend and master, it was, as he revealed later on (in 1945), out of shame for what had happened to the Jews in the meantime. In an (in)famous report on Eduard Baumgarten, the nephew of Max Weber and a liberal-democrat, Heidegger refers to Baumgarten's links with 'the Jew Fraenkel', professor of classical philology. In 1931, however, Heidegger had already rejected Baumgarten's candidacy to a post of assistant in favour of Werner Brock, himself a Jew. It is the same Brock for whom he arranged a research fellowship at Cambridge University when he could no longer keep him on as his assistant. When he became rector, he broke off his contacts with his Jewish colleagues and friends, and declined to supervise the doctoral theses of Jewish students. At the same time, he tried to prevent the dismissal of Eduard Fraenkel (the 'Jew Fraenkel', as he once wrote to blacken Baumgarten) and Georg von Hevesy, professor of physical chemistry, by writing to the Ministry of Education. In the letter, he refers to them strategically as 'Jews of the better sort, men of exemplary character', and professors 'whose extraordinary scientific standing was beyond doubt'.[16] The most disturbing piece of evidence is in the form of a letter discovered in 1989, written by Heidegger in 1929 and addressed to the acting president of the Hardship Committee for German Science, an organization for the granting of scholarships. To my knowledge, it is the only document that reveals a trace of genuine anti-Semitism on his part (and by that, I mean one that cannot be attributed to mere opportunism or rivalry). He writes: 'There is a pressing need for us to remember that we are faced with the choice of either bringing genuine autochthonous forces and educators into our German spiritual life, or finally abandoning it to the growing Judaisation in the wider and narrower sense.'[17] Unlike some, I cannot even begin to try to diminish the sense of outrage one has in reading these words.[18] According to Toni Cassirer, the widow of Ernst Cassirer (himself a Jew), Heidegger's 'inclination to anti-Semitism' was known by 1929. At the same time, and for all his opposition to Heidegger from 1936, Karl Jaspers, whose wife was Jewish, never took Heidegger for an anti-Semite. Similarly, a deeply rooted anti-Semitism would be hard to reconcile with his passion and intellectual esteem for Hannah Arendt, as well as his friendship with Max Scheler and, to an extent, Husserl. In short, it seems impossible to conclude that Heidegger was deeply anti-Semitic, that is, committed to a

vision of the Jewish people as a race (rather than a religion), and an inferior one
at that. Equally, though, it seems impossible to exonerate him from the charge
of having failed some of his Jewish friends and colleagues, as well as his respon-
sibilities as an academic, at a time when his support would have made a difference. We would hardly want to hold Heidegger the man as a role model.
Can we hold a different view of Heidegger the thinker? I shall turn to this
question in a moment.

Before that, let me touch briefly on how his own colleagues viewed
Heidegger the rector. For those who knew him well, like Karl Jaspers, or Karl
Löwith, the reactions ranged from surprise and disbelief to shock and outrage.
Löwith, commenting on the immediate effect of the rectorial address, remarked
that it was not quite clear whether one should begin to study the pre-Socratic
philosophers or join the SA. In their last meeting in Heidelberg in June 1933,
Jaspers recorded how Heidegger had seemed to him like 'a man intoxicated,
with something threatening emanating from him'.[19] Jaspers could not understand how the 'new reality' Heidegger spoke of could have such a philosophical significance. In the case of both Löwith and Jaspers, the perplexity came
from their respect for Heidegger as a philosopher and their inability to reconcile his thought with his political stance. Most of the professors in Freiburg,
though, according to Safranski, regarded their rector as 'a visionary gone
wild',[20] and were mostly annoyed at the loss of seminar or lecture time to para-
military exercises and labour service organized by the SA students under
Heidegger's rectorship. At the same time, others found the whole persona
Heidegger fabricated for himself somewhat comical, if not altogether grotesque. The military allure and martial attitude he adopted did not sit well
with his war service record confined to postal censorship and a meteorological
observatory. Outside Freiburg, and given the polycentrism of the Nazi power
apparatus, it is difficult to say how Heidegger was perceived exactly. Some, like
the prominent philosopher Alfred Baeumler, believed he was a loyal servant of
the National Socialist cause, whilst others, especially the hard-line Nazi ideo-
logues, such as the philosopher Ernst Krieck and the psychologist Erich
Jaensch (to say nothing of the arch-ideologue Alfred Rosenberg), considered his
thinking to be 'schizophrenic', 'nihilistic' and essentially Jewish in character
('talmudist-rabbinic'). In any case, all agreed in thinking that Heidegger's philosophy was in no way espousing the Nazi world-view. In it, Krieck wrote,
'there is nothing about nation and state, about race, or any of the values of our
National Socialist ideology'.[21] It was a shared assumption that Heidegger's
version of National Socialism was personal, even private (it is the private nature
of this National Socialism that I shall want to examine and evaluate), and that,
in the words of Safranski, he was 'playing at National Socialism'.[22] Still, he was
taken seriously enough to be offered a chair at the University of Berlin in
September 1933, and one at the University of Munich in October of the same
year. After serious consideration, he declined both offers.

In April 1934, Heidegger resigned from his post. Why? Not, as he claimed
in a letter to the rector of the University of Freiburg dated 4 November 1945,

out of solidarity with the dismissal of Wilhelm Möllendorf, a dean and a Social Democrat; not, then, because he wanted to save the old university's spirit, the *universitas*, but because, in his mind, the party policy was not revolutionary enough. The revolution, he had come to realize, could not be saved from academic conservatism and the technologization of German universities. His own version of National Socialism (what he would soon call its 'inner truth and greatness') was not to prevail. His resignation did not mean the end of his political career, or that of his allegiance to Hitler. It did mean the beginning of the end, though. He gradually loosened his ties with politics over the next few months. By the summer of 1934, he was back at work, lecturing on 'logic' and Heraclitus.[23] These lectures were followed, in the winter semester 1934–5, by his first lectures on the great and, at the time, much celebrated poet Hölderlin.

After the war, Heidegger appeared before a de-Nazification committee, which charged him with four things: having an important position in the Nazi regime; engaging in Nazi propaganda; introducing the Führer principle at the university; and inciting students against allegedly 'reactionary' professors. The debate over the report stretched well into 1946 and finally broke Heidegger's health. He suffered a depressive episode and spent three weeks at a sanatorium. The hearings of the committee ended in March 1949. They declared Heidegger a Nazi 'fellow traveller' (*Mitläufer*) and banned him from any future teaching. The ban was lifted in 1951 and Heidegger given emeritus status. He taught and lectured on and off into the 1960s.

THE MOTIVATIONS

So much for the historical and biographical background. The question, now, is one of knowing what Heidegger saw and sought in the revolution, and why he embraced it as a philosophical, as well as a political, enterprise. The question, then, is not one of knowing whether he had Nazi ties, but how and why his thought became mixed up with this odious regime. This, of course, assumes that his thought is not primarily political, and least of all Nazi, that is, rooted in questions of race, blood and vital space. At the same time, though, and for a few months at least, Heidegger allowed these *völkisch* motifs to find their way into his own thought. The question, then, amounts to asking the following: given the nature of Heidegger's thought, and what we have said of it thus far, what exactly enabled the author of *Being and Time* to lend his unconditional support to the National Socialist revolution, and drive him to take an active part in the overthrow of the most fundamental democratic values and the most basic civil liberties? Also, given that Heidegger's thought does not promote the biologism nor the imperialism inherent to Nazi ideology, we need to ask what exactly prohibited it from recognizing the atrocities perpetuated under the banner of National Socialism, and the systematic extermination of the Jewish people in particular? The fact that Heidegger never saw the persecution of minorities (the Jewish one in particular) and the question of the final solution as a philosophical problem in its own right signals a certain incapacity on the part of that thought (a thought centred around the concept of the event in its onto-historical dimension) to open itself to this decisive historical event. If there is a failure here, beyond that of character and personality (beyond the failure of ethics), it is a failure of thought, that is, a failure to address this event *philosophically*.[24]

If we are to begin to understand the motivations behind Heidegger's whole-hearted embracing of National Socialism, we need to bear in mind the way in which, following the method and the aims of *fundamental* ontology set out in *Being and Time*, he never ceased to subordinate politics to ontology. It is the specific way in which the relation of precedence of the philosophical over the political was established and reformulated, but never called into question, that made his support for Nazism possible and, at once and simultaneously, irreducible to it. Because of his philosophical presuppositions, Heidegger was able to see in Nazism a historical event that was never there (a response to the essence of our time as dominated by planetary technology and calculation in place of thought) and was never able to see, even after the war, what was really there (an essentially totalitarian, repressive and criminal regime). Not only did Heidegger's political involvement constitute the 'greatest stupidity' of his life; it also and primarily revealed a certain blindness of his thought.[25] I've attempted to write the story of this blindness elsewhere.[26] Here, I can only limit myself to a few comments, and highlight the most decisive issues and the most problematic passages.

Where do we need to look in order to trace the origins of Heidegger's support of National Socialism? It would seem natural to turn to his major work, in a search for clues. The project of fundamental ontology was explicitly developed against a conception of philosophy as world-view and as based on an investigation of human values. It was to be an ontology, not an anthropology. It was to be descriptive, not prescriptive. At the same time, and from the start, Heidegger recognizes that one does not philosophize in a vacuum, but from a factical, and this means historical, cultural, religious, ethical and political position. *Being and Time* recognizes the historically and culturally situated aspect of human existence, as well as its essentially collective nature. 'I' am always a 'we', and this 'we' is never neutral. It is embedded and incarnate, living in a particular place and at a particular time, in a specific historical and socio-economic context. As a project, fundamental ontology does not set out to define the set of conditions under which it is preferable to live one's life. It does, however, reveal the structures on the basis of which such decisions and value judgements can be made. Its analysis is *a priori*, even regarding history. This means that it aims to show the essential historical and collective character of human existence – what it calls its historicity – without engaging critically with the times. In that respect, *Being and Time*, and the whole project of fundamental ontology, can be said to be not so much a- as pre-political. The 'pre-' in question needs to be thought of as delimiting the ontological and temporal conditions of possibility of politics (the ontological *a priori*).

That being said, Karl Löwith recalls how, when he and his former professor met for the last time in Rome in 1936, he suggested to Heidegger that his involvement with National Socialism stemmed from the very essence of his philosophy. Löwith was somewhat surprised when Heidegger agreed with him 'without reservations' and made it clear 'that his concept of "historicity" was the basis for his political engagement'.[27] And so, following Heidegger's own clue, which, to an extent, goes against the explicit aims of fundamental ontology, let me show how the sections on historicity from *Being and Time* can be seen to mark an opening onto his own politics, how, in other words, they can be seen to frame his interpretation of National Socialism in 1933.

According to *Being and Time*, human existence is historical not because it unfolds in time, but because it is a 'destiny' (*Geschick*). Destiny, Heidegger writes, 'is not something that puts itself together out of individual fates', any more, he adds, than our being-with-one-another is made of a random collection of subjects.[28] Rather, destiny means that our fates have been guided in advance, by virtue of the world we share, and the definite possibilities to which we open ourselves resolutely. Destiny stems from our fateful being, and by that we need to understand our factical, thrown being, on the basis of which we are confronted with possibilities, and on which we act together. As such, History is the scene on which our freedom and collective existence is played out. Yet, he adds, 'only in shared communication [*Mitteilung*] and struggle [*Kampf*] does the power [*Macht*] of destiny become free'.[29] The power of destiny can be released only through communication, negotiation, persuasion and struggle. Of those, Heidegger will eventually retain struggle only. Struggle will become the measure of all things. With the end of democracy, the only communication left will be that of the struggle for essence, and the leadership of the Führer, around which the people (*Volk*) or the community (*Gemeinschaft*) as a whole will be gathered. As a whole? Not really. For those not included in the vision will be sidelined, and eventually exterminated. When it eventually became a question of opening oneself resolutely to the Führer, 'the sole reality and law of Germany', as Heidegger once wrote, then the only form of communication he could envisage was massive, hysterical, fusional and total. This mode of communication is a far cry from the ideal (increasingly ignored) of democratic communication, based on persuasion (as opposed to demagogy), arguments (as opposed to propaganda) and checks and balances (as opposed to blind following). It is precisely this democratic ideal Heidegger was (perhaps always) suspicious of. In his book on Nietzsche written 1936–7, we find this:

> Europe always wants to cling to 'democracy' and does not want to see that this would be a fateful death for it. For, as Nietzsche clearly saw, democracy is only a variety of nihilism, that is, the devaluing of the highest values, in such a way that they are only values and no longer form-giving forces.[30]

Further indication of this erosion of core democratic values is to be found in Heidegger's use of the words *Volk* and *Gemeinschaft*. It is perhaps useful to recall that, at the time Heidegger was writing *Being and Time*, these words were contrasted with what appeared as their complementary yet often antithetical modes of social organization, namely, the state (*der Staat*) and society (*die Gesellschaft*). One finds versions of this distinction between *Gemeinschaft* and *Gesellschaft* in the works of historians, sociologists and philosophers such as Spengler, Weber and Scheler.[31] Yet all such versions can be traced back to the publication in 1887 of Ferdinand Tönnies' *Gemeinschaft und Gesellschaft*,[32] the reprinting of which in 1912 was to have a decisive influence on a whole generation of social scientists. Whilst Tönnies' book is not profoundly original (most of its concepts can be traced back to Aristotle's *Politics*), it displays distinct qualities, such as its Germanic rootedness, a romanticized vision of the country life and the Middle Ages, as well as a deep scepticism regarding democracy and the effects of the industrial revolution on the traditional modes of social organization and production. These are traits that became the focus of concern for many at the turn of the twentieth century, and eventually served to feed a reactionary ideology, often referred to as the conservative revolution, or the *völkisch* (national–racist) movement.

According to Tönnies, the history of the West is marked by the combination of two types of social organization, communities and societies, each type being characterized by basic geographical, economic and sociological patterns. Communities are characterized by ties of blood, place and spirit. As such, they are limited to the family and to the village, which is itself the place where agricultural labour, natural and customary law and the worship of deities converge. The community's economy is domestic and rural; its spiritual life is one of friendship and religion. As an organic and natural unity, it is a *Volk*. Its spiritual life as a whole is identified as *Kultur*. Unlike the *Gemeinschaft*, the *Gesellschaft* is an artificial association based on a free contract motivated by interest. As the platform for the development of commerce and trade, the society's place is the city. Its ties are purely practical and conventional, and its law is contractual. The life of the city is spiritless, since it is governed by public opinion, calculative thinking and cosmopolitan newspapers. Where passion, sensuality, courage, genius, concord, piety and imagination prevail in the community, lust for pleasure and power, greed, self-interest, ambition, calculation, vanity and spiritlessness dominate amongst societies. Where the community appears as a harmonious totality governed by need and mutual interest, the society appears as a mechanistic and anonymous organization governed by money, profit and exploitation. Given that, as a result of the development of capitalism, societies have tended to dissolve traditional communities, Tönnies concludes his book by claiming that, 'in the course of history, the culture of the people has given rise to the civilisation of the state'.[33] And we have now reached the point where 'the entire culture has been transformed into a civilisation of state and society, and this transformation means the doom of culture itself if none of its scattered seeds remain alive and again bring forth the essence and idea of community, thus secretly fostering a new culture amidst the decaying one'.[34]

A further elaboration of Tönnies' fundamental thesis regarding the decay of culture in civilization can be found in Spengler's *Years of Decision* and in his famous and influential *The Decline of the West*. Even if not through a direct reading of Tönnies, Heidegger was exposed to the motifs of *Gemeinschaft*, *Volk* and *Kultur* through the cultural historian Spengler, whom he was reading and teaching in the 1920s. The following passage resonates with Tönnies' pathos:

> If the Early period is characterised by the birth of the city out of the country, and the Late by the battle between city and country, the period of civilisation is that of the victory of city over country, whereby it frees itself from the grip of the ground, but to its own ultimate ruin. Rootless, dead to the cosmic, irrevocably committed to stone and to intellectualism, it develops a formal language that reproduces every trait of its essence . . . . Not destiny, but causality, not living direction, but extension now rules.[35]

I am not suggesting that Heidegger is borrowing his concepts of community, people and destiny directly from Tönnies or Spengler.[36] Nor am I saying that it is the use of such a vocabulary alone that made Heidegger's political involvement possible (if only because some of the most prominent figures of the conservative revolution, like Jünger or Spengler, refused to embrace National Socialism). I do believe, however, that, through the use of such a vocabulary in the years preceding his rectorship and his official entry into the Nazi party, Heidegger was laying the ground for a positive assessment of the ongoing 'revolution'. In the intellectual context of the time, the use of such a vocabulary testifies to a specific understanding of what binds a people or a nation together, one that is directed against the liberal view that articulates the meaning of communal life in terms of society and state, with which democracy is essentially linked.[37] It is, I believe, highly significant that, in his reply to Löwith, Heidegger locates the philosophical content of his future political engagement in that context and in those aspirations, and not, for example, in considerations regarding the nature of the social contract, social justice and the relation between classes. It is this ideological background that Heidegger will mobilize in order to support a conception of Germanness emphasizing soil, blood, sacrifice, struggle and science at the service of a higher, spiritual goal (what the Nazis referred to as the *Volksgemeinschaft*).

Two (no doubt rather anecdotal) testimonies regarding Heidegger's ideological stance in the late 1920s seem to confirm the scarce indications revealed in *Being and Time*. This is the way Max Müller, a student of Heidegger's in the late 1920s, describes his teacher:

> Heidegger cultivated an entirely different style with his students than the other professors. We went on excursions together, hikes and ski trips. The relationship to national and popular culture [*Volkstum*], to nature, and also to the youth movement were, of course, talked about then. The

word *völkisch* was very close to him. He did not connect it to any party.
His deep respect for the ordinary people [*Volk*] was also linked to certain
academic prejudices, for example the absolute rejection of sociology and
psychology as big-city and decadent ways of thinking.[38]

The second testimony comes from Hans Jonas, another former student of
Heidegger's:

[Y]es, a certain 'blood-and-soil' point of view was always there: he
[Heidegger] emphasised his Black Forest roots a great deal; I mean his
skiing and the ski cabin up in Todtnauberg. That was not only because
he loved to ski and because he liked to be up in the mountains; it also
had something to do with his ideological affirmation: one had to be close
to nature, and so on. And certain remarks, also ones he sometimes made
about the French, showed as sort of (how could I say it?) primitive
nationalism.[39]

And how, in the light of these two testimonies, can we not mention the short
text Heidegger wrote in 1934, after having been invited to take up a chair in
Berlin, and then in Munich? The text is entitled 'Why do we stay in the provinces?' and resonates with the rural and communitarian pathos of Tönnies
and Spengler. This is how Heidegger describes his work at the cabin in
Todtnauberg, which is in total symbiosis with the elements and surrounding
nature:

On a deep winter's night when a wild, pounding snowstorm rages
around the cabin and veils and covers everything, that is the perfect time
for philosophy. Then its questions must become simple and essential.
Working through each thought can only be tough and rigorous. The
struggle to mould something into language is like the resistance of the
towering firs against the storm.

And this philosophical work does not take its course like the aloof
studies of some eccentric. It belongs right in the middle of the peasant's
work. When the young farm boy drags his heavy sled up the slope and
guides it, piled high with beech logs, down the dangerous descent to his
house, when the herdsman, lost in thought and slow of step, drives his
cattle up the slope, when the farmer in his shed gets the countless shin-
gles ready for his roof, my work is of the same sort. It is intimately rooted
in and related to the life of the peasants.

. . . The inner relationship of my own work to the Black Forest and
its people comes from centuries-long and irreplaceable rootedness in the
Alemanian-Swabian soil.

. . . At most, a city-dweller gets 'stimulated' by a so-called stay in the
country. But my whole work is sustained and guided by the world of
these mountains and their people.[40]

Regarding Heidegger's thought prior to 1933, and those sections of *Being and Time* devoted to the historicity of human existence in particular, my conclusion is that, whilst not displaying any Nazi tendencies whatsoever, they reveal an affinity, or a family resemblance, with the most identifiable, conservative, revolutionary (*völkisch*) motifs. As such, they lay the ground for Heidegger's subsequent hasty and unproblematic burial of some of the most basic tenets of democracy, and the no less hasty embracing of a single leader around which the German people will be gathered and given an ultimate direction.

However important such a pre-orientation may be, it does not suffice to account for Heidegger's enthusiastic embrace of National Socialism. It may lay the ground for an easy and remorseless dismissal of the democratic values and principles of the Weimar Republic, but it is not enough to account for Heidegger's decision to support actively the specifics of Nazism. We need to identify the truly positive, historical possibilities that he saw in the 'revolution'.

These have to do with Heidegger's specific interpretation of the rise of National Socialism precisely in terms of a revolution, that is, of a total upheaval of the very *being* of the German nation. What he saw in it was, first and foremost, a chance for the German people, and possibly the West as a whole, to reawaken itself to its own, forgotten origin. What he saw was the possibility of carrying out at the level of an entire nation, and possibly an entire continent, the programme he had initially laid out for the singular human existence. However strange this may sound, the revolution in question was, for him, ontological. Politics was only a way of achieving a goal and a programme set out in his work, and in his desire to ground ontology anew in particular. It was, in a sense, a way of bringing about this state of 'authenticity' and 'resolute disclosedness' described in *Being and Time*, only now at the level of the German people as a whole. 'Authenticity', we recall, signified this attempt to reawaken life to itself. It designated this unique and singular possibility for life of becoming alive to its own singular destiny, which is to be open and receptive to the Open itself.

It would seem that Heidegger began to formulate the possibility of such a communal and even political interpretation of authenticity and resolute disclosedness in his lecture course from 1929–30. This, I believe, is where the ground for his subsequent positive appraisal of National Socialism was first laid. In that lecture course, he gives a clear interpretation of the nihilistic forces that, according to him, have taken hold of the nation and the epoch as a whole. Our situation, he writes, is one where

> no one stands with anyone else and no community stands with any other in the rooted unity of essential action. We are all servants of slogans, adherents to a programme, but no one is the custodian [*Verwalter*] of the inner greatness of Dasein and its necessities.[41]

In this time of confusion and crisis (most visible, perhaps, in the agonizing Weimar Republic), it has become necessary to seek, if not yet a *Führer*, at least a 'custodian' able to bring out and gather the 'inner greatness' of the German Dasein. Against the problems, the concerns, the difficulties and the solutions of the Weimar Republic (indeed in a state of complete crisis and virtual implosion at the time of the lecture course), a certain preference, a certain inclination for an authoritative and saving figure begins to emerge. It is as if the 'hero' political communities are bound to choose for themselves, the necessity of which Heidegger had evoked in *Being and Time* (§ 74), is now beginning to be given a recognizable face. Whilst becoming more openly political, Heidegger never discusses traditional political questions, such as the role and place of government, the nature of political representation, the balance of powers or social justice. In other words, the political turn that his thought is taking around 1929–30 does not translate into an interest in political philosophy. In a way, he goes so far as to say that these traditional questions are precisely those that need to be neutralized, and its advocates given a lesser role. Our epoch, he argues, is indeed 'able', it even raises many interesting questions and problems. But 'competencies' and 'talents' are not what we need. Lacking are the strength (*Kraft*) and the power (*Macht*), which all the competencies in the world cannot replace. And if anything is achieved with this accumulation of competencies, he goes on to say, it is rather 'the suffocation of all such things'.[42] Away, then, with this expertise and this competence; the time has come to bring about peril, strength and power – in short, oppression! And for this, a new custodian (*Verwalter*), a different light is needed.

Our age, Heidegger laments in his lecture course, is characterized by a lack of genuine direction and goals. Yet, from the heart of our absolute spiritual destitution, a voice can be heard. It is the voice that appeals to our essence and that demands of man that 'he necessarily shoulder once more his very Dasein, that he explicitly and properly takes this Dasein upon himself'.[43] This demand, Heidegger is quick to add, has nothing to do with putting forward something like a human ideal, or with reviving a moribund humanism. Unless, of course, one understands humanism differently, as Heidegger himself did, most explicitly perhaps in his letter to Jean Beaufret from 1946, that is, unless one understands humanism as the 'liberation of the Dasein in man'.[44] Yet, as I already suggested in connection with the phenomenon of 'resolute disclosedness', this liberation hardly amounts to getting rid of something within Dasein. Least of all does it amount to wresting Dasein from its own condition. Rather, it is a matter of freeing Dasein for its own freedom, or for its disclosedness to the world as such. And so, it is a question for Dasein of assuming its own Dasein as 'an actual burden', as this never-ending task and demand. It is in this very decision for existence – 'resoluteness' – that Dasein is first opened to its ownmost possibilities of thought and action, that it becomes free for its own freedom. And it is this very state of urgency and neediness that, indirectly, the contemporary state of crisis and destitution establishes.

Now if questioning, thinking in the most genuine sense, is indeed for Heidegger the ultimate expression of this oppression in which Dasein is revealed to itself as metaphysical animal, it would also seem that philosophizing has its limitations and that this urgency may be introduced through other means, amongst which politics would figure prominently. As soon as it becomes a matter of awakening to its essence no longer just an individual Dasein, but an entire epoch and a community, the gate of politics is opened. And where politics is concerned, a guide, a custodian, a leader is needed:

If, in spite of all our neediness, the oppressiveness of our Dasein still remains absent today and the mystery still lacking, then we must principally concern ourselves with preparing for man the very basis and dimension upon which and within which something like a mystery of his Dasein could once again be encountered. We should not be at all surprised if the contemporary man in the street feels disturbed or perhaps sometimes dazed and clutches all the more stubbornly at his idols when confronted with this challenge and with the effort required to approach this mystery. It would be a mistake to expect anything else. We must first call for someone capable of instilling *terror* [*Schrecken*] into our Dasein again.[45]

Of course, in the context of *Being and Time* especially, this 'someone' capable of instilling 'terror' within us could be Dasein itself. Terror itself is not primarily a political phenomenon in the context of the lecture course: it is a specific attunement, a shock to our existence that is required in order for it to experience the 'bliss of astonishment' and the sense of awe and wonder in the face of beings as a whole that is a precondition for philosophy.[46] With hindsight, however, and given Heidegger's enthusiasm for Hitler only a few years later, we can only shiver at the thought that he may have seen the Führer as the one man capable of reawakening Germany to its own essence and destiny. When terror did eventually come about, and spread through virtually the whole of Europe, Heidegger began by mistaking it for a chance to reawaken Europe to its forgotten origin, and for a sign of the coming about of the 'other beginning'. Soon, though, but too late, and certainly too timidly, he was able to recognize it for what it was. The important point regarding the passage I've just quoted, though, is its recognition that Dasein is no longer alone, absolutely individualized in the task of reawakening itself to its own essence. The task has become historical. And, where history is concerned, as Hegel had already made clear, there is only so much that questioning can *do*: terror, revolutions and the unleashing of passions can sometimes achieve far more. Of course, Goethe's valet, or the Heideggerian equivalent, namely the 'contemporary man in the street', might be somewhat disoriented and lost when confronted with the challenge of history. But never mind the man in the street. Never mind his idols and his existential gadgets. With a bit of terror coming from the right leader, everyone will get his share of the burden – although, as we all know, when the *Führer* did eventually make his entrance, some were made to take upon themselves a burden with allures of death and ashes, and the terror that shook Europe bore little resemblance to the 'basic disposition' of the 'other beginning' Heidegger hoped for.

We are now in a better position to understand how, in Heidegger's view, with Nazism, and after thousands of years of errancy, the unique chance of a turning within history itself, of a total transformation of the course of history, and the German Dasein, finally emerged. This is a chance he did not want to waste, and an event he was not about to witness without taking part. This part, as we saw, he played with utter conviction and zeal. His role – his calling – was to be rector and ruler (*Führer*) of the University of Freiburg. It was to be at the level of the university what Hitler was at the level of the nation as a whole: a guide, a light, a beacon, the tip at which the resolve and the fate of the people was to be gathered.

This calling is best revealed in his rectorial address of May 1933.

The address marks an attempt to gather the essence of the German nation as a whole by way of a repetition of the uniquely historical beginning of Ancient Greece.[47] This general awakening, which was to mark a new beginning for European history, is almost entirely gathered in the Greek word *techne*, which Heidegger translates as science (*Wissenschaft*). But how does Heidegger understand 'science?' Not in its modern, experimental and mathematical sense, not as *method*, then, but as *questioning*. In the context of the address, and of Heidegger's work at the time, 'science' refers precisely to the forgotten ability to *question* beings with respect to their being, to relate to beings from beyond the abandonment and the forgottenness that characterizes our time. 'Science' in the genuine sense of the term is precisely opposed to the calculation and domination that is the distinctive trait of our relation to the world today, and which Heidegger traces back to the techno-scientific origins of modern thought in Descartes, Galileo and Newton. By *techne*, we need to understand the emergence of a thinking and questioning relation to the whole of being (and not simply to this or that being). This scientific attitude is metaphysics proper. For the first time, in Ancient Greece, man rises up against the totality of what is and stands upright in the midst of that totality through his questioning attitude. In a fundamental or archaic sense, questioning refers to a distinct possibility of existence itself, one that was first realized in Ancient Greece. Specifically, it refers to the very transcendence of existence itself, that is, to the fact that existence *is* this singular being for which its own being is always at issue for it, and so the being for which being itself is a question. And what Heidegger is calling for in his address is the repetition – at the collective level, that is, at the level of an entire people – of the Greek beginning. Following the Greek man, the German man is now given the historical chance to stand again in the midst of the whole of being, and to address beings with respect to their being. No doubt, Heidegger's rectorship was the perversion and caricature of this rectitude or this standing erect that characterizes the genuinely scientific (or questioning) attitude. Heidegger wanted to build the university of transcendence and of finitude, the university of the meta-physical ground in which all disciplines are rooted. We can't blame him for having wanted to bring the university back to the place of its forgotten essence. But we can blame him for having tried to enforce it by adhering to the policies and the rhetoric of National Socialism.

The 'new' university was to reflect this historical turning (or this repetition of the first beginning). It was to turn its back on the technological, highly specialized university, in which thinking had come to be associated with calculation and quantification, and be administered according to principles of production and efficiency. In passing, there is perhaps something to be said in favour of that programme, in favour of at least subjecting to rigorous questioning the implicit techno-scientific decision that is driving contemporary research, irrespective of the field to which it is applied. Today, research is driven by, and administered through, targets, strict planning, output; it is constantly monitored, and quantified. In taking up the rectorship, Heidegger saw the historical possibility of reawakening the university (and hopefully the country as a whole) to a fundamental attitude towards the world, of bringing back the forgotten dispositions of 'wonder', 'awe' and 'admiration'. He hoped to take the university beyond its contemporary technical–scientific interpretation, which is responsible for the fragmentation of knowledge into a manifold of now largely disconnected fields and disciplines. Genuine questioning alone, Heidegger claims, 'will shatter the encapsulation of the various fields of knowledge into separate disciplines' and 'ground science once again directly in the fruitfulness and blessing of all the world-shaping forces of man's historical existence'.[48]

In short, the revolution was not (just) a political event for Heidegger. In fact, it was not primarily political. Its political aspect was only superficial. It was a historical event, but historical in Heidegger's sense: an event that announced a turning within history itself, and the possibility for the people as a whole to turn once again to the truth of being, thus matching the greatness of the Greek beginning. And in that historical revolution the university was to lead the way. To the extent that it is able to carry out the most extreme form of questioning, the university was to guide and enlighten the people with respect to its essence and destiny. As the site of 'science', the university could claim to guide the guides and guardians of the nation. It was to orient and give meaning to the other spheres of social and political life: in a gesture reminiscent of Plato's *politeia,* Heidegger's address subordinates the two services of work and defence to that of knowledge. In the Platonic republic, the workers and the defenders of the city were united under, and guided by, the power of knowledge, and the leaders themselves were lead by the light of the Good and the True. In his address, Heidegger merely revives this Platonic programme, subordinating the classes of the workers and the warriors to that of knowledge understood in his own, very precise sense. The programme Heidegger develops in his address is that of a technocracy, and even of an arch-technocracy: the supreme power is to be given to those who 'know', that is, to those who are attuned to the highest principles. Yet knowing, as we have already begun to see, means something quite specific for Heidegger. It means the ability to question, and to question with respect to the whole of being. It means to question beings from beyond the abandonment of and by being that characterizes contemporary science, and that takes the form of calculation, measuring and domination. Knowledge in the highest sense is philosophy understood as attunement to the truth of being.

Ultimately, then, it would seem that the true guide is not the Führer, but Science itself. Yet if Science itself is the Führer, it demands obedience and discipline. The discipline in question is the self-discipline of the disciple, that is, of he or she who follows the law of science as rooted in the truth of being. And the various 'disciplines' are such to the extent that they remain open to the law of their essence. Otherwise, they will only be the fragmented and isolated set of fields they have become under the demands of contemporary technology. In that respect, the address seems to express rather clearly the nature of Heidegger's Nazism – a very 'private' one indeed. Why? To the extent that the highest instance, to which the Führer himself is to be subordinated, is that of 'science' as questioning. The guiding principle, which was to have guided the guide himself, was philosophy. And this is the guiding principle Heidegger set out to clarify in his address, and implement in his rectorship. His 'failure' as a rector was primarily his failure to carry out a vision of the university that no one in the party shared, and his failure to convince his fellow Nazi collaborators of the need to subordinate the politics of the Reich to the 'scientific' mission of the German people in the European context.

Yet the address is also a text in which Heidegger allows his own voice to resonate with the cheap rhetoric of National Socialism and with its ideology of blood, soil, race and will. It is a text in which Heidegger compromises his own thought, lends his prestige and authority to a regime that will immediately turn out to be ignominious. I will not draw up the list of the many National Socialist motifs Heidegger mobilizes and inscribes within his own thought. They can be found in the many addresses, tracts, speeches, etc. Heidegger wrote in 1933–4, and which I began by reviewing. Let me simply, by way of example, quote from the rectorial address, in many ways the (politically and ideologically) most restrained of Heidegger's texts from that period. Having asserted that what the German people needs is a 'spiritual world', Heidegger goes on to define 'spirit' in the following terms:

> [I]t is the power that comes from preserving at the most profound level the forces that are rooted in the soil and blood of a *Volk*, the power to arouse most inwardly and to shake most extensively the *Volk's* existence.[49]

And this is the way in which the newly appointed rector justifies the abolition of the academic freedom that had been fought for and gained only some 100 years before, and provides a philosophical justification for what the alignment of the German university as a whole that he was himself so keen to promote:

The much praised 'academic freedom' is being banished from the German university; for this freedom was false, because it was only negative. It meant predominantly lack of concern, arbitrariness in one's intentions and inclinations, lack of restraint in everything one does. The German student's notion of freedom is now being returned to its truth. Out of this freedom will develop for German students certain bonds and forms of service.[50]

Academic freedom no longer weighs much in the eyes of this *other*, more decisive freedom to which Heidegger hoped to reawaken students and colleagues alike, and which was to serve as an example for the nation as a whole. In this enterprise, Heidegger believed he had the support of the *Führer* himself, as well as that of the 'movement' as a whole. In that, he was gravely mistaken.

Could he have really been mistaken to such an extent? Can he really have picked the wrong man, and, in a way, the wrong revolution, welcoming Hitler himself as the genuinely historical figure whose destiny was to liberate us from our existential torpor by introducing oppression, danger, incertitude, strength and power in politics? Can he really have believed in National Socialism as in this unique possibility of overcoming Europe's metaphysical nihilism, of repeating the Greek beginning and initiating the 'other beginning'? Can he have genuinely seen in Nazism the possibility of freeing the essence of man and of constituting it in an authentic community? I believe so. It is striking to see the extent to which the terms with which he embraced the forcing into line (*Gleichschaltung*) of the German university in his rectorial address are virtually identical with the ones he developed in the 1929–30 lecture course, for example. In both instances, what is most urgent is to wrest twentieth-century Europe from its torpor and its indifference to what is philosophically and historically most decisive, namely, our exposedness as human beings to the ontological difference, or the truth of being. It is, in other words, about, opening history to the power of the whole of being once again, of holding it and maintaining it there, in short, of acting in such a way that the epoch become philosophical again by reawakening itself to the sense of wonder and awe before the essence of truth. To believe, if only for a second, that Hitler and his 'movement' may have had the slightest intention of realizing such an ideal, amounts to an obvious and particularly worrying form of blindness. But equally worrying is the fact that, at least for a while, Heidegger believed that such a historical turning could be brought about by a political regime, whatever its nature. To expect from any movement, party or government that they reawaken us to our essence as ek-sistent beings amounts to a political fault: it is at once too ambitious and naive, too theological and messianic. But this is perhaps, for us, the lesson that can be drawn from the many political disasters of the twentieth century: too many believed in politics as in a saving and redemptive power, as a form of uncritical messianism and, at times, fanaticism. Heidegger himself will not be caught at this twice: having burnt his fingers in politics, and lost his illusions in the failure of Nazism to carry out a project of onto-destinal significance, his hopes will turn to the hidden resources of thought, art and poetry, all deemed to carry a historical and destinal power far greater than that of politics.

NOTES

1 Edited, with a Foreword by Joseph Margolis and Tom Rockmore, translated by Paul Burrell and Gabriel Ricci (Philadelphia: Temple University Press, 1989).

2 René Char and Heidegger first met in Paris in 1955 and subsequently in Provence. Paul Celan and Heidegger met on several occasions between 1967 and 1970, the year Celan took his life. George Steiner's stern rejection of the interviewer's (Antoine Spire) invitation to condemn Heidegger's philosophy (and not just his action as rector) was made in the context of a programme called 'A voix nue', broadcast on France Culture in January 1997. The two CDs of the interviews are now available under the title *Barbarie de l'ignorance* (Paris: Compacts Radio France, 1998). Hannah Arendt's most explicit tribute to her former teacher and lover was written for his eightieth birthday, and was originally published as 'Martin Heidegger at Eighty' in *The New York Review of Books* (October 1971). Derrida's own subtle engagement with Heidegger's Nazism is to be found in *Of Spirit. Heidegger and the Question,* trans. Geoffrey Bennington and Rachel Bowlby (Chicago: University of Chicago Press, 1989).

3 Rüdiger Safranski, *Martin Heidegger. Between Good and Evil*, trans. Ewald Osers (Cambridge, MA: Harvard University Press, 1998), p. 230.

4 The testimony of Karl Jaspers, once a close friend of Heidegger's, and one of Germany's foremost philosophers, is, in that respect, illuminating. See K. Jaspers, *Philosophische Autobiographie* (Piper: Munich, 1977), p. 101. See also Safranski, *Martin Heidegger*, p. 231.

5 K. Jaspers, *Philosophische Autobiographie*, p. 101.

6 Hugo Ott, *Martin Heidegger: A Political Life*, trans. Allen Blunden (New York and London: Basic Books/HarperCollins, 1994); Bernd Martin (ed.), *Martin Heidegger und das 'Dritte Reich'* (Darmstadt: Wissenschaftliche Buchgesellschaft, 1989).

7 See Rüdiger Safranski, *Martin Heidegger*, pp. 238–9.

8 Quoted in B. Martin (ed.), *Heidegger und das 'Dritte Reich',* p. 166.

9 All of these speeches, articles and tracts can be found in R. Wolin (ed.), *The Heidegger Controversy* (Cambridge, MA: MIT Press, 1993), pp. 40–60.

10 See Rüdiger Safranski, *Martin Heidegger*, p. 253.

11 Quoted in H. Ott, *Martin Heidegger: A Political Life*, trans. Allen Blunden (London: HarperCollins, 1994), p. 229.

12 Ibid.

13 If anything, and especially from the 1930s onward, Heidegger had become anti-Catholic, if not altogether anti-Christian.

14 Unfortunately, I don't have the space to introduce the relevant evidence regarding this question. It can be found in my *Heidegger and the Political* (London: Routledge, 1998), Chapters 3 and 4 especially. I have tried to show how, beginning in 1934, Heidegger turns to Hölderlin's poetry in order to develop a reflection on Germanness (*das Deutsche*), away from considerations of blood and soil, and towards the question of language, thus arguing in favour of a nationalism without ethnical or biological foundations. Apart from Farias, the vast majority of historians and Heidegger scholars are in agreement regarding the absence of anti-Semitic traits in Heidegger's work. See Ott's *Martin Heidegger*, pp. 187ff., Safranski, *Martin Heidegger*, Chapter 14 ('Is Heidegger anti-Semitic?').

15 Rüdiger Safranski, *Martin Heidegger*, p. 256.

16 Quoted in Ott, *Martin Heidegger*, p. 108.

17 The letter, published by Ulrich Sieg, appeared in *Die Zeit*, no. 52 (22 December 1989).

18 After a long footnote on the history of anti-Judaism and anti-Semitism, the French Heideggerian François Fédier attempts – unsuccessfully, in my view – to attenuate the effect of Heidegger's declaration. See M. Heidegger, *Écrits politiques*, ed. F. Fédier (Paris: Gallimard, 1995), pp. 275–86.

19 K. Jaspers, *Philosophische Autobiographie*, p. 101.

20 Rüdiger Safranski, *Martin Heidegger*, p. 267.

21 Quoted in Rüdiger Safranski, *Martin Heidegger*, p. 268.

22 Rüdiger Safranski, *Martin Heidegger*, p. 269.

23 That summer, Heidegger gave a lecture series entitled 'The State and Science'. It drew a very large audience, as people were curious to hear what he had to say in his first lectures since his resignation from the rectorship. The title of the series was deceiving, though: Heidegger abstained from making any comments of a political nature. After the first lecture, his audience was reduced to only those interested in philosophy.

24 I can only signal the question here, and point to various studies devoted to it. See T. Rockmore, *Heidegger's Philosophy and Nazism* (Berkeley: University of California Press, 1992); Berel Lang, *Heidegger's Silence* (Ithaca, NY: Cornell University Press, 1996); P. Lacoue-Labarthe, *La Fiction du Politique: Heidegger, l'art et la politique* (Paris: Christian Bourgois, 1987); trans. Chris Turner, *Heidegger, Art, Politics* (Oxford: Blackwell, 1991); J. F. Lyotard, *Heidegger et 'les juifs'* (Paris: Galilée, 1988); trans. Andreas Michael and Mark Roberts, *Heidegger and 'the Jews'* (Minneapolis: Minnesota University Press, 1990); Miguel de Beistegui, *Heidegger and the Political* (London: Routledge, 1998), Chapter 6.

25 Cited by Heinrich W. Petzet in his preface to Martin Heidegger-Erhart Kästner, *Briefwechsel* (Frankfurt: Insel Verlag, 1986), p. 10.

26 In *Heidegger and the Political*, Chapter 6 ('And Into Silence . . .').

27 K. Löwith, *Mein Leben in Deustchland vor und nach 1933* (Stuttgart: Metzler, 1986), p. 57.

28 SZ, 384/436.

29 SZ, 384/436.

30 GA 43, 193.

31 Oswald Spengler, *Der Untergang des Abendlandes* (Munich: Beck, 1920). English translation by Charles F. Atkinson, *The Decline of the West* (London: George Allen & Unwin, 1926), Vol. II, Chapters XI–XIV. Max Weber, *Wirtschaft und Gesellschaft. Grundriss der verstehenden Soziologie* (Tübingen: J. C. B. Mohr [Paul Siebeck], 1956). English translation under the supervision of Guenther Roth and Claus Wittich (eds), *Economy and Society* (New York: Bedminster Press, 1968), Vol. I, pp. 40–3. Max Scheler, *Der Formalismus in der Ethik und die materiale Wertethik* (Bern: Francke, 1963), *Gesammelte Werke*, Vol. 5, pp. 524–36.

32 Ferdinand Tönnies, *Gemeinschaft und Gesellschaft. Grundbegriffe der reinen Psychologie* (Darmstadt: Wissenschaftliche Buchgesellschaft, 1963). Translated by Charles P. Loomis, *Community and Association* (London: Routledge and Kegan Paul, 1955).

33 F. Tönnies, *Community and Association*, 243/263.

34 F. Tönnies, *Community and Association*, 251/270.

35 O. Spengler, *The Decline of the West*, Vol. II, 58/48.

36 In fact, Heidegger takes his distance from Spengler and from what he calls *Kulturphilosophie* in his lecture course on *The Fundamental Concepts of Metaphysics* from 1929–30. See GA 29/30, 103–7/69–71. The philosophy of culture, he argues in that lecture course, goes only so far in diagnosing the destitution and crisis of our time in terms of a conflict between life, or soul, and spirit, or between culture and civilization. It fails to understand the problem in metaphysical terms, and to ask about how the epoch as a whole has become so bored with itself, how we, human beings, have become so alienated from ourselves – and this, of course, with a view to asking how we can

become interested in our own essence again, how we can awaken ourselves to our own humanity. This is the point at which the question of nihilism begins to be articulated in meaningful terms.

37 Heidegger's critique of the state, which, beginning immediately after his resignation from the rectorship, he sees as the modern, political and most effective form of organization of the will to power, and which he contrasts with the Greek *polis*, especially as it appears in the chorus from Sophocles' *Antigone* (line 370), takes place in a number of texts between 1935 and 1945. See EM (117/152), GA 53 (§§ 14–15, 18), 54 (§ 6), 55 (6–10) and 69 (179–98). The latter text is a meditation on the totalitarian nature of machination, or technology, which spares no nation and no people, including the German one. By that time (1940), his break with politics, which he understands as the politics of power, or as the military and economic arm of the technological will to power, has become irreversible.

38 M. Müller, 'A Philosopher and Politics: A conversation', in G. Neske and E. Kettering (eds), *Martin Heidegger and National Socialism* (New York: Paragon House, 1990), p. 178.

39 H. Jonas, 'Heidegger's Resoluteness and Resolve' in *Martin Heidegger and National Socialism*, p. 200.

40 'Why do I stay in the Provinces?' (1934). Translated by Thomas Sheehan in Martin Heidegger, *Philosophical and Political Writings* (Continuum: New York/London, 2003), pp. 16–17. The original text ('*Warum bleiben wir in der Provinz?*') is published in GA 13, 9–13.

41 GA 29/30, 244/163.

42 GA 29/30, 245/164.

43 GA 29/30, 254/171.

44 GA 29/30, 255/172.

45 GA 29/30, 255/172. My emphasis.

46 This attunement of 'terror' is one that Heidegger will keep referring to, especially in connection with the 'other beginning', of which it is said to be the 'basic disposition'. See, for example, GA 45, Appendix I. If 'wonder' before the 'miracle of beings', that is, before their very presence, designated the basic disposition of the first beginning, especially in Greek philosophy, it is a disposition that can no longer be experienced today, such is the 'obviousness' that characterizes our relation to beings as a whole, and our 'domination' over them. We are now so far from being able to *question* beings (with respect to their being), so deeply immersed in a relation of calculation and domination with them, that they can no longer appear as a miracle. 'Terror' is the disposition that heralds an altogether different relation to beings: 'In wonder, the basic disposition of the first beginning, beings first come to stand in their form. Terror, the basic disposition of the other beginning, reveals behind all progress and all domination over beings a dark emptiness of irrelevance . . .' (GA 45, 197/169).

47 On repetition, and the nature of the relation between the 'first' and the 'other' beginning, see Chapter 3.

48 SDU, 13/33.

49 SDU, 14/33–4. Derrida has provided a remarkable analysis of the sudden and worrying resurgence of the motif of 'spirit' in Heidegger's rectorial address in *Of Spirit*.

50 SDU, 34–5/15.

RECOMMENDED READING

Kettering, Emil and Neske, Gunther (eds) *Martin Heidegger and National Socialism. Questions and Answers*, trans. Lisa Harries (New York: Paragon House, 1990). This is a collection of some of Heidegger's politically oriented texts and interviews. It also includes testimonies, interviews and essays from a number of scholars and philosophers.

Sheehan, Thomas, 'Heidegger and the Nazis', *New York Review of Books*, 16 June 1988: 38–47.

Wolin, Richard, *The Heidegger Controversy* (Cambridge, MA: MIT Press, 1993). A good complement to the previously cited collection, it includes Heidegger's political texts and speeches, as well as testimonies and appreciations of his political engagement from scholars and philosophers.

Janicaud, Dominique, *The Shadow of that Thought: Heidegger and the Question*, trans. Michael Gendre (Evanston, IL: Northwestern University Press, 1996). A fine, nuanced and insightful interpretation of Heidegger's politics in relation to his philosophy.

Concluding Remarks

In a way, the last thing I want to do is conclude. I want to go on, naturally, as I believe I have barely scratched the surface of a thought that, after every reading, reveals yet another layer of complexity, yet another world of riches. Following Leo Strauss, I would be tempted to say that 'the more I understand what Heidegger is aiming at, the more I still see how much still escapes me'.[1] This, perhaps, is all the more surprising, given the fact that Heidegger claimed to have had one thought and one thought only. Yet, as he also claimed, it is perhaps that one thought, and the question it sought to solve, that is the most difficult to penetrate. Time and again, with relentless energy, he returned to that very question, taking it further each time. At times, he appears hesitant. At other times, he is fast and bold. Each time, though, he clears new paths. In doing so, he multiplies encounters and dialogues with other thinkers and other disciplines – with the philosophical tradition, with science, technology, logic, the arts, ethics, politics and psychotherapy. Each time, he considers and questions these disciplines in the light of what he takes to be the single most decisive, yet forgotten question. There is something profoundly and irreducibly untimely about his thought, for its inspiration comes from the depths of our history. This untimeliness is not an anachronism, though. It is on the basis of this untimeliness that Heidegger was able to engage with our time in such a radical and compelling manner, and develop a free relation to the present. Does this mean that we, in turn, should follow him all the way, and blindly? Of course not. We must ourselves adopt a questioning attitude. But where does this ability to question come from? What, exactly, generates and provokes thinking? Ultimately, we need to decide for ourselves whether Heidegger's own and only question, namely, the question concerning the meaning and truth of being, is one that we wish to make our own. If we do, then the meaning of thinking, of the world, of our relation to it and to our fellow human beings finds itself irreversibly transformed.

Far from wanting to conclude, then, I want to invite the reader to use what I have said here as a point of departure, as an invitation to explore Heidegger's thought further, without falling into the trap of either piety and adulation or hasty dismissal and condemnation. If anything, I hope to have shown the originality of that thought, and the impossibility, therefore, of judging it simply on the basis of previously established philosophies and principles of thought. This, once again, does not mean that we should refrain from questioning it, that we should remain content with repeating it. What we must do, what is expected of us, readers and thinkers, is to *engage* with it. The rules of engagement are not inscribed in stone, however, and have not been defined in advance. In a way, every genuine thinker redefines them, thereby making our task more difficult, forcing us to find a negotiating ground between the old rules and the new. This is a negotiation that we have to carry out for ourselves. The rules of engagement with the philosophical tradition that Heidegger himself defined were gathered mostly in the words 'phenomenology', 'hermeneutics' and 'de(con)struction'. We saw – albeit very briefly – how some of the thinkers I introduce in the Appendices extended this task, at times, as in the case of Derrida, subjecting Heidegger's own texts to its rigour. These are only possible modes of engagement, however. The only thing that matters, in the end, is that we elevate ourselves to the level at which 'the battle of giants over being', to use Plato's famous definition of philosophy, takes place, and join in the battle itself. Too often, the philosophical debates resemble cocktail-party conversations. They can be very civil, mildly ironic and at times amusing. Most often, though, they consist of pointless rivalries, bitter disputes and false accusations. In either case, they are singularly unphilosophical, despite their being carried out by professional philosophers. The *real* battle I am talking about, the tight negotiations and the struggles I have in mind, only testify to the fact that philosophical debates are neither *divertissements* for the idle and the intellectually gifted, nor platforms for the display of large egos, but the stuff of life itself. It is over life as such, its meaning, its value and its potential, that philosophers fight. Their fight is itself born of the greatest desire to measure up to the possibilities of life. It is not fuelled by animosity, ambition and resentment, but by the extraordinary power of thought to delve into the depths of life. Heidegger was one such philosopher, for whom life and thought were indistinguishable. Upon entering the battlefield, we must strive to emulate this proximity.

Before parting company, and as a mere indication of a possible strategy of engagement with Heidegger's thought, inspired in part by some of his most astute readers, let me say a few words about the dangers of his uncompromising view regarding our contemporary conception of life, whether biological, political or ethical. Life, he claims in a book from 1939–40, and published only recently, is now envisaged exclusively technologically and machinically.[2] What we call materialism, vitalism and spiritualism are *metaphysically* identical. It is the same *image* of the world that is mobilized, one that systematically favours causality and production over truth in the sense that Heidegger seeks to revive. Christian doctrine, political endoctrination, the technical interpretation of life, fundamentally unchanged by the various attempts to add to it a spiritual dimension, all partake of the same technologization of beings and life. They all presuppose the total mobilization of the whole of being for the *Machenschaftiche*, for what can be made, and for *Machenschaft*, or machination. This is the radical and uncompromising nature of Heidegger's claim: we think we are making real decisions, establishing decisive distinctions, between

various beliefs, world-views and courses of action. But in fact, we are only ever
responding to a historical decision that's already been made for us. In fact, we
are only ever carrying out a metaphysical project initiated a long time ago, and
one that only a considerable amount of philosophical work can reveal. In the
same highly significant and emblematic text, Heidegger claims something as
scandalous as this: from the point of view of their onto-historical origin, there
is no *real* or *fundamental* difference between the Christian doctrine and
Bolshevism, between the biologism and imperialism of Nazism and the forces
of capital (which, today, have permeated all spheres of life), and between vitalism and spiritualism. This, I believe, is at once the strength, and the extraordinary weakness and limitation of Heidegger's position. For on the one hand
it allows us to establish continuities and complicities where we thought there
were incompatibilities, and to shift the weight of difference to a different
terrain (that of the 'meaning' or the 'truth' of being). On the other hand,
though, by revealing such differences as *pseudo*-differences, he also neutralizes
the decisions and choices they often call for, thereby erasing the traditional
space of politics and ethics. He himself would not and could not establish a
real difference, that is, a difference that would be *historically decisive* in his sense,
between, say, mechanized agriculture and the death camps, between Western
democracies and totalitarian regimes, between the victims of Nazism and
those of the Berlin blockade.[3] He would not and could not distinguish
between Communism and Christianity. For he envisaged them all as episodes
– however catastrophic and lamentable – of the same, 'first' beginning. The
only real, decisive difference he *did* recognize was that between the 'first' and
the 'other' beginning, between metaphysics (and its consummation in contemporary techno-science, techno-discourse and techno-politics) and thought,
between the total occlusion of truth in contemporary culture and the possibility of a genuine openness to it in a historical turning and a form of engagement he tried to elaborate throughout his life. This is the lesson I'd like to
draw from this: whatever our commitment to the deconstruction of metaphysics, and to the struggle for new possibilities of thought and action beyond it,
or perhaps in its margins, we continue to live within the metaphysical, technical framework, and so must remain committed to taking seriously, and discriminating between, the many differences, choices and situations we are faced
with at the historical, political, religious and artistic level. We must engage
in critique (from the verb *krinein*, to distinguish) as well as in deconstruction.
Otherwise, and simply as a result of having declared our time one of alienation, we risk a total alienation from alienation itself. The free relation to technology Heidegger advocates may, after all, also involve an active participation
in intra-metaphysical processes, and not just a meditation of its essence. For
within technology, there are differences that matter, and to which we cannot
and must not – remain blind. With one critical eye, and the other deconstructive, we may be better equipped to navigate the often treacherous waters of
our time.

NOTES

1 Leo Strauss, 'An Introduction to Heideggerian Existentialism', in Thomas L. Pangle
   (ed.), *The Rebirth of Classical Rationalism. An Introduction to the Thought of Leo Strauss*
   (Chicago: University of Chicago Press, 1989), p. 30.
2 GA 69, 179–98 ('Koinon. Aus der Geschichte des Seyns').
3 Heidegger's now famous remark regarding the similarity of essence between the death
   camps and mechanized agriculture was made on 1 December 1949, in a lecture entitled 'Das Ge-stell'. His exact words were as follows: 'Agriculture is now a motorised
   food-industry – in essence, the same as the manufacturing of corpses in gas chambers
   and extermination camps, the same as the blockading and starving of nations, the same
   as the manufacture of hydrogen bombs.' The English translation of those remarks,
   along with an explantory footnote, appears in Thomas Sheehan, 'Heidegger and the
   Nazis', *New York Review of Books*, 16 June 1988, pp. 41–2. As Sheehan rightly points
   out, 'all but the first five words of the sentence are omitted from the published version
   of the lecture', in TK, 14–15/296.

Appendix 1: A Brief, Philosophical Biography

Heidegger once began a lecture on Aristotle, on whom he lectured and wrote extensively, with the lapidary sentence: 'He was born, he worked, and he died.' This shows the insignificance, in his mind, of matters biographical for philosophy. As a philosopher, he himself aspired to live for philosophy and disappear within it. Philosophy is what his life is really about. Yet even the life of the philosopher is shaped and influenced by the environment in which it develops, by family, places, encounters, and events that are not immediately philosophically relevant.

Heidegger was born on 26 September 1889, in the Swabian town of Messkirch, Germany. His father was a master cooper and a sexton at St Martin's Catholic Church in Messkirch. His origins were modest, rural and catholic. They remained a source of inspiration and pride throughout his life.

It is only through the material and financial support of the Church that Heidegger gained access to secondary and higher education. He attended the Gymnasium in Constance on a scholarship (1903–6), and boarded in the Catholic school. There, he prepared himself for a clerical career. Heidegger's early Catholicism, and his complex and tormented relation with it, and with Christianity in general, cannot be underestimated. Between 1906 and 1909, he attended the Gymnasium and the archiepiscopal convent in Freiburg. In 1909, he entered the novitiate with the Jesuits in Tisis near Feldkirch (Austria), and was discharged after only two weeks because of heart problems. Between 1909 and 1911, he studied theology and philosophy in the Philosophy Department at the University of Freiburg in preparation for the archdiocesan priesthood, with residence at the archdiocesan Theological Seminary. There, he wrote anti-modernist articles in Catholic periodicals. In the winter semester of 1911–12, he withdrew from the Theology Department and the Theological Seminary for health reasons and abandoned his career plans for the priesthood. He transferred to the Department of Natural Science and Mathematics with the initial intention of reading mathematics and taking the state examination granting the degree required for a teaching career in secondary school. Shortly thereafter, he considered moving to the University of Göttingen to study with Edmund Husserl, but remained in his new department for financial reasons, with the intention of majoring in philosophy, while attending courses in the Departments of Philosophy, Theology and Classical Philology. He took classes in many different areas: in mathematics (in analytic geometry of space, differential and integral calculus, algebraic analysis and advanced algebra), experimental physics and chemistry, but also in logic and epistemology, epistemology and metaphysics (with the Neo-Kantian Heinrich Rickert), the history of philosophy, theology (dogmatic theology, Gospel of John), Hellenic mystery religions and art history. In July 1913, he obtained his doctorate ('Theory of Judgement in Psychologism: Critical and Positive Contributions to Logic'). Immediately thereafter (August 1913), he applied to the Freiburg Archdiocesan Chancellery Office for a grant in order 'to dedicate himself to the study of Christian philosophy and to pursue an academic career' through work on the post-doctoral degree (*Habilitation*) and license to teach in German universities as a lecturer (*Privatdozent*). He was awarded a scholarship for two years with the expectation that the applicant 'would remain true to the spirit of Thomistic philosophy'. In 1915, he submitted his post-doctoral thesis ('The Theory of Categories and Meaning in Duns Scotus'), directed by Rickert.

He began to lecture at the University of Freiburg in 1915. That first year, he applied for a third, consecutive Von Schaetzler Grant to work on the publication of the post-doctoral thesis, as well as of a related investigation dealing with 'the logic and psychology of Late Scholasticism', with the aim of making a contribution to 'the future struggle for the Christian ideal of life in Catholicism'. He obtained the grant, and published his thesis (now in GA 1). As a young doctor and scholar, then, Heidegger was still very much committed to Catholicism, and to contributing to Christian philosophy. That same year, he met Elfride Petri, a Protestant, whom he married in 1917, thus bringing the plans for priesthood to an effective end. In 1916, Husserl had arrived in Freiburg, and began to collaborate with the young philosopher only a year later, despite Heidegger's eagerness to establish a working relationship with the founding father of phenomenology. Around that time, Heidegger wrote and lectured on the phenomenology of religion, finding inspiration not only in Husserl, but also in Luther, Kierkegaard and contemporary Protestant theology. The Heideggers' son, born in 1919, was not baptized as a Catholic. 1919 marks the year Heidegger broke with what, in a letter to his friend from the early teens, Father Engelbert Krebs, he called 'the system of catholicism'.[1] That same year, he became Husserl's assistant, and lectured extensively on phenomenology, whether in connection with the questions of value, of intuition and expression, with religion and the religious Life, with historical figures such as Descartes, Augustine and the Neo-Platonists or, more importantly still, Husserl himself (*Logical Investigations*) and Aristotle. It is the teaching on Aristotle that struck the greatest chord with his audience, and gave him a national reputation, which resulted in an appointment as Associate Professor in Philosophy at the University of Marburg in 1923. Husserlian phenomenology progressively emerged as the crucial tool that allowed Heidegger to unlock the mystery of the unifying sense of being identified by Aristotle, and to take his own thought in the direction of what he eventually called a 'fundamental ontology'. His fame as a lecturer, and a thinker in his own right, started to grow, and students began to come from all over Germany to study with him, especially after his appointment in Marburg. A number of them (H. Arendt, H. G. Gadamer, L. Strauss, H. Jonas, K. Löwith, M. Horkheimer, H. Marcuse and E. Levinas), profoundly marked by Heidegger's teaching, became important philosophers in their own right, often developing strands of their teacher's own thought, allowing it to find its way outside Germany (in France in the early 1930s, and in the United States in the mid-30s, where some of them, often Jewish, found refuge from Nazism).

At this point, Heidegger hadn't published a book for over ten years. It had been known in the academic world that he was preparing a major work. At the time, though, he was not yet regarded as a systematic philosopher, but as an unusually gifted interpreter of the philosophical tradition, which he brought to life like no one else. It was only at the explicit request of the University of Marburg, which wanted to promote him to a full professorship, and the Ministry of Culture, that Heidegger agreed to publish an unfinished manuscript in the 'Annual for Philosophy and Phenomenological Research', edited by Husserl and Max Scheler. The book bore the title *Being and Time*. This is the book that propelled Heidegger to international fame, the book for which he is still recognized as a revolutionary thinker and with which generations of students and philosophers have struggled; it is one of the most acclaimed works of the twentieth century. In 1928, Heidegger returned to Freiburg to take up Husserl's old chair. He taught in Freiburg for the rest of his career. He died in Freiburg in 1976 at the age of 87.

Had it not been for his involvement in favour of National Socialism, and his rectorship as the first Nazi rector of the University of Freiburg, Heidegger's life in Freiburg would have been relatively uneventful. I deal with this crucial and lamentable episode in Chapter 6 ('Politically Adrift: The Affair with National Socialism').

NOTES

1 The letter in question can be found in J. van Buren (ed.), *Supplements*, 69–70.

RECOMMENDED READING

Heidegger, Martin, 'My Way to Phenomenology', in Martin Heidegger, *On Time and Being*, trans. Joan Stambaugh (New York: Harper & Row, 1972). German version in SD.

Ott, Hugo, *Martin Heidegger: A Political Life*, trans. Allen Blunden (New York and London: Basic Books/HarperCollins, 1994).

Petzet, Heinrich Wiegand, *Encounters and Dialogues with Martin Heidegger, 1929–1976*, trans. Parvis Emad and Kenneth Maly (Chicago: University of Chicago Press, 1993).

Safranski, Rüdiger, *Martin Heidegger. Between Good and Evil*, trans. Ewald Osers (Cambridge, MA: Harvard University Press, 1998).

Appendix 2: Existential Philosophy and Psychotherapy

Should we recognize in Heidegger's description of our occasional longing to escape life a new interpretation of what Freud called the death drive? Could the origin of our (more or less occasional) desire to be dead, inert matter, lie with our ontological structure, as opposed to our psychic apparatus? It is not by chance that the vocabulary I am using here borders on that of psychopathology. At issue, however, in Heidegger's thought, is the possibility of interrogating anew this reality we call the *psyche* (along with its relation to this other reality we call the *soma*, or the body). These are realities we have come to take for granted. They are born of a certain scientific turning within our conception of nature as a whole, however. This turning can be traced back to Galileo and Newton, and consists of reification, and an objectification of natural 'phenomena'. According to this conception, reality is essentially mechanistic; it consists of a series of causes and effects. Understood 'scientifically', the mind is, according to Heidegger, a projection and an extension of this epistemic world-view. Freud himself, with his idea of the psychic apparatus, transfers scientific, mathematical–physical causality, and its concept of energy, to the understanding of our relation to the world and others, and to the various ways in which it can break down. Similarly, the body that is envisaged in relation to the psyche, in what amounts to a reworking of the Cartesian dualism of body and soul, of material and psychical reality, is primarily an object, a thing that I, as a living, existing being, can never experience. It is an idealization, and so a form of abstraction. Heidegger makes a distinction here, inherited from his master Husserl, and taken up subsequently by the French phenomenology of the body (Sartre and Merleau-Ponty), between corporeality (*Körper*) and the lived body (*Leib*). The point of departure, in examining abnormalities and dysfunctions in one's life, must not be the relation between *psyche* and *soma*, or between the mind and the body posited separately and abstractly, and connected, as Freud argued, via the basic drives and instincts, but the fundamental phenomenon of incarnate existence (*leibliche Dasein*), which characterizes us in our being. Behind and beneath the projection of who we are as unity of body and soul, or corporeality and psyche, lies the reality of existence, understood as being-in-the-world. This is the phenomenon that needs to be interrogated. From this follows the possibility of interpreting, and ultimately treating, pathologies as diverse in character as the meaninglessness of existence felt by some, and the intolerable boredom that accompanies it, depression, melancholia, anorexia, acute stress and even schizophrenia. On boredom, for example, and the existential as well as onto-historical background from which it stems, see Heidegger's detailed and fascinating analyses in *The Fundamental Concepts of Metaphysics* (GA 29/30).

Husserlian phenomenology began as a critique of empirical psychology, which claimed to solve the enigma of human consciousness by developing models of representation borrowed from the natural sciences. Instead, Husserl insisted, what was needed was a pure science of consciousness, or a transcendental psychology, based on the principle of intentionality, and the infinite correlations that it made possible. Instead of looking at actual innerworldy states of consciousness, Husserl suggested we look at the way in which these states are given, at how they present themselves to consciousness, and describe them in the most rigorous way, without any *a priori* restrictions regarding what may or may not count as a genuine phenomenon for consciousness. Whilst very much influenced by Husserl, and by his critique of psychologism, Heidegger believed his master had not gone far enough. Why? Because, he thought, Husserl still believed in consciousness (albeit as pure, or transcendental) as the originary site of our encounter with the world and its myriad of phenomena. Inevitably, and as a corollary, he could not quite move away from a certain dualism of subject and object. So long as we think of ourselves primarily in terms of consciousness, we are positing ourselves against a world that is ontologically different from us. Heidegger's effort to understand who we are as *Dasein* (and no longer as *Bewusstsein*), or as being-*in*-the-world, was his response to the problem he identified in Husserl. Philosophy, as phenomenology, needed to be existential and ontological, and not psychological. What we see in Heidegger, then, is a radicalization of the Husserlian critique of psychology.

It is perhaps not surprising, then, that Heidegger's philosophy eventually made its way into psychiatry and psychopathology. Under the influence of the Swiss psychiatrists Ludwig Binswanger and Medard Boss, both trained in psychoanalysis and both close to Freud, a school of analytic psychiatry known as Daseinanalysis began to develop in the 1940s. Whilst very critical of Binswanger's 'phenomenology of love', which, in his opinion, stemmed from a profound misunderstanding of the entire project laid out in *Being and Time*, Heidegger actively supported Boss' enterprise. Boss and Heidegger began to correspond in the late 1940s. Beginning in 1959, and for a full decade, a series of annual, two-week seminars took place in Boss' home in Zollikon, Switzerland, and involved the participation of colleagues of Boss and psychiatry students. What both Binswanger and Boss saw in Heidegger's work was a way out of, or beyond, the metaphysics of subjectivity and the ontological dualisms (subject and object, consciousness and world, consciousness and body, mind and matter) governing Freudian psychology and psychiatry. Medard Boss saw in Heidegger's new approach to the question 'Who are we?' the possibility of treating 'mental' illness as a mode of being of a being whose essence, or distinct trait, is to be in the world amidst beings, or to be this *openness* that Heidegger describes in *Being and Time* and elsewhere. Naturally, this mode of being can only be seen as deficient, and as signalling something like a breakdown of the structures through which existence normally operates within the world. Boss saw the possibility of approaching mental illness precisely not from the point of view of the 'mind' (the existence of which we should not take for granted), or consciousness (and its Freudian corollaries, the ego, the id and the superego), but from that of a totality called being-in-the-world, and on the basis of which, retrospectively as it were, and somewhat abstractly, something like a *psyche* and a *soma* can be extracted. Boss thought that neurotic and psychotic patients suffered from a 'blockage' of their world-openness. This could take the form of a bodily-jamming, for example, through which an individual refused a world-relation. There was no effort on Boss' part to explain *why* human beings may behave in such a way. The effort focused on the description of *how* it happens. Health and illness are ways in which a person finds himself or herself immediately with beings. In a letter addressed to Heidegger for his eightieth birthday, which was initially published in the *Neue Zürcher Zeitung* in 1969, and subsequently reproduced as the Afterword to the *Zollikon Seminars*, Boss writes: 'In the basic structures of the way of human existing which you elaborated, I recognised the most reliable outline of an art of healing, which I had glimpsed till then during my wanderings through the history of philosophy and medicine and during my expeditions to the Far East and the Far West. Since that time, you have also become the most genuine representative of basic research in medicine for me. It is only with the background of your thinking that the results of modern biology, anatomy, physiology, psychology and pathology can be understood in their essential significance' (365/294). Among the people 'in need of help' was Heidegger himself, who suffered from depression after having been dismissed from the university and banned from teaching by the French de-Nazification committee after the war.

Today, Daseinanalysis has far exceeded its Swiss origin, and is studied, practised and discussed in a number of countries, universities, schools and journals across the world.

RECOMMENDED READING

Boss, M., *Psychoanalysis and Daseinanalysis*, trans. L. B. Lefebre (New York: Basic Books, 1962); *Existential Foundations of Medicine and Psychology*, trans. S. Conway and A. Cleaves, with an introduction by P. J. Stern (New York: J. Aronson, 1979).
—, 'Martin Heidegger's Zollikon Seminars', trans. B. Kenny, *Review of Existential Psychiatry and Psychology*, 16 (1978–9), 7–20.
Cohn, H., *Heidegger and the Routes of Existential Therapy* (London: Continuum, 2002).
Guignon, C., 'Authenticity, Moral Values, and Psychotherapy', in *The Cambridge Companion to Heidegger* (ed.) C. Guignon (Cambridge: Cambridge University Press, 1993), pp. 215–39.
Heidegger, M., *Zollikon Seminars: Protocols – Conversations – Letters* (Evanston, ILL: Northwestern University Press, 2001). Edited by Medard Boss and translated from the German and with notes by Franz Mayr and Richard Askay. This volume contains the protocols of the seminars organized by Boss for colleagues and students in psychiatry in Zollikon, Switzerland, between 1959 and 1969, as well as records of conversations with

Heidegger (1961–72) and letters from Heidegger (1947–71). See also Boss' Afterword, as well as Richard Askay's Afterword, 'Heidegger's Philosophy and its Implications for Psychology, Freud, and Existential Psychoanalysis'.

Hoeller, K. (ed.), *Heidegger and Psychology* (Seattle: Review of Existential Psychology and Psychiatry, 1988).

Richardson, W., 'Heidegger among the Doctors', in *Reading Heidegger: Commemorations* (Bloomington: Indiana University Press, 1993), pp. 49–63.

Scott, C. E., 'Heidegger, Madness and Well-Being', in *Martin Heidegger. Critical Assessments* (ed.) C. Macann (London: Routledge, 1992), 4, 279–98.

Appendix 3: Heidegger and the Greeks

Heidegger's fame began as a teacher in the 1920s in Freiburg and Marburg. His teaching covered large areas of philosophy and spanned its entire history. It was his reading of the Greeks, though, and of Aristotle in particular, that really captivated his audience. Many students of his, who became philosophers in their own right, and not just followers, have expressed their debt and gratitude to Heidegger's teaching. I shall mention only three here: Hans-Georg Gadamer, the prominent hermeneutic philosopher (see also Appendix 4); Hannah Arendt, who was Heidegger's lover whilst her student and who, as a Jew, fled Nazism to settle in the United States and become one of the most prominent political philosophers of the twentieth century; Leo Strauss, another Jew, also exiled to the US, and another political philosopher whose thought stemmed from his detailed and careful interpretation of, amongst others, the Greek classical texts. All three philosophers stress the significance of Heidegger's teaching, and his relation to the Greeks especially, as crucial for their own philosophical development. What, exactly, was so striking, and so new, about Heidegger's approach?

For Gadamer, it was the role of *phronesis* in Aristotle's *Nicomachean Ethics*, Book VI that turned out to be decisive. In his presentation of Heidegger's report to Natorp from 1922, a copy of which he once possessed, and subsequently lost, and which was accidentally found again in the 1980s, Gadamer recounts its decisiveness for his own development. The manuscript in question was devoted to a phenomenological interpretation of Aristotle's *Nicomachean Ethics*, *Metaphysics* and *Physics*, and of the notion of *phronesis* ('prudence') in particular. This is the notion, he says, that was to serve as the way into the thematic of the self-explanation of life and of what, at the time, Heidegger called 'factical life'. Most striking, then, was Heidegger's ability to turn to Aristotle not as a historically important object, but as a way of clarifying the most pressing and urgent question of the time, namely, that of life. In his writings, and more so even in his teaching, Heidegger was able to make the Greeks speak *as if for the first time* by anchoring their thought in the fundamental experiences of human existence. His phenomenological and hermeneutical approach brought the canonical Greek texts back to life by bringing them back into the concrete life-world of our own experience (the 'factical life'). It was no longer a matter, as was still the case with the idealists and the neo-Kantians, of approaching the problems from afar and inscribing them within systematic constructions, but of using the history of philosophy to make those questions comprehensible and lively, to turn them into 'our own'. Heidegger's students had the impression that the Greeks were speaking to them directly, across the ages, and that the questions of the Greeks were – or had to become – their own. This, in effect, was the source of what Gadamer called the 'fundamental hermeneutic experience', which became the focus of his own philosophy.

Like Gadamer, Arendt gained from Heidegger a phenomenological method, which brought together a genealogy of philosophical notions inherited from the tradition and their rootedness in specific and concrete experiences. This method implies a central aspect of Heidegger's thought, to which Arendt was more sensitive than Gadamer, namely, the deconstruction of the many schemas and concepts carried over by the philosophical tradition and used naively, that is, without paying attention to the phenomena to which they correspond and the experiential soil from which they grow. This deconstruction has two sides, one negative, which consists in denouncing fallacious associations and combinations, and one positive, which consists in bringing to light the very phenomenal distinctions that these associations erase. Arendt went to apply this method to the political field by examining the concepts inherited from Greek philosophy and the conception and practice of political life they reveal. What is remarkable about Arendt is that she uses tools she first learned from Heidegger in order to highlight shortcomings and confusions in Heidegger's own thought. She uses Heidegger's tools against Heidegger in order to develop a different conception of philosophy, and of philosophy's relation to the political life. For example, on the basis of a close reading of Aristotle's *Ethics*, and in direct opposition to their Heideggerian interpretation, which she witnessed first hand, she distinguishes very carefully between the concepts of labour and production, of production and action, within the sphere of what she calls the *vita activa* (itself distinguished from the *vita contemplativa*). Directly related to those concepts is the question of time, the centrality of which Heidegger had done much to reveal. The temporality Arendt thematizes, though, differs significantly from that of Heidegger, and is based on her distinction of the various spheres of life. She distinguishes between the cyclical time of labour and necessity, the linear time of production and, finally, the time of action, which is free (this is what distinguishes it from the time of labour), fragile (this is what distinguishes it from the time of production), as well as irreversible (and this is what distinguishes it from labour and production). To a large extent, Arendt's thought is a confrontation with that of her teacher and lover. Yet this is a confrontation that has its methodological roots in what she learned from him.

Leo Strauss was a doctoral student when he first heard Heidegger speak in 1922. Up to that time, he recalls in a lecture on 'Heideggerian Existentialism' from the 1950s, he had been particularly impressed, as many of his contemporaries, by Max Weber.[1] In comparison with Heidegger, however, he was an 'orphan child in regard to precision and probing and competence' (p. 28). Never, Strauss goes on to say, had he witnessed such 'seriousness, profundity, and concentration in the interpretation of philosophic texts', an attitude that was to leave its mark on Strauss forever. It became obvious to all who heard Heidegger that 'there had been no such phenomenon in the world since Hegel' (p. 28) and that, in 1950, Heidegger remained 'the only great thinker in our time' (p. 29). Yet Strauss is far from being a follower or a disciple of Heidegger. He describes himself as a mere scholar, whose work does not reach the 'inaccessible heights and mists' of the great thinker. At the same time, however, he stresses Heidegger's political engagement, and his deep suspicion regarding ethics, as an obstacle that is not easily overcome. Strauss' own relation to the classical tradition, and to Greek philosophy especially, can be seen as an attempt to avoid the pitfalls into which Heidegger had fallen, whilst retaining the lesson of intellectual rigour and profundity learned from him. The fact that Strauss spent so much time (re)reading the very texts Heidegger himself had laboured over is no coincidence, and testifies to his desire to let the Greeks speak for us *differently*. Where he remains indebted to Heidegger, though, is in the possibility of returning to the Greeks in order to address our *present* situation, beyond the epistemology of the neo-Kantian school and the phenomenology of consciousness of Husserl.

For that generation – as for Heidegger himself, naturally, Greek philosophy meant this way out of – and beyond – the dead-ends of modernity: beyond the dualisms of subject and object, of mind and body, beyond epistemology and positivism, and into the concreteness of factical life.

NOTES

1 Leo Strauss, 'An Introduction to Heideggerian Existentialism', in *The Rebirth of Classical Rationalism. An Introduction to the Thought of Leo Strauss* (ed.) Thomas L. Pangle (Chicago: University of Chicago Press, 1989), p. 27. The following references are from the same lecture.

RECOMMENDED READING

Arendt, Hannah, 'Heidegger at Eighty', in *The New York Review of Books*, October 1971. Reprinted as 'For Martin Heidegger's Eightieth Birthday', in *Martin Heidegger and National Socialism* (eds) Gunther Neske and Emil Kettering (New York: Paragon House, 1990), pp. 207–17.

Gadamer, Hans-Georg, 'Introduction' to Heidegger's 'Natorp-Report', *Dilthey-Jahrbuch*, 6, 1986.

—, *Truth and Method*, trans. Joel Weinsheimer and Donald G. Marshall (New York: Continuum, 1993). See the sections on 'Heidegger's project of a hermeneutic phenomenology' (254–64) and the 'fundamental hermeneutic problem' (307–24) especially.

Strauss, Leo, 'An Introduction to Heideggerian Existentialism', in *The Rebirth of Classical Rationalism. An Introduction to the Thought of Leo Strauss* (ed.) Thomas L. Pangle (Chicago: University of Chicago Press, 1989).

Taminiaux, Jacques, *Sillages phénoménologiques. Auditeurs et lecteurs de Heidegger* (Brussels: Ousia, 2002).

Appendix 4: Hermeneutics after Heidegger: The Philosophy of Hans-Georg Gadamer

In *Truth and Method*, a seminal book published after decades of a very active philosophical life, Gadamer developed his own version of hermeneutics, influenced in part by Heidegger's teaching from the early 1920s on Aristotle and his attempt to establish a fundamental ontology with the help of Husserlian phenomenology. Heidegger's analysis of facticity offered Gadamer a powerful means of overcoming the initial isolation of the knower from tradition that was central to earlier hermeneutical theory. Gadamer's contribution, in part inspired by Heidegger, was to ask whether the knower can ever leave his own present situation, transcend his prejudices, in order to access another situation and transpose himself into a horizon of understanding altogether different from his own. If our own historicity is not merely accidental, but is constitutive of our very being, as Heidegger suggests, then our access to the past will always and irreducibly be informed by our present situation. Our prejudices will themselves orient and free our relation to the past, open it up as such. Following Heidegger's suggestion that our hermeneutic situation is a structural feature of our being, or an ontological trait that cannot be reduced, 'Gadamer takes the knower's boundness to his present horizons and the temporal gulf separating him from his object to be the productive ground of all understanding rather than negative factors or impediments to be overcome'.[1] Shaped by the past in an infinity of unexamined ways, the present situation is the 'given' in which understanding is rooted, and which the reflection of the interpreter can never hold at a critical distance, or objectify. There is, in other words, an absolute limit to knowledge in the social sciences, one that Gadamer characterizes as the 'hermeneutical situation'. As soon as the past, or history, is involved in an operation of understanding, that understanding will always and irreducibly be informed by a present situation, the ramifications and roots of which can never be fully clarified. Because the social sciences deal with ourselves, or this being that we are, they can and should never be 'objective'. The process of understanding that characterizes the hermeneutical attitude differs significantly from the controlled investigation of an object by a subject. The latter characterizes the classical model of the natural sciences. Hermeneutics, on the other hand, is more akin to a dialogue between persons, or a game between players, through which both parties evolve and are transformed. Understanding is this movement to and fro between text (or situation) and interpreter, between an 'I' and a 'Thou'.

NOTES

1 David E. Linge, Editor's Introduction to Hans-Georg Gadamer, *Philosophical Hermeneutics* (Berkeley and Los Angeles: California University Press, 1976), p. xiv.

RECOMMENDED READING

Gadamer, Hans-Georg, *Truth and Method* (see Appendix 3).
—, *Philosophical Hermeneutics*, (ed.) David E. Linge (Berkeley and Los Angeles: California University Press, 1976).
—, *Philosophical Apprenticeships*, trans. Robert R. Sullivan (Boston: MIT Press, 1985).
Heidegger's Ways, trans. John W. Stanley (Albany, NY: SUNY Press, 1994).

Appendix 5: Philosophy and Architecture

Heidegger's thinking of the being of the being human as dwelling informs his own meditation on architecture, which he develops from the 1930s onward. This meditation, in turn, had a certain influence on the theory and philosophy of architecture, and on the works of Christian Norberg-Schulz and Kenneth Frampton in particular. These theorists focus on Heidegger's onto-logical interpretation of place and regionality, which in turn allows them to call into question aspects of modernist and postmoderninist architecture. Dwelling, Heidegger will insist throughout, is indicative of and made neces-sary by the openness to this excess that marks the human in its essence, and not by, say, the building itself, or the economy that it harbours. Never can a building, no matter how well it is built, 'how well planned, easy to keep, attractively cheap, open to air, light and sun'[1] assure us that *dwelling* takes place therein. Dwelling in the Heideggerian sense presupposes the openness to – and the experience of – that which throws us beyond the familiarity of things into the uncanny of the Open as such, where we find ourselves primar-ily not-at-home. Dwelling in the most fundamental sense begins with *Unheimischkeit*. A distinction therefore needs to be made between dwelling and residing. Residence presupposes a certain economy, whether of needs and shelter (from the cold, the heat, the rain, the sun, wildlife, others, etc), or sym-bolic, and even encompasses the aesthetic, ornamental dimension of architec-ture. But dwelling belongs to a different order altogether. It belongs in the order of being as such. To be, Heidegger will suggest, is to dwell. We humans inhabit the world as dwellers. And so, architecture will appear as a technical solution to a problem or a question which itself is nothing technical, but ontological. If the question of dwelling, and subsequently of building is to make any sense for Heidegger, it will be on the basis of a conception of space that brings us back to the originary existential–ontological phenomenon of space as *spacing*, to existence as the very site or proto-place of presence, and to dwelling in the world not as things amidst a neutral and indifferent container, but as beings who, in their very being or existence, always encounter their own being or essence as something that matters to them. Does architecture *today* provide a place for such beings? If the modern conception of space, inherited from Descartes and Newton, indeed corresponds to Heidegger's description, does it prevail in modern and contemporary architecture, in such a way that existence would no longer be in a position to dwell authentically, and this means on the basis of its own essence? Does architecture free a space for existence, or does it force it to become a thing, in a world where there is space (and time) for things only?

NOTES

1   'Building Dwelling Thinking', in PLT, 146.

RECOMMENDED READING

Frampton, Kenneth, 'Towards a Critical Regionalism: Six Points for an Architecture of Resistance', in Hal Foster (ed.), *The Anti-Aesthetic: Essays on Postmodern Culture* (Port Townsend, WA: Bay Press, 1983).
Norberg-Schulz, Christian, *Genius Loci: Towards a Phenomenology of Architecture* (London: Academy Editions, 1980).

Appendix 6: Derrida and Deconstruction

The most rigorous and relentless practitioner of this approach after Heidegger is the French philosopher Jacques Derrida who, despite his indebtedness to the German philosopher, sees aspects of Heidegger's own philosophy as still caught within the very metaphysics of presence it seeks to neutralize. This 'failure' alone, Derrida believes, testifies to the need to adopt a slightly different, more duplicitous, deconstructive strategy. For Derrida, to philosophize will always mean to run the risk of falling back into the very metaphysical presuppositions one is trying to avoid; it will always involve a tight negotiation with the vocabulary, the concepts and the oppositions of metaphysics, and the training of an eye for the exact moment at which a given, metaphysical text reveals the conditions of its own (im)possibility by indicating the excess (the reality beyond presence) that governs it, and which it cannot master. In so doing, the text carries out its own transgression, and points to an irreducible alterity within its own identity. Prior to – and at the very core of – the constitution of the metaphysical text in its identity and self-presence, and prior to its commitment to presence as the meaning and ground of being, there is a differential economy, and a logic of radical alterity (of the trace), which deconstruction sets out to free in every instance. Far from being a merely playful, and purely textual exercise, deconstruction is the constant and relentless effort to liberate the voice of difference and radical alterity that speaks from the depths of our metaphysical destiny. It is the forever renewed attempt to provide a space from within metaphysics itself for a reality 'older' than metaphysics. It is an ethics as much as it is a philosophical strategy, a politics as much as it is a reading of philosophical (or literary, anthropological, theological, legal, etc.) texts. Derrida is certainly one of the most prolific philosophers of the last hundred years. His influence in and outside philosophy has been perhaps as great as that of Heidegger himself, and testifies to the profound originality and radical nature of his thought.

RECOMMENDED READING

The following reading list only mentions a small number of his texts, and the ones that deal with Heidegger's thought explicitly:

Derrida, Jacques, *Positions*, trans. Alan Bass (Chicago: Chicago University Press, 1981). A series of interviews from 1972. A good introduction to Derrida's work, and to his relation to Heidegger.

—, '*Ousia* and *Grammè*: Note on a Note from *Being and Time*', in *Margins of Philosophy*, trans. Alan Bass (Chicago: Chicago University Press, 1982). Derrida's first 'deconstructive' reading of Heidegger. It focuses on a note from *Being and Time* devoted to Aristotle and the so-called linear.

—, 'Geschlecht: sexual difference, ontological difference', *Research in Phenomenology*, 13, 1983. Interrogates the sexual neutrality of Dasein and the relationship between the ontological difference and the sexual difference.

—, *The Postcard. From Socrates to Freud and Beyond*, trans. Alan Bass (Chicago: Chicago University Press, 1987). A remarkable – and remarkably entertaining – meditation on the economy of sending and receiving that goes to the heart of Heidegger's later thought, and his concept of *Ereignis* in particular.

—, *Of Spirit*, trans. Geoffrey Bennington and Rachel Bowlby (Chicago: Chicago University Press, 1989). A close reading of the metaphysical motif of 'spirit' in Heidegger's work, and its relation to Heidegger's Nazism.

—, *Aporias. Dying – awaiting (one another at) the 'limits of truth'*, trans. Thomas Dutoit (Stanford: Stanford University Press, 1993). Includes a long, detailed and compelling reading of Heidegger's analysis of being-towards-death in *Being and Time*.

Appendix 7: Human vs Artificial Intelligence

The most applied and focused critique of technology, and of the cybernetic paradigm in particular, to have come out of a reading of Heidegger is that formulated by Hubert Dreyfus. Dreyfus applies Heidegger's thought to a very specific problem, and a specific area, namely, artificial intelligence. Can machines think? Everything, of course, depends on what we mean by 'thinking'. Interestingly enough, Dreyfus does not take his point of departure in Heidegger's explicit critique of technology, and of the cybernetic paradigm, but in the early work, and in the first division of *Being and Time* in particular. This is perhaps no coincidence, as the division in question reveals a conception of everyday, average human understanding that, to this day, computers are still struggling to imitate.

Focusing on the claim of artificial intelligence to represent, and so somehow explain, human intelligence by modelling it on the operation of a complex but limited set of precise algorithms, Dreyfus defends the thesis of a human reason altogether different from artificial reason. In his influential *What Computers Still Can't Do: A Critique of Artificial Reason*, Dreyfus advocates a 'critical caution in the behavioural sciences',[1] and the need to take into account aspects of human comportment, such as embodiment, practical involvement in ongoing activity, feelings, context and a sense of belonging to a totality, which all operate at an immediate, pre-representational level. This is the very level that, according to Dreyfus, artificial intelligence cannot reproduce, and which Heidegger so aptly describes. Intelligence, Dreyfus argues, requires understanding, and understanding requires giving a computer the background of common sense that human beings have by virtue of having bodies, interacting skilfully with the material world and being part of a given culture. It is not chess-playing, in which machines have indeed become great masters, such is their ability to compute and process extremely large quantities of information, but everyday life, which is the ultimate testing ground for artificial intelligence. In our everyday world, Dreyfus claims in the Introduction to the MIT Press edition of his book (1992), 'we are all masters'.[2] This is precisely the existential–ontological world that Heidegger had set out to describe in *Being and Time*. Our global familiarity with our surroundings enables us to respond to what is relevant and ignore what isn't, without having to process representations that are without purpose or facts that are without context.

What is given to us in any given situation are not discrete facts, which we somehow arrange in a meaningful totality, as the method adopted by Artificial Intelligence (AI) to simulate human intelligence reveals. Rather, we encounter specific facts and make them explicit within a context or situation of which we have from the start, immediately as it were, a definite and concrete – albeit only implicit – understanding. Furthermore, what enables human beings to zero in on the relevant facts, without having to exclude others that might become relevant, has to do with the way we are at home in the world, the way we have it wrapped around ourselves, so to speak.[3] Unlike the world of machines, ours is not packed like a trunk full of objects, or even carefully indexed like a filing cabinet. Rather, it is 'there', at the tip of our fingers, and all around us. In fact, as Heidegger claimed, we *are* it. This objection is inspired by Heidegger's analysis of the worldhood of the world and understanding as fundamental structures of human existence (see *Being and Time*, §§ 15–18, 31–2). For artificial intelligence theorists, Dreyfus argues, 'details of the everyday world – snapshots, as it were, of tables, chairs, etc. – are perceived by the mind. These fragments are then reassembled in terms of a model built of other facts that the mind has stored up. The outer world, a mass of isolated facts, is interpreted in terms of the inner storehouse of other isolated, but well catalogued, facts – which somehow was built up from earlier experiences of this fragmented world – and the result is a further elaboration of this inner model.'[4] In reality, however, mind, or rather, intelligence, and world are not dissociated in this way. My personal plans and my memories, for example, are not stored in my mind. Rather, 'they are inscribed in the things around me just as are the public goals of men in general. My memories are stored in the familiar look of a chair or the threatening air of a street corner where I was once hurt. My plans and fears are already built into my experience of some objects as attractive and others as to be avoided.'[5]

Thanks in part to Dreyfus' critique, a recent development in Artificial Intelligence, known as 'interactionism', has become sensitive to the Heideggerian critique of the use of symbolic models of the world, and has attempted to turn Heidegger's account of what Dreyfus calls 'ongoing skilful coping' into an alternative research programme. At MIT, where this approach was developed, it is even sometimes referred to as Heideggerian AI! This approach, associated with the work of Philip Agre and David Chapman, attempts to produce programs that interact intelligently with a micro-world without using either context-free symbolic representations or internal, model-based planning. Following Heidegger, Dreyfus argues, these 'interactionists' note that in our everyday coping we experience ourselves not as subjects with mental representations over against objects with fixed properties, but as absorbed in our current situation, responding directly to its demands.[6] If a computer program is to reproduce such a 'knowledge' of the world, it must abandon representational models altogether, and turn the machine into a worldly entity. But how? Can machines have a world in the sense of being-in-the-world? This supposes that the effort of programmers shift from a representation of a world of objects, with fixed properties, to a configuration of a world of current functions (what Heidegger called 'in-order-tos' in *Being and Time*). But beyond this initial stage, we would need a system that has the ability to learn, and by that we need to understand a system that learns on its own how to cope with the environment and modifies its own responses as the environment changes. But isn't this tantamount to saying that computers must now integrate time as their central feature, that they must somehow be given the ability to evolve, whether we take evolution in its biological, specific sense, or in its individual, experiential sense? Should machines not become temporal beings themselves?

NOTES

1 *What Computers* Still *Can't Do: A Critique of Artificial Reason* (Cambridge, MA: MIT Press, 1992), p. xxvii.
2 *What Computers* Still *Can't Do*, p. xxviii.
3 *What Computers* Still *Can't Do,* p. 260.
4 *What Computers* Still *Can't Do*, p. 267.
5 *What Computers* Still *Can't Do*, p. 266.
6 *What Computers* Still *Can't Do*, p. xxxi.

RECOMMENDED READING

Dreyfus, Hubert L, 'From Micro-Worlds to Knowledge Representation: AI at an Impasse', in John Haugeland (ed.), *Mind Design: Philosophy, Psychology, Artificial Intelligence* (Cambridge, MA: MIT Press, 1981).
—, *Being-in-the-World: A Commentary on Heidegger's* Being and Time, *Division 1* (Cambridge, MA: Harvard University Press, 1991).
—, *What Computers* Still *Can't Do: A Critique of Artificial Reason* (Cambridge, MA: MIT Press, 1992).
—, 'Philosophy of Artificial Intelligence: Response to My Critics', Terrell Ward Bynumn and James H. Moor (eds), *The Digital Phoenix: How Computers are Changing Philosophy* (Oxford: Basil Blackwell, 1998).

Bibliography

WORKS BY HEIDEGGER

A full bibliography of the *Gesamtausgabe*, or the Complete Works to date, in German and in translation, is updated every year in the journal *Heidegger Studies*. Included in my list are only those texts I have referred to in this book. The majority are included in the 'List of Abbreviations' at the beginning of the book.

Briefwechsel. Martin Heidegger-Erhart Kästner, edited by Heinrich Wiegand Petzet (Frankfurt: Insel Verlag, 1986).

'My Way to Phenomenology', in Martin Heidegger, *On Time and Being*, trans. Joan Stambaugh (New York: Harper & Row, 1972).

Philosophical and Political Writings, edited by Manfred Stassen (London: Continuum, 2003).

Zollikon Seminars: Protocols – Conversations – Letters, edited by Medard Boss and translated from the German with notes by Franz Mayr and Richard Askay (Evanston, ILL: Northwestern University Press, 2001).

WORKS ON HEIDEGGER

Arendt, Hannah, 'Martin Heidegger at Eighty', *The New York Review of Books*, October 1971. Reprinted as 'For Martin Heidegger's Eightieth Birthday', in Gunther Neske and Emil Kettering (eds), *Martin Heidegger and National Socialism*, pp. 207–17.

de Beistegui, Miguel, *Heidegger and the Political* (London: Routledge, 1998).

Cohn, H., *Heidegger and the Routes of Existential Therapy* (London: Continuum, 2002).

Fédier, François (ed.), Martin Heidegger, *Écrits politiques* (Paris: Gallimard, 1995).

Gadamer, Hans-Georg, 'Introduction' to Heidegger's 'Phenomenological Interpretations in Connection with Aristotle', *Dilthey-Jahrbuch*, 6, 1986.

Hoeller, K. (ed.), *Heidegger and Psychology* (Seattle: Review of Existential Psychology and Psychiatry, 1988).

Jonas, Hans, 'Heidegger's Resoluteness and Resolve', in Gunther Neske and Emil Kettering (eds), *Martin Heidegger and National Socialism*.

Lang, Berel, *Heidegger's Silence* (Ithaca, NY: Cornell University Press, 1996).

Lacoue-Labarthe, Philippe, *La Fiction du Politique: Heidegger, l'art et la politique* (Paris: Christian Bourgois, 1987), trans. Chris Turner, *Heidegger, Art, Politics* (Oxford: Blackwell, 1991).

Lyotard, Jean-François, *Heidegger et 'les juifs'* (Paris: Galilée, 1988), trans. Andreas Michael and Mark Roberts, *Heidegger and 'the Jews'* (Minneapolis: Minnesota University Press, 1990).

Martin, Bernd (ed.), *Martin Heidegger und das 'Dritte Reich'* (Darmstadt: Wissenschaftliche Buchgesellschaft, 1989).

Neske, Gunther and Kettering, Emil (eds), *Martin Heidegger and National Socialism*, trans. Lisa Harries (New York: Paragon House, 1990).

Ott, Hugo, *Martin Heidegger: A Political Life*, trans. Allen Blunden (New York and London: Basic Books/HarperCollins, 1994).

Petzet, Heinrich Wiegand, *Encounters and Dialogues with Martin Heidegger, 1929–1976*, trans. Parvis Emad and Kenneth Maly (Chicago: University of Chicago Press, 1993).

Richardson, W., 'Heidegger among the Doctors', in *Reading Heidegger: Commemorations* (Bloomington: Indiana University Press, 1993), pp. 49–63.

Rockmore, Thomas, *Heidegger's Philosophy and Nazism* (Berkeley: University of California Press, 1992).

Safranski, Rüdiger, *Martin Heidegger. Between Good and Evil*, trans. Ewald Osers (Cambridge, MA: Harvard University Press, 1998).

Scott, C. E., 'Heidegger, Madness and Well-Being', in C. Macann (ed.), *Martin Heidegger. Critical Assessments* (London: Routledge, 1992), 4, 279–98.

Sheehan, Thomas, 'Heidegger and the Nazis', *New York Review of Books*, 16 June 1988, 38–47.

Strauss, Leo, 'An Introduction to Heideggerian Existentialism', in Thomas L. Pangle (ed.), *The Rebirth of Classical Rationalism. An Introduction to the Thought of Leo Strauss* (Chicago: University of Chicago Press, 1989).

Taminiaux, Jacques, *Sillages phénoménologiques. Auditeurs et lecteurs de Heidegger* (Brussels: Ousia, 2002).

Wolin, Richard (ed.), *The Heidegger Controversy* (Cambridge, MA: MIT Press, 1993).

OTHER WORKS CITED

Atlan, Henri and Koppel, Mark, 'The Cellular Computer DNA: Program or Data?', *Bulletin of Mathematical Biology*, 52, (3), 335–48.

Bateson, Gregory, *Steps to an Ecology of Mind* (Chicago: University of Chicago Press, 2000).

Bergson, Henri, 'The Possible and the Real' (1930), trans. Mabelle L. Andison, in *The Creative Mind* (New York: Citadel Press, 2002).

Bijvoet, Marga, 'How intimate can art and technology really be? A survey of the Art and Technology movement of the Sixties', in *Culture, Technology and Creativity in the Late Twentieth Century* (ed.) Philip Hayward (London: John Libbey and Company, 1990).

Boss, Medard, *Psychoanalysis and Daseinanalysis*, trans. L. B. Lefebre (New York: Basic Books, 1962).

—, 'Martin Heidegger's Zollikon Seminars', trans. B. Kenny, *Review of Existential Psychiatry and Psychology*, 16 (1978–9), 7–20.

—, *Existential Foundations of Medicine and Psychology*, trans. S. Conway and A. Cleaves, with an introduction by P. J. Stern (New York: J. Aronson, 1979).

Bryant, B., 'Nature and Culture in the Age of Cybernetic Systems', *CyberNatures/ CyberCultures: Redefining Natural and Cultural Borders*, American Studies Association Annual Meeting, Detroit, Michigan, 12–15 October 2000.

Carnap, R., 'The Elimination of Metaphysics through Logical Analysis of Language' (1931), trans. A. Pap, in *Logical Positivism* (ed.) A. J. Ayer (Glencoe, Scotland: Free Press: 1959).

Churchland, Paul M., *Matter and Consciousness* (Cambridge, MA: MIT Press, 1988).

Crick, Francis, 'On Protein Synthesis', *Symposium of the Society of Experimental Biology*, vol. 12, 1958.

—, 'The Genetic Code: III', *Scientific American*, 1966.

Critchley, Simon, *Continental Philosophy. A Very Short Introduction* (Oxford: Oxford University Press, 2001).

Derrida, Jacques, *Positions*, trans. Alan Bass (Chicago: Chicago University Press, 1981).

—, '*Ousia* and *Grammè*: Note on a Note from *Being and Time*', in *Margins of Philosophy*, trans. Alan Bass (Chicago: Chicago University Press, 1982).

—, 'Geschlecht: sexual difference, ontological difference', *Research in Phenomenology*, 13, 1983.

—, *The Postcard. From Socrates to Freud and Beyond*, trans. Alan Bass (Chicago: Chicago University Press, 1987).

—, *Of Spirit*, trans. Geoffrey Bennington and Rachel Bowlby (Chicago: Chicago University Press, 1989). A close reading of the metaphysical motif of 'spirit' in Heidegger's work, and its relation to Heidegger's Nazism.

—, *Aporias. Dying – awaiting (one another at) the 'limits of truth'*, trans. Thomas Dutoit (Stanford: Stanford University Press, 1993).

Descartes, René, *Œuvres et Lettres* (Paris: Gallimard, Bibliothèque de la Pléiade, 1953).

Dreyfus, Hubert L., *What Computers Can't Do: A Critique of Artificial Reason* (New York: Harper & Row, 1972).

—, 'From Micro-Worlds to Knowledge Representation: AI at an Impasse', in John Haugeland (ed.), *Mind Design: Philosophy, Psychology, Artificial Intelligence* (Cambridge, MA: MIT Press, 1981).

—, *Being-in-the-World: A Commentary on Heidegger's* Being and Time, *Division 1* (Cambridge, MA: Harvard University Press, 1991).

—, *What Computers Still Can't Do: A Critique of Artificial Reason* (Cambridge, MA: MIT Press, 1992).

—, 'Philosophy of Artificial Intelligence: Response to My Critics', in Terrell Ward Bynumn and James H. Moor (eds), *The Digital Phoenix: How Computers are Changing Philosophy* (Oxford: Basil Blackwell, 1998).

Frampton, Kenneth. 'Towards a Critical Regionalism: Six Points for an Architecture of Resistance', in Hal Foster (ed.), *The Anti-Aesthetic: Essays on Postmodern Culture* (Port Townsend, WA: Bay Press, 1983).

Freud, Sigmund. *The Standard Edition of the Complete Psychological Works* (ed.) James Strachey (London: Hogarth Press, 2001).

Gadamer, Hans-Georg, *Truth and Method*, trans. Joel Weinsheimer and Donald G. Marshall (New York: Continuum, 1993).

—, *Philosophical Apprenticeships*, trans. Robert R. Sullivan (Cambridge, MA: MIT Press, 1985).

—, *Heidegger's Ways*, trans. John W. Stanley (Albany, NY: SUNY Press, 1994).

—, *Philosophical Hermeneutics*, trans. David E. Linge (Berkeley and Los Angeles: California University Press, 1976).

Grinevald, J., 'Progrès et entropie, cinquante ans après', in J. M. Besnier and D. Bourg (eds), *Peut-on encore croire au progrès?* (Paris: Presses Universitaires de France, 2000).

Guignon, C., 'Authenticity, Moral Values, and Psychotherapy', in C. Guignon (ed.), *The Cambridge Companion to Heidegger* (Cambridge: Cambridge University Press, 1993), pp. 215–39.

Haraway, Donna J., 'A Cyborg Manifesto', in *Simians, Cyborgs, and Women* (London: Free Association Books, 1991).

Hegel, G. W. F., *Ästhetik* (ed.) Friedrich Bassenge (West Berlin: Verlag das Europäische Buch, 1985). English translation by T. M. Knox, *Hegel's Aesthetics: Lectures on Fine Art* (Oxford: Oxford University Press, 1975).

—, *Hegel's Phenomenology of Spirit*, trans. A. V. Miller (Oxford: Oxford University Press, 1977).

Heims, S. J., *The Cybernetics Group, 1946–1953. Constructing a Social Science for Post-war America* (Cambridge, MA: MIT Press, 1991).

Hölderlin, Friedrich, *Poems and Fragments*, trans. Michael Hamburger (Cambridge: Cambridge University Press, 1980).

Ince, K., *Orlan. Millennial Female* (Oxford: Berg, 2000).

Irigaray, Luce, *The Forgetting of Air*, trans. Mary Beth Mader (London: Athlone, 1999).

Jacob, François, *The Logic of Life. A History of Heredity* (1970), trans. Betty E. Spillmann (London: Penguin Books, 1989).

—, (with Monod, Jacques), 'Genetic Regulatory Mechanisms in the Synthesis of Proteins', *The Journal of Molecular Biology*, 3, 1961.

Jaspers, K., *Philosophische Autobiographie* (Munich: Piper, 1977).

Kamenka, E. (ed.), *The Portable Karl Marx* (London and New York: Penguin Books, 1983).

Knorr Cetina, Karin, *Epistemic Cultures* (Cambridge, MA: Harvard University Press, 1999).

Lafontaine, C., *L'empire cybernétique. Des machines à penser à la pensée machine* (Paris: Seuil, 2004).

Löwith, K., *Mein Leben in Deustchland vor und nach 1933* (Stuttgart: Metzler, 1986).

Mayer, Ernst, 'Cause and Effect in Biology', *Science*, 154, 1961.

Nancy, Jean-Luc, *The Experience of Freedom*, trans. Bridget McDonald (Stanford: Stanford University Press, 1993).

Nietzsche, Friedrich, *Thus spoke Zarathustra*, trans. R. J. Hollingdale (London: Penguin, 1969).

—, *The Will to Power*, trans. W. Kaufmann and R. J. Hollingdale (New York: Vintage Books, 1968).

Norberg-Schulz, Christian, *Genius Loci: Towards a Phenomenology of Architecture* (London: Academy Editions, 1980).

Sallis, John, *Double Truth* (Bloomington: Indiana University Press, 1995).

—, *Force of Imagination* (Bloomington: Indiana University Press, 2000).

Scheler, Max, *Der Formalismus in der Ethik und die materiale Wertethik. Gesammelte Werke*, vol. 5 (Bern: Francke, 1963).

Schrödinger, Emil, *What is Life?* (Cambridge: Cambridge University Press, 2002).

Spengler, Oswald, *Der Untergang des Abendlandes* (Munich: Beck, 1920), trans. Charles F. Atkinson, *The Decline of the West* (London: George Allen & Unwin, 1926).

Steiner, George, *Barbarie de l'ignorance* (Paris: Compacts Radio France, 1998).

Stelarc, 'Parasite Visions: Alternate, Intimate, and Involuntary Experiences', in T. Druckrey (ed.), *Ars Electronica: Facing the Future* (Cambridge, MA: MIT Press, 1999).

Tönnies, Ferdinand, *Gemeinschaft und Gesellschaft. Grundbegriffe der reinen Psychologie* (Darmstadt: Wissenschaftliche Buchgesellschaft, 1963), trans. Charles P. Loomis, *Community and Association* (London: Routledge and Kegan Paul, 1955).

Virilio, Paul, *The Information Bomb*, trans. Chris Turner (London: Verso, 2000).

Weber, Max, *Wirtschaft und Gesellschaft. Grundriss der verstehenden Soziologie* (Tübingen: J. C. B. Mohr (Paul Siebeck), 1956), translation under the supervision of Guenther Roth and Claus Wittich (eds), *Economy and Society* (New York: Bedminster Press, 1968).

Wiener, Norbert, *Cybernetics or Control and Communication in the Animal and the Machine* (Cambridge, MA: MIT Press, 1948).

—, *The Human Use of Human Beings. Cybernetics and Society* (Garden City, NY: Doubleday Anchor Books, 1950/1954).

Index